COMMUNITY DEVELOPMENT
through
TOURISM

COMMUNITY
DEVELOPMENT
through
TOURISM

SUE BEETON

LAND
LINKS

National Library of Australia Cataloguing-in-Publication entry
    Beeton, Sue.
    Community development through tourism

    Bibliography.
    Includes index.
    ISBN 0 643 06962 3.
    ISBN 978 0643069 62 6.

    1. Tourism – Australia. 2. Community development –
    Australia. I. Title.

    338.47910994

Published by and available from
Landlinks Press
150 Oxford Street (PO Box 1139)
Collingwood VIC 3066
Australia

Telephone: +61 3 9662 7666
Local call: 1300 788 000 (Australia only)
Fax: +61 3 9662 7555
Email: publishing.sales@csiro.au
Web site: www.landlinks.com

Landlinks Press is an imprint of **CSIRO** PUBLISHING

Front cover
Images by istockphoto

Set in 10.5/13 Minion
Cover, text design and typeset by James Kelly
Printed in Australia by BPA Print Group

Contents

Chapter 3: Strategic tourism planning for communities 57

Chapter 4: Community-inclusive tourism strategies 79

Acknowledgements

This book has taken over nine years to materialise. During that time, an incalculable number of people and groups have assisted me in my own personal and professional development, particularly in relation to community development and tourism's place in it.

The many communities who have welcomed me and given me the opportunity to learn from them must also be thanked, as the book would not have its strong ethnographic research base without their generosity.

The communities of Shepparton, Dookie and Bendigo all played an enormous role, as I lived in each of them over this period. While not realising it at the time, my induction into the world of community radio in Shepparton was a turning point in my understanding of what communities are, can be and how the various roles of power and influence are played out. Thanks to all at ONE FM.

My students, both in the courses of Rural Tourism and Community Tourism have been instrumental in guiding the structure and information included in this book. Their comments and responses to the world of tourism and community development have been a critical driving force in actually getting all of this down on paper.

The influence of my colleagues, friends and mentors in the fields of tourism and community development is immeasurable. Through many discussions, debates and simply sharing our thoughts I have been able to articulate my own beliefs and also learn about other, multiple perspectives. While it is really impossible to list all of them, Associate Professor Gayle Jennings deserves special recognition for her feedback on my proposal for this book and her professional support as a sounding board.

And thanks once more to the music without which I cannot work effectively. In this case, the musicians of Cuba and New Orleans provided the environment for much of my time when I was shut away putting pen to paper as well as Australians Bruce Mathiske, Bernie McCall and Sweet Mona's Choir. And of course, community radio stations, Triple R and 3PBS in Melbourne and WWOZ in New Orleans, were always there when I was not able to access my collection.

1

Communities and tourism

Globalisation may be dead (Saul 2005)[1], but internationalisation certainly prevails. In an age where communications technology encompasses the world, enabling us to sit in our lounge rooms and participate in others' lives through our television sets and communicate with them via the Internet, those with the ability to visit other places want to experience something that technology can't provide.

What that 'something' is, is debatable. However, many of those searching for that difference are looking to the people at the places they visit – the local communities. Tourism has had a close connection with the local communities, particularly as hosts and guides, but the opening up of travel to the mass market from the 1960s propelled the development of the package holiday that in effect removed the tourist from the community. With tour leaders from their own country, specialised transport and hotels, the visitors' interaction with their hosts became moderated to the extent where the local community became objectified as a quaint picture opportunity. Yet as these masses increased their travel experience, and learnt more about the world from the television, the desire for interaction increased.

However, before such interaction can be positively achieved, we need to understand what is not possible as well as what is in terms of meaningful tourist–host interaction. Unfortunately, as tourism has grown organically in most places with limited planning, some people have been burnt and they now reject tourism as a viable community asset. On the other hand, many believe that tourism is the answer to 'everything' and the only means for developing their community. Understanding the capabilities of tourism so that the correct decisions can be made in terms of community development is what this book is about.

This chapter introduces the main contention and theme of the book, namely the possibility of (or potential for) developing our communities through the judicious application of tourism. After an overview of the book, the terms 'community' and 'tourism' are described and discussed. We consider community in terms of those constructed communities of the 20th century (including theme parks) as well as those that have formed organically. The remainder of the chapter looks at tourism in general and introduces some of the main issues that communities have to face when considering their future in relation to tourism. This includes some discussion of one of the primary paradoxes of tourism – it carries within itself the seeds of its own destruction. This is particularly pertinent to the focus on community development, as is the presence of many truths (multiple realities), which is also discussed.

The chapter concludes with a common format for each chapter with an empirical case study that demonstrates some of the principles or theories discussed. In this case, we look at different approaches to tourism from two indigenous communities that occurred primarily as a response to the complications and even dangers that tourism may bring with it.

Outline of the book

Tourism in communities is not simply a case of whether to encourage visitors or not, but also what type of visitors and what type of tourism the community decides it wants and needs. Each chapter builds on the understanding gained from the previous chapters, and while they do not necessarily need to be read in strict order, such an approach would benefit the reader new to this field. Others may find it more beneficial to dip in and out of the chapters as required.

Chapter 2 takes this discussion into the theoretical realm, outlining some of the most pertinent tourism, community development and business theories. This chapter underpins the book and argues that an understanding of theory is crucial for any activity, regardless of its nature.

Community tourism planning and development are considered over the next three chapters, that move from strategic to community-inclusive planning and then to marketing. The main aspects covered include strategic planning for community development, the concept of the triple bottom line, capacity building and the notion of community empowerment. Chapters 3 and 4 directly relate to each other, moving from general areas of strategic planning (Chapter 3) to some of the more specific aspects relating to tourism and community development planning, which include the notion of capacity building and the important aspect of the power relations in a community and their influence on tourism (Chapter 4). The reader may well find that these two chapters need to be read in conjunction and referred to regularly. The planning chapters finish with Chapter 5 that focuses on marketing community tourism and some of the specific issues involved, such as how to use marketing to control visitor numbers and behaviour.

Chapter 6 looks in more detail at tourism in rural communities while Chapter 7 moves into the critical area of disaster and crisis management. The concluding chapter brings together material from the previous chapters and considers them in terms of the future of community development through the (judicious) use of tourism, outlining concepts such as corporate social responsibility, poverty alleviation through tourism (Pro-Poor tourism) and private philanthropy. This chapter demonstrates how we can move from taking a cultural imperialist stance of 'knowing what is best' for others to listening to them and working cooperatively to achieve shared goals.

Each chapter includes a piece entitled 'From theory to practice', which outlines a case study pertinent to its theme. These cases primarily come from personal (often ethnographic) field research. This empirical approach enables the reader to see how things work in the 'real world', and ways that various theories can be and have been applied. As they are real-life instances, many of the cases will include elements discussed in other chapters, as it is impossible to describe an empirical case purely in terms of the very arbitrary divisions of these chapters without heavily editing them to the extent where they are no longer 'real'.

Why 'Community'?

It has been argued that, as a response to the increasing alienation individuals were experiencing due to the impersonal effects of globalism and what has been coined by Ritzer (1993) as the 'McDonaldization' (or homogenisation) of culture and societies, there has been a desire to return to the 'community'. Simply put, Ritzer maintains that McDonald's restaurants operate along the lines of five basic principles: efficiency, calculability, predictability, control, and the concept of rationality, and that these principles have also become more prevalent in other parts of society. Others argue that there is more choice and difference in the world – yet many of these consumer choices are provided by a fewer number of global/international/multinational corporations.

'Community' is a term that is used by politicians, social commentators, religious leaders, academics and media reporters. However, it is rarely defined – rather it seems to be a given that we all know what is meant by the term. This is a problem, as communities can be defined in many ways, and I often suspect that what a politician may mean when using the term is very different from my own interpretation.

The word 'community' is derived from the Latin *communitas*, which refers to the very spirit of community, or an unstructured community in which people are equal. (It is the first part of this definition that we are primarily interested in here.) It also has special significance in relation to community development as a term that has been appropriated for particular use in cultural anthropology and the social sciences. In the 1960s, Turner (1969) described *communitas* as relating to a community in process – 'a whole group of people cross[ing] a threshold and together enter[ing] a liminal time and space – that is, an in-between that is neither past nor present, and a space that is neither here nor there.' (Turner 1969: vii.). While this term may appear to be a long way from the theme of this book of community development through tourism, as you progress through the various discussions of communities, tourism and development, you will see how important this anthropological notion of *communitas* really is. We re-visit this later in this chapter where we discuss issues of postmodernism and communities, as well as in Chapter 8.

Taking the above notion of *communitas* into account, we start to see that communities can be described in many different ways. The most common uses of the term in today's culture tend to see communities defined geographically as in a valley, mountain range or water catchment, or politically as in towns, cities and countries. The expression, 'local communities' often refers to small towns or units of an urban centre such as suburbs. Differences between urban and rural (or even regional) communities, however, are more than merely geographical or political – access to services, education and the natural environment, as well as differing social issues, levels of homogenisation and personal preferences influence such communities quite differently.

Family groups also form a particularly powerful type of 'community', especially in those cultures based on strong family ties, responsibilities, reciprocity and respect, referred to in Chapter 8 as 'authoritative communities'. Many indigenous communities are based on a complex hierarchy of familial ties, which for many tourists from Western cultures where extended family ties are diminishing is a fascinating concept that they wish to view, experience and understand. Even the most culturally sensitive visitors to such communities tend to view them as 'inferior' in the sense that they need protection from the outside world, so we can continue to enjoy the spectacle. Such tourism smacks of cultural imperialism, and the notion that these (usually) poor indigenous communities have 'got it right' (particularly in social and environmental terms) and should remain in stasis is anathema to the inevitability of cultural change. Often the tourist, who has had the means to travel by aircraft to get there, wears clothes made from materials not seen before and demonstrates a level of education not attainable by people living in the host community, does not desire those visited to have similar access to the world. I often find myself asking the question, 'Who are we to decide what others can and cannot have?' Nevertheless, visiting and experiencing traditional indigenous communities is a popular form of tourism that we must acknowledge and consider in terms of community development.

Apart from the communities of family at a destination, there are groups of tourists who travel in a family group, which has its own cultural influence and needs. In fact, travellers in general form their own communities while in the act of visiting others. This is not an aspect that is covered in much detail in this book, but it certainly needs to be acknowledged that each community (the host and the guest) influences the other. This is partly discussed in Chapter 2 when we look at the theory of social exchange and the marketing discourse in Chapter 5.

Finally, we have 'communities of interest', such as the artistic community and academic community, as well as professional communities of doctors, lawyers and so on. These communities can have a geographic or spatial component, but can also transcend physical borders. The changing nature of communication has also influenced our notion of communities, with virtual communities of common interest existing outside of any physical place – in cyberspace.

In summary, a community is an amalgamation of living things that share an environment. What truly delineates a community are the acts of sharing reciprocity and interaction, which can be realised in a number of ways. In human communities, intent, belief, resources, preferences, needs and a multitude of other conditions may be different for some community members, which in turn influence the mixture of that community. Nevertheless, the definitive driver of community is that all individual subjects in the mix have something in common. Such complexity can be seen in any community group, particularly those based on geographic boundaries (which is often the case in tourism as people tend to visit *places* or *destinations*), as their members are continually changing, evolving and developing.

Constructed communities – an oxymoron?

Many of the world's cities are planned cities, notably Washington, DC in the United States, Abuja in Nigeria, Brasília in Brazil, Canberra, Perth and Adelaide in Australia, New Delhi in India, and Islamabad in Pakistan. It was also common in the European colonisation of the Americas to build according to a plan and it can be argued that the ancient cities of Peru and others were also planned.

While cities have been planned for many years (dating back to Roman times and before), it was during the early 20th century that the first so-called 'planned' *communities* were constructed, where an attempt was made to create a sense of place and *communitas* in an artificially constructed environment. Early attempts to create public housing 'communities' were dismal failures, with their consequences still being felt today in terms of the concrete ghettos they created. The first of these so-called modern community-creation movements is arguably the

Garden City movement of Europe and the United Kingdom, followed by the post World War II New Town movement in the UK.

Inspired by Utopian desires for a return to nature and the 19th century Romantic desire for a rural idyll (all strong tourism drivers – see Chapter 6 for more on the rural idyll), the Garden City movement began in England in the late 1800s as an approach to urban planning and a reaction to the increased urbanisation related to industrialisation. Garden Cities were to be planned, self-contained communities surrounded by greenbelts, containing carefully balanced areas of residences, industry and agriculture. This idea of the Garden City was influential in German worker housing, the United States and again in England after World War II, when the New Towns Act triggered the development of many new communities based on this egalitarian community vision. Following World War II, 28 towns were designated under the 1946 Act as New Towns, and were developed in part to house the large numbers of displaced people who had lost homes during the War.

Ultimately, these New Towns did not centre around the Romantic, rural idyll of the Garden Cities, instead becoming tributes to post-war development, featuring a car-oriented layout with many roundabouts and a grid-based road system. Construction of the New Towns was often rushed, and the inhabitants were generally plucked out of established communities, instead of the displaced people they were intended for, developing a reputation as the home of 'New Town Blues'. The results of such community 'experiments' should also be heeded by those wishing to capitalise on tourism's interest in communities – rarely can they be constructed, whereas they can be so easily destroyed.

In Australia, after the separate states formed a Commonwealth Federation at the beginning of the 20th century, there was much dispute as to which of the country's two major cities (Melbourne or Sydney) would be the nation's capital. To resolve this impasse, and in a nod to the New Towns movement of Europe (and a reflection of Australia's place in the British Commonwealth), it was decided to create a new capital city of Australia. The site of the nation's capital, Canberra, was pronounced in 1908 at a site almost equidistant from Melbourne and Sydney on farmland that had not before seen a town or city. In 1912, after an extensive planning competition was completed, American planner Walter Burley Griffin's concept, based on the New Town and Garden

City movements, was chosen for this planned community. Unlike most Australian cities, the road network, suburbs, parks and other elements of the city were designed in context with each other, rather than the organic growth witnessed in much of Sydney. However, many Australians argue that Canberra has no 'soul' or sense of community, and has difficulty in attracting tourists, demonstrating the difficulties surrounding created communities.

The era of the modern planned city in the United States began in 1963 with the creation of Reston in Virginia, sparking a revival of the New Town concept. Reston incorporated higher density housing in order to conserve open space, as well as mixed-use areas for industry, business, recreation, education and housing. The first residential section of the community, Lake Anne Plaza, emulated a European village on a lake – a totally constructed site not unlike the recreated places of today's theme parks.

It is the development of theme parks in the United States that is of particular interest in terms of tourism and constructed communities. The Disney parks are the most famous American theme parks, replicating a Romantic notion of small town America. This is particularly so for Disneyworld in Florida with its re-creations of other American towns such as New Orleans – in a far cleaner and safer environment than the real place. Even the 'residents' are constructed, either as staff coming in each day for work or with residential 'communities' being constructed in conjunction with (usually adjacent to) the modern-day theme park. In Florida, Disney constructed the modern residential community of Celebration in Orlando, 10 minutes from Disneyworld.

Eventually, inexorably, Disney began to move to other parts of the world, including Paris and more recently Hong Kong. The story of the constructed community surrounding Disneyland Resort Paris (originally called Euro-Disney) is in itself a fascinating study of communities and tourism, leading on from the construction of Celebration in Florida.

Disneyland Resort Paris is a vacation and recreation resort near Paris, featuring two Disney theme parks, Disneyland Park (usually called Disneyland Paris) and Walt Disney Studios. The theme park officially opened as Euro Disneyland in 1992, but attendance was disappointingly low – 500 000 visitors were expected on opening day, but only a fraction of this number turned out, with numbers falling further after the first three months. So, Euro Disneyland and Euro Disney Resort changed their name to Disneyland Resort Paris, inferring that it is more akin to a resort than simply a theme park. As a result of the name change, the reconstruction of the complex to better appeal to European tastes and the addition of more 'relevant' attractions, Disneyland Resort Paris finally turned a (small) profit in 1995. After this re-start, Disneyland Resort Paris has become the most visited tourist destination in Europe with more than 12 million visitors per year.

As with Celebration in Disneyworld in Florida, there is a created urban area known as Val d'Europe – a 'high standard' housing area with a large (75 000 metre^2) shopping mall, a shopping village dedicated to *haute couture* and 'Aquarium Sea Life' – an aquarium where visitors can journey from the River Seine to the Atlantic, then beyond to the Caribbean. The question that comes to mind when we consider these constructed, theme-park-related communities is, are people living in or simply visiting this 'community'? Do they contribute to the *communitas* of the place?

As with the French example above we are even seeing shopping malls becoming their own constructed community, not unlike theme parks. The development of the 'Mall of America' in Bloomington has a Lego Space Station, a medieval castle and a series of theme-park-based rides. At the (supposedly) world's largest shopping mall, West Edmonton Mall in Canada, shoppers can gamble at roulette tables, soak in a spa near a volcano or view sharks from a submarine (and go shopping!) (Goeldner *et al.* 2000). The line between places to live, work and play is becoming extremely blurred – a fact that anyone involved in community development and/or tourism needs to remember.

In an interesting work that considers the consequences of such blurring of roles, Hannigan (1998) introduces the concept of a 'Fantasy City'. He describes many of these constructed communities (and theme parks and shopping malls) as having six main features. The 'Fantasy City':

- is based around a single or multi-theme (drawn from popular entertainment, sport, history or the city's geographic locale);
- is aggressively branded with sponsors and highly reliant on licensed merchandise sales;

- operates day and night;
- is modular (mixing and matching an array of standard components such as themed restaurants, cinema megaplexes and high tech amusements);
- is solipsistic (that is, self-contained and physically, economically and socially isolated from its locale); and
- is postmodern in that it is constructed around simulations, virtual reality and the 'thrill of the spectacle' (Hannigan 1998, pp. 3–4).

And finally, the exponential growth in controlled, 'gated' communities (not unlike the theme parks discussed previously and Hannigan's Fantasy City) can be seen as today's equivalent of the Garden City and New Towns movements. This time, the communities are based on safety and security, arguably among the primary human motivations (see Maslow's 'Hierarchy of Needs' in Chapter 2). How this relates to tourism is problematic, as tourists may be prevented from even entering these 'secure' sites to interact with the community.

Sense of community

While most communities, as we generally perceive them, have grown organically, there are various attempts to develop planned communities as outlined above, with varying degrees of success. It is argued that many planned communities actually lack a 'sense of community'.

'Sense of community' is itself imbued with individual meaning and related to the notion of *communitas* presented earlier. It is often seen as a feeling of belonging to a group (community) and a shared faith that members' needs will be met together, primarily through informal social channels. McMillan and Chavis (1996) identify four factors: membership, influence, shared emotional connection, and integration and fulfilment of needs. In addition, the notion of 'empowerment' is also central to a sense of community. Others define sense of community as an environment in which people interact in a cohesive manner, continually reflecting upon the work of the group while always respecting the differences individual members bring to the group (Graves 1992). These various descriptions present the most essential elements of community as:

- empowerment;
- the existence of mutual interdependence among members;
- having a sense of belonging, connectedness, spirit, faith and trust;
- possessing common expectations, shared values and goals.

Indigenous communities

As noted in an earlier publication, the descriptions of communities introduced in the various discussions above

> ... can be applied to both indigenous and non-indigenous communities, large and small. It is important to recognise that most of the elements of a community revolve around emotional rather than physical aspects, such as the sense of belonging, heritage, sense of place and social organisation. It is easy to overlook these more intangible areas when considering a tourism development (which includes guided tours and activities, not just resorts) as they are not easily quantifiable. However, to have a sustainable tourism industry that is around for many years to come these aspects of community must be carefully considered (Beeton 1998, p. 35.)

While not given separate attention in this publication, all of the elements discussed in the book relate to indigenous communities in varying degrees, and some of the examples and cases are taken from such groups. However, what we tend to see when looking at indigenous communities that exist within a different, dominant culture (usually a 'Western' hegemony) is that the level and degree of complexity of the issues they face are multiplied. This is particularly so in terms of the various power relations and notions of 'empowerment', which is discussed briefly below and in more detail in Chapter 4.

In any wide-ranging publication such as this, it is necessary to generalise, however it is important to acknowledge that all communities (indigenous and non) have their own specific circumstances. As a case in point, the case study outlined at the end of this chapter looks at two geographically related indigenous communities and their differing historical relationship with tourism and tourists.

The use of 'community' in this publication

While we have established there are many different ways to look at communities, the primary focus in this book is on communities defined spatially or geographically – often the members of a small town or region, which in tourism terms is a destination. So, we are looking primarily at 'destination communities'. Yet many of the arguments and ideas presented can be applied to other types of communities (many of which are often located in a certain place), which at times will be noted when they are particularly significant.

Destination communities are alternatively referred to as host communities (which can also relate to other types of non-geographic communities), local or even residential communities. A problem with using the term 'resident' is that it ignores the homeless and itinerant residents who are very much a part of any community, particularly in tourism terms where often many of the encounters with locals are with the homeless and itinerant. It is assumed throughout this book that they are part of the community and must not be ignored in community and tourism development and the processes of consultation and empowerment.

Community empowerment

'Community empowerment' has become the buzzword of the 21st century. How has this come about, and what is so important about it? In his book, *Empowerment for Sustainable Tourism Development*, Trevor Sofield (2003) not only defines the concept, but also traces the development of the notion as well as providing real-life, in-depth cases for critical analysis and discussion. This comprehensive publication is referred to throughout this book, particularly when talking about the empowerment of communities through (and for) tourism in Chapter 4. He observes that '… the concept of empowerment by and of communities is at once a process and an outcome' (Sofield 2003, p. 8). This is an important aspect of empowerment – the process of empowering people (and communities) is just as important as the actual final outcome. I believe that it is often more important.

In this book, when referring to the term community empowerment, I am adopting Sofield's approach and understanding. It is not possible to provide a glib, simple definition that students (or even someone trying to impress others at a dinner party) can rattle off, parrot-fashion. In an earlier publication, Sofield talks of two main components of the empowerment process – the government and the community (Sofield 2001). This inclusion of government is significant, as many theoretical discussions of community empowerment fail to acknowledge the role of government and the associated power relations in actually achieving an empowered community. Without political will and support, communities remain 'empowered' in name only, yet with it run the risk of being misappropriated by the more powerful government interests that may not be in the locals' best interest.

Sofield's concept of empowerment and the issues involved in understanding the various power relations are considered in detail in Chapter 4.

Why tourism?

The first form of recorded tourism is arguably that of pilgrimages to sacred sites. Many of these sites resided in and were tended by a local community that either already existed or actually developed to serve the pilgrims and manage the site. Where the communities became compromised with an abundance of visitors, we have witnessed dramatic changes, particularly if the residents have had little input into the site's development. This is the case in many host communities, but is particularly evident at pilgrimage sites, which were not planned. However, even tourism that has been planned requires a community to support it – either one that already exists or one that is created for that purpose. In some developing countries, resorts have been built as enclaves where tourists are 'contained' in the area of the resort. Paradoxically, tourists also want to have some sense of the place they are visiting, even if it is by proxy through constructed communities at the resorts.

'Tourism' has been variously defined and described in terms of the traveller, the businesses servicing the traveller and the places (communities) in which the traveller goes to and through. Many of the theoretical models in Chapter 2 consider the structure of tourism as an industry and an experience. For the benefit of clarity in this publication, and because of its inclusive description, I have adopted Williams and Shaw's approach to understanding tourism as:

... crucially important. In most countries tourism is 'statistically invisible' and, usually, only the most obvious sectors or those exclusively devoted to tourists are enumerated in official tourism data. Inevitably, this tends to be the accommodation sector and, perhaps, cafés and restaurants. Yet the tourism industry is far larger than this. Tourists also spend money directly on recreational facilities, tourist attractions, shops and local services. In turn, these have indirect effects on agriculture, wholesaling and manufacturing, while secondary rounds of spending of tourism create induced linkages in the economy (Williams and Shaw 1998, cited in Hall 2003a, p. 13).

From the previous discussion of the definition of community, it is clear to see that where people gather to work, live and play, they form some type of community. Tourists themselves form a temporary community within that host community, particularly if they are on a tour or in any other group configuration. Simply put, tourism exists **in** communities, not outside them.

Tourism platforms

One of the first academics to actively study tourism is Jafar Jafari. In 1973 he founded the first academic journal in tourism, *Annals of Tourism Research*, which remains the pre-eminent journal in the field. In 1988 Jafari published one of his seminal articles that outlined the development of how we perceive, study and approach tourism in the world, nominating four themes or 'platforms': advocacy, cautionary, adaptancy and knowledge-based. While Jafari used this to describe the development of tourism research and theory over a period of time, all of the platforms are still relevant today – not everyone has taken the journey from advocacy to knowledge-based, and for some, their political/personal situation will not permit them to do so. Due to the continued relevance of Jafari's platforms, it is important to outline them here:

1 Advocacy platform
Those who focus on the advocacy platform are generally trying to advance the interests of tourism and the industry in general, claiming

that tourism is beneficial, particularly in economic terms. This is based on post World War II economic reconstruction. Such a stance was particularly important when trying to convince others that tourism is an industry in its own right and should be treated as such, particularly in terms of government support and assistance. Tourism is presented as the 'saviour', particularly for rural, regional and remote communities. Those who still follow the advocacy platform tend to come from the commercial areas as well as many government and non-government tourism agencies.

2 Cautionary platform

This platform came out of the 1970s with the growing interest in broader issues beyond the economic and increased writings by thinkers and researchers who were saying 'Yes, it CAN be beneficial, but it is also very damaging.' The impacts of tourism were becoming acknowledged, particularly by sociologists and environmentalists.

3 Adaptancy platform

The adaptancy platform is in many ways a mid-point between the first two groups, where its proponents believe that certain forms of tourism can bring economic and other benefits without the same level of environmental damage that other types of enterprises might. This opened up the concepts in the 1980s of alternative forms of tourism, using terms such as green, soft, nature-based and ecotourism. This period also saw the emergence of community-centred tourism where local resources are deployed. Proponents of the adaptancy platform maintain that tourism can benefit both the hosts and the guests. You will find many examples of the adaptancy platform throughout the book, however this publication is actually based on the following platform.

4 Knowledge-based platform

The final platform that Jafari identified comes out of the three preceding it and attempts to build on previous work by taking a multi-disciplinary approach to the study of tourism. There is a focus on the discovery and development of scientific knowledge about tourism and tourism-related issues while maintaining bridges with the other platforms. This is the preferred platform of many tourism professionals and academics and is the basis of this book, building on theory and research knowledge along with practical experience in order to further improve the quality of life for people in various communities as well as enhance the visitor experience.

So what do we mean by 'community' and 'tourism'?

As tourism relies on visiting places and people, it cannot exist outside a community. So, both tourism and the communities it is in must be viewed simultaneously – any change to one will affect the other. Consequently, tourism is one of the most significant community development tools, particularly in marginal or peripheral communities such as indigenous, remote and rural communities.

The earlier quote regarding tourism from Williams and Shaw (cited Hall 2003a) demonstrates the intricacies of understanding tourism and its links with the communities in which it occurs. There is increasing recognition of the intrinsic role that the host community (or destination community) plays in the creation and delivery of tourism experiences, so many have combined these terms into the term 'community tourism'. It has been variously described as:

Tourism in which local residents (often rural, often poor and marginalized) are active participants as land-managers/users, entrepreneurs, employees, decision-makers and conservators (Ashley n.d.).

An industry which uses the community as a resource, sells it as a product and, in the process, affects the lives of everyone (Murphy 1980).

Community tourism shifts the focus away from the tourist and their experience to the host community and THEIR experience (Kelly 2002).

Reflecting Sofield's (2003) comments regarding the process of community empowerment is the following quote from the Business Enterprises for Sustainable Tourism's (BEST) Community Tourism Summit, where they conclude that 'community tourism is a process rather than a product' (BEST 2003).

In spite of the use of the term, I am not entirely comfortable in using 'community tourism' as it has connotations of tourists visiting a community to observe (or gaze at) the lives of the community members – the community becomes the entire tourism 'product'. Tourism does more than simply gaze upon communities – it can assist in the development of communities in terms of their economic, social and environmental wellbeing, while at the same time can have the opposite effect. This is the premise of this book, which considers how tourism can (and can not) contribute to the development of sustainable, healthy communities; hence I will avoid using the term 'community tourism' per se, even though it may occasionally slip in.

Tourism: Maintaining the status quo or bringing change?

Tourism is a major agent of change, and while it is often promoted by those with a positivist (advocacy platform) perspective as a force for positive contributions to society, economy and natural environment, such change can arrive unnoticed.

The cost of change can be high, particularly if it is not recognised – too often the negative impacts of tourism are realised only once the damage has been done. This is due to the fact that much change is incremental and difficult to isolate and measure. Residents may simply feel overwhelmed by the sheer number of tourists. Some of the more commonly reported costs include role conflict and social problems where women and even children may be earning more than the traditional male breadwinner. This can result in loss of pride and a sense of helplessness, resulting in increasing social problems such as depression and even suicide.

Tourism is more complex than many people believe it to be. There is a general unspoken belief in Western culture that as most of us have been on a holiday, consequently we understand tourism. Such a simplistic notion would be laughable if it was not so common. It was not many years ago when a group of tourism researchers were in the audience of a late-night popular American TV chat show where the ('famous') host derided tourism research as not 'serious' or 'real research'.

Tourism is intricately woven into a community's regular activities, as locals often utilise tourist facilities, while visitors also utilise locals' facilities. In addition, the growing interest in many tourists for experiential encounters can result in loss of privacy or the commodification of the community.

Environmental and economic issues also come into play in many ways in communities, depending on numerous social as well as economic variables. A focus on the natural environment by tourists can encourage its conservation and constructive management, whereas too many visitors run the risk of 'loving it to death'. The section below considers the main issues surrounding the social impacts of tourism development on community development.

Social impact issues of tourism development

A multitude of impacts that tourism development has on communities has been identified and is well documented by researchers including

Table 1.1 Reported social impacts of tourism

Tourism development	Modifies the internal structure of the community
	Divides the community into those who have/have not relationships with tourists
	Has colonialist characteristics
	Employment in tourism offers more opportunities for women
	Instigates social change
	Improves quality of life through infrastructure development
	Increased pressure on existing infrastructure
Tourist–host interactions	The nature of contact influences attitudes/ behaviour/ values relating to tourism
	Young locals are most susceptible to the demonstration effect
	Cultural exchange/increased understanding and tolerance
	Increased social interaction increases communication skills
	Hosts adopt foreign languages through necessity
	Hosts develop coping behaviour and avoid unnecessary contact
Cultural impacts	Arts, crafts and local culture revitalised
	Acculturation process likely to occur
	Assumed negative effects of commodification of culture
	Meaning/authenticity not necessarily lost

Source: Beeton 2005a, p. 122.

Murphy (1981), Craik (1991), Robinson and Boniface (1997), Bramwell and Lane (2000), Singh *et al.* (2003b), to name but a few. Table 1.1 outlines the range of these impacts in terms of the development, interactions and cultural impacts. The list does not judge whether the impacts are positive or negative or better or worse than each other, as they will often be both, for different people, or in different circumstances. In addition, the magnitude of the impacts will vary, depending on the rate of change in a community and its capacity (willingness) to embrace such change, as well as the actual community being considered.

One of the issues with the negative elements of tourism development is that it is often not until after some time that the negative impacts become evident. It may well be too late to correct some of these impacts, particularly when they affect local community attitudes and beliefs, which are difficult to consciously alter. This hidden and irreversible nature of some of the negative effects is the greatest danger of any blind acceptance of tourism as a sole development tool.

Yet, when it works, tourism is an outstanding community development tool. The case study at the end of this chapter is of two related yet different indigenous communities' responses to the various impacts of tourism.

Postmodernism, communities and multiple realities

The term 'postmodern' has become one of the most used and abused words in English today. Those who understand little of its meaning and application in the world are often the most vociferous in its denigration. Others feel that the concept is far too complex and removed from them to understand it, so they rarely bother. This was my own attitude until a few years ago when I was required to read on the topic and 'discovered' that so much of what I was thinking, believing and saying about tourism (and the rest of my life and culture) was from a postmodern perspective. As with any evangelist, I now feel that everyone should at least understand, if not embrace, some of the basic tenets of the postmodern paradigm.

Simply put, postmodernism is 'a rejection of many, if not most, of the cultural certainties on which life in the West has been structured over the past couple of centuries' (Sim 2005, p. vii). In other words, it is a reaction against the 20th century concepts of modernism and modernity and their social and political failings. This more widely accepted usage of the term was not apparent until the latter half of the 20th century, when it was used in architecture as a reaction against the so-called 'modern' International Style architecture of concrete and glass with little orna-mentation. Today, postmodernism is committed to 'dissent, pluralism, cultural difference, and skepticism towards authority' (Sim 2005, p. xi).

Postmodernists accept that there is no single, universal truth or 'grand narrative' (nor should there be an 'International Style') and embrace scepticism about what our 'culture' stands for. However, grand narratives that explain everything still speak meaningfully to many, a pertinent example being the reassertion of religious fundamen-talism where institutional authority is accepted without question, and conformity, not difference, is sought (Sim 2005).

Postmodernism acknowledges the existence of multiple realities, where the same thing or incident may be seen by many people in different ways, depending on the 'lens' through which they view it (Beeton 2005a). In many cases, the same person may also have a multitude of realities on the same thing, depending on his or her current position. For example, if I am going to an extremely crowded concert with very loud music, as a fan of that music my reality is that this is a great thing. However, if my children are attending, my reality now shifts to that of 'responsible adult' where I may be concerned about the concert in terms of its effect on their personal safety and their hearing. This is an extremely simple example, but one that holds true in many circumstances.

In addition, the notion of 'reality' is challenged in that a model or representation may be as real as the 'real thing' that it represents (Baudrillard 1983). This is particularly the case when we look at theme parks – they are constructed and controlled representations of the 'real' world, yet they exist in time and space and many people actually celebrate the fact that they are 'fake', acknowledging a different type of reality. Las Vegas takes notions of representation and simulacra to yet another level.

In terms of tourism, postmodernism has been described as 'post-tourism' by some (Ritzer and Liska 1997), representing a particular type of tourist and way of interpreting tourism experiences from a post-modern perspective. What this means is that 'tourism is seen as an end in itself, not as a means to the loftier goals of personal development, cultural interaction or education' (Beeton 2005a, p. 177). Urry (1990, p. 100) supports this notion, stating that 'the post-tourist knows that they are a tourist and that tourism is a game … with multiple texts and no single, authentic tourist experience'.

If this is how those visiting our communities perceive tourism, then this will affect how our community can benefit from tourism and develop in the ways it desires. This is an important planning and marketing issue, which is re-introduced in Chapter 5.

The notion of Hannigan's (1998) 'Fantasy City' comes from a post-modern perspective, particularly in the way that he acknowledges the receding space between 'authenticity' and 'illusion' in relation to theme parks and movies. Tourists to theme parks and film sites rarely expect to see something authentic, rather they are looking for simulacra and representations, often searching for the 'fake'. This is where many of those involved in community tourism fall down when they fail to acknowledge or understand that their version of 'authenticity' may be very different from the tourist's who may not be looking for 'authenticity' at all!

The discussion here on postmodernism has been purposely kept brief so as to simply introduce some of the terms and concepts that are presented throughout this publication. For a more comprehensive outline of postmodernism and its relationship with tourism, see John Urry (2002) which has an excellent, readable synthesis of postmodernism from a sociological tourism perspective.

While not specifically postmodern, the following case study illustrates some of the issues facing indigenous communities and their responses to them. This is particularly based on what type of community they desire and what type of visitor they are prepared to host and is informed by their interpretation (reality) of past experience. The message in this case study is from the Knowledge-based Platform with a cautionary focus.

From theory to practice: A case of the wrong type of tourism, or just too much?

There are hundreds of American Indian tribes, each with their own community structure and relationship with tourism, from intense to virtually zero. Much has been written on gaming on Indian lands and its associated pros and cons, both in terms of economics, tourism and community development. This case study is not looking at this issue, but at two different responses to tourism in general from two neighbouring, yet very different communities, namely the Hopi and Navajo Indians.

The Hopi and Zuni Indians migrated north from Aztec and Mexico 900 years ago and settled in Northern Arizona, not far from modern-day Flagstaff. They were a horticultural community, settling in where the earliest indigenous peoples, the Anasazi, had lived over 1000 years ago. Along with the Apaches, the Navajo Indians migrated south from Canada's Subarctic around 500 years ago. They were primarily hunter-gatherers, and the Navajo lands took in much of Northern Arizona as well as parts of Utah and New Mexico, including some of the Hopi lands. Both tribes used similar tracts of land – the Hopi tilling the poor soil, while the more mobile and aggressive Navajo hunted over the same lands. Today, the much smaller Hopi Reservation is surrounded by the significantly larger Navajo land.

The Hopi Reservation consists of three mesas edging the Painted Desert, where at 6000 feet above sea level the annual rainfall is between 10 and 13 inches. The Reservation was ceded to the Hopi in 1943, but is extremely small to support the 8500 residents, consequently overuse of the land has resulted in poor soil and erosion. Nevertheless, from an early date in terms of Indian tourism, the Hopi community welcomed and cared for the visitors attracted to their unusual culture.

The Hopi became particularly famous for their Kachina Cult and their dances, in particular the Snake Dance, where young men in a trance danced with poisonous snakes. The Hopi believe that Kachinas are supernatural beings who visit Hopi villages during the first half of the year. They bring rain, punish offenders and act as a link between gods and mortals. They provide pleasure and amusement as well as play a more serious religious role. At many ceremonies, masked impersonators in traditional costume are believed to take on supernatural qualities, becoming the Kachina.

Visitors were welcomed at these ceremonies. However, by the 1950s there were so many lay anthropologists visiting and imposing on the Hopi community, that it was only a matter of time before there was a reaction from the Hopi people. This came during a Snake Dance around 1956, where the flash bulbs of the tourists' cameras disturbed the snakes in the Snake Dance, killing two of the community's young men. Immediately, all tourists were banned.

Today, the Hopi community continues to be extremely sensitive of its culture, with their pueblos (villages) varyingly open or closed to tourists, depending on local circumstances, such as sacred dances and events. All visitors are restricted as to where they can go and photographing or sketching any Hopi people is strictly forbidden. In order to limit the number of sightseers, there are no signs announcing that the traveller has entered Hopi Land, unlike the Navajo who proudly announce their Navajo Nation (which surrounds the Hopi Reservation). However, the Hopi people themselves remain extremely welcoming of tourists who do visit and respect their culture, which they are determined to retain. While many of their youth move away to study, they return to assist at harvest time and to contribute back to their community. Maintaining the Hopi traditional ways is not only a link to their past, but grounds them in today's modern society.

The American Indians of the Arizona region are among the poorest in the nation, apart from those who adopted gaming as a source of tourist income. The Navajo Nation has the largest Indian reservation in the United States, covering some 17.5 million hectares (27 000 square miles) with a population of around 160 000. The land is extremely barren, with the average income of its population standing around US$4400 per annum, making them one of the poorest of the Indian groups in the poorest region. Apart from tourism, their primary sources of income are from coal mining and the filming of commercials in the striking desert regions and badlands of Arizona.

The Navajo council decided, in spite of the attractive financial arguments and their own poverty, not to allow gaming on their land, relying on their natural resources as a source of tourism. Part of their land includes Monument Valley and Canyon de Chelly – both strong natural and cultural attractions. Their tourism tends to rely on these iconic sites, along with so-called 'Trading Posts' throughout their land selling artefacts and crafts. Many of these Trading Posts are historical sites and attractions in their own right and have become must-see stopovers for visitors. While they desire more visitors, the travel distances are vast and are reliant on vehicle-based transport to get there.

However, they do little to encourage visitors into the communities, which are dispersed and poor, in a barren environment with little to attract the tourist. Consequently, they retain some privacy, but the benefits of tourism rarely trickle down to many of these communities.

Travelling through this region, the different responses to tourism from these two groups is marked – the Hopi who have an enormous tourism appeal are trying to limit their tourism, while the Navajo, with limited tourism appeal and dispersed sites are keen to encourage it. Such is the contrary nature of tourism and communities. If we want to develop communities through tourism, care must be taken and the requirements of those communities taken into consideration.

Endnote

1   This comment from economist John Raulston Saul is based on his understanding of globalisation as the outwards expansion of a single dominating culture, resulting in a single global economy that is dominated by Western-style capitalism. Saul argues that this is no longer true and that the Western capitalist economy has failed as a homogenous global force.

2

Tourism theories and their relevance to communities

The whole notion of using theory to better understand what we do, how we do it and even what may happen continues to be contested by so-called 'practitioners'. Some claim that there is nothing to learn from theory – that one needs to be out there actually doing things to understand them. Such comments do have a certain amount of relevance in that one of the primary aims of those developing theories is that they need to be not only applicable, but also applied. Unfortunately, these comments have been appropriated by those wanting to condemn theoretical study as purely 'academic' (another misused term). But, if we think back to many of the tasks that we do every day of our lives, we had to learn how to do them, and once we had developed our communication skills, all have some degree of theory attached. Often we are given the theory followed by a demonstration before we are permitted to attempt a procedure for the first time.

For example, a person learning to drive a car is initially told about the process – put the key in the ignition, check all mirrors, depress the clutch, turn the key, put the car into gear, release the brake and ease off the clutch. This is the 'theory'. Then the process is demonstrated, and eventually the learner is allowed to 'practise' it themselves. Even those who attempt to do this without prior explanation have observed others and developed their own 'theoretical model' to understand and explain what needs to be done. The more complex the task, the more complex the process becomes, creating an even greater need to be able to express it in an abstract, theoretical manner.

Most (if not all) theories are developed by observing what is happening in the world and then converting those observations into a communicable format, such as a model, diagram or written description. The way that theories are developed is to study (or 'research') a process, describe it and then test it for accuracy.

When we look at the notion of research, the term 'relevant research' is being constantly thrown at academic researchers (one of the main groups of theory developers) as a criticism of what they *don't* do. What critics often mean is that they feel academics should undertake research whose results can be immediately used; what in academic terms is applied research. This is a valid type of and use for research, but it is not the only one. Other forms of research assist in the development of theories and theoretical models that are often not considered 'relevant' in today's lexicon. However, without useful theory development there is a limited base framework from which students (a term that includes anyone interested in learning) can build their knowledge.

Unfounded, spurious claims that denigrate the importance of theory and development are extremely dangerous. I hope I am never faced with the prospect of going for a drive with someone who has no concept of how to operate a vehicle such as a motor car!

One of the areas that may have confused the critics of theory is that there are various types of theory and theoretical models. I have already referred to the theory that explains how to do something – the models or diagrams that are used to illustrate these theories are explanatory models. They describe things as they are.

The second type of theory is the causative model, which shows what will happen if a certain action is taken, or a certain thing occurs. For example, if a nation's currency exchange rate drops, international tourism to that country often increases as it becomes more economic to do so. In this example the exchange rate and international visitor numbers are directly related.

The third type (and often the most controversial) is the predictive theoretical model. These models attempt to predict what will occur in the future. They are closely related to the first two, particularly the second one, but tend to take a longer time perspective. In tourism, we have models that attempt to predict the number of visitors to a particular region over the next 10 years, their economic contribution or even future infrastructure needs. For example, the Tourism Forecasting Committee (previously the Tourism Forecasting Council), Australia's primary tourism prediction organisation with members from the finance, property, export and tourism industry (private and public sectors), presents regular forecasting reports. It is an independent body that develops forecasts based on consensus from 'experts', including researchers and economists as well as the tourism industry. The Committee primarily focuses on international and domestic tourism's economic value. The theories used here are primarily economic forecasting models that are based on historical data as well as future projections. These results are presented in graphs and tables such as Table 2.1.

Such forecasts can indicate future opportunities as well as issues that a community may have to deal with in terms of tourism growth (or lack of), and need to be considered in all planning exercises.

Other groups that conduct similar forecasts include the Pacific Asia Travel Association (PATA), the Tourism Research Council New Zealand and the International Air Transport Association (IATA).

Tourism theory

In direct contrast to some of my earlier comments regarding practitioners and academics, it is interesting to note that many of the theories that underpin the study of tourism were developed by 'practitioners', many of whom continue to operate in the commercial world, not the academic world.

Any introductory tourism text presents a number of basic theories that many students will be familiar with. Nevertheless, it is important that we re-visit some of them, not only for those who have not studied tourism, but for those familiar with such theories, as we will be considering them in light of their contribution to improving our

Table 2.1 Total Australian tourism visitation and forecasts

Year	Inbound arrivals	Change on previous year (%)	Domestic visitor nights (000s)	Change on previous year (%)	
2000	4931.4	10.6	239 384.0	−0.3	
2001	4855.7	−1.5	289 644.0	−1.3	
2002	4839.1	−0.3	298 657.0	3.1	
2003	4744.6	−2.0	294 111.0	−1.5	
2004	5215.0	9.9	296 878.0	0.9	
2005	**5574.8**	**6.9**	**297 483.8**	**0.2**	
2006	**5924.8**	**6.3**	**300 483.5**	**1.0**	
2007	**6291.9**	**6.2**	**303 303.1**	**0.9**	
2008	**6660.8**	**5.9**	**306 171.4**	**0.9**	
2009	**7051.4**	**5.9**	**309 065.1**	**0.9**	
2010	**7453.6**	**5.7**	**311 992.5**	**0.9**	
2011	**7873.5**	**5.6**	**314 947.7**	**0.9**	
2012	**8324.2**	**5.7**	**317 547.5**	**0.8**	
2013	**8797.6**	**5.7**	**320 168.7**	**0.8**	
2014	**9297.2**	**5.7**	**322 811.6**	**0.8**	
Average annual growth (%) 2005 to 2014					
	5.8	–	0.9	–	

Numbers in **bold** are forecasts
[a] TIEV: total inbound economic value; [b] TDEV: total domestic economic value
Source: TFC 2005.

understanding of community development through tourism. Murphy and Murphy (2004) support this approach, noting that

> Regardless of the definitions and theoretical approach taken, few deny the need to concentrate more on the development of theory in the area of community tourism. If the growing academic and practical interest in community tourism is to take on a more solid form it needs the structure of a theoretical framework (Murphy & Murphy 2004, p. 30).

Outbound departures	Change on previous year (%)	TIEV[a] (real) ($bn)	Change on previous year (%)	TDEV[b] (real) ($bn)	Change on previous year (%)
3498.2	9.0	18.1	9.0	59.4	3.2
3442.6	-1.6	18.8	3.8	58.4	-1.7
3461.0	0.5	18.4	-1.9	58.1	-0.4
3388.0	-2.1	16.9	-8.4	55.9	-3.8
4368.7	28.9	17.5	4.1	55.3	-1.1
4661.9	6.7	18.5	5.4	56.4	1.9
4850.2	4.0	19.6	5.8	57.0	1.2
5054.8	42	20.7	5.8	58.0	1.7
5237.2	3.6	21.8	5.5	58.9	1.5
5393.4	3.0	23.2	6.1	59.9	1.7
5556.9	3.0	24.6	6.1	60.7	1.5
5718.1	2.9	26.1	6.4	61.4	1.1
5879.2	2.8	27.9	6.7	62.1	1.1
6023.5	2.5	29.9	7.1	62.4	0.5
6163.8	2.3	32.1	7.6	62.4	0.1
3.2	–	6.3	–	1.1	–

The tourism theories that I am interested in here in terms of their continued use in tourism and their relevance to community planning and development include Butler's Tourist Area Life Cycle, Leiper's Industrial Tourism System, Hall's Tourism Market System, Murphy's Ecological Model of Tourism Planning, Maslow's Hierarchy of Needs, Push and Pull Motivations, Plog's Psychographic Segmentation, Iso-Ahola's Travel Motivation Model and Doxey's Irridex. The theoretical discussion ends with an outline of Social Exchange Theory and Chaos (or

Complexity) Theory and how all of these theories relate to communities as well as tourism.

This is a purely selective and personal choice of theories, and while it may seem that they do not relate to each other, many are intricately connected – to the extent that their proponents (and at times, detractors) have combined elements from each to improve their own models. Also, some of these theories are not specific to tourism and may not have even been developed with it in mind. This is not a comprehensive list of tourism theory, even in the context of community development, but those that I have found to be most pervasive and persuasive in my own (theoretical and applied) work.

Understanding the process: Butler's Tourist Area Life Cycle (TALC)

Any tourism text from the Western world (and some others) of any worth includes some explanation of Butler's TALC. Due to this wealth of information, the description below is cursory. Developed in 1980 by Richard Butler, this life cycle is based on the product cycle concept. In his seminal article presenting his model, Butler acknowledges the contribution of others who have perceived a similar cycle in the real world (Butler 1980). Of particular interest is his quote from Christaller who, as early as 1960, stated:

> The typical course of development has the following pattern.
> Painters search out untouched and unusual places to paint. Step
> by step the place develops as a so-called artist colony. Soon a
> cluster of poets follows, kindred to the painters: then cinema
> people, gourmets, and the jeunesse dorée. The place becomes
> fashionable and the entrepreneur takes note. The fisherman's
> cottage, the shelter-huts become converted into boarding houses
> and hotels come on the scene. Meanwhile the painters have fled
> and sought out another periphery – periphery as related to space,
> and metaphorically as 'forgotten' places and landscapes. Only
> the painters with a commercial inclination who like to do well in
> business remain: they capitalize on the good name of this former
> painter's corner and on the gullibility of tourists. More and more
> townsmen choose this place, now in vogue and advertised in the
> newspapers. Subsequently the gourmets, and all those who seek

real recreation, stay away. At last the tourist agencies come with their package rate travelling parties: now, the indulged public avoids such places. At the same time, in other places the same cycle occurs again: more and more places come into fashion, change their type, turn into everybody's tourist haunt (Christaller 1960, cited Butler 1980, pp. 5–6).

Butler's Tourist Area Life Cycle (TALC) is illustrated in Figure 2.1.

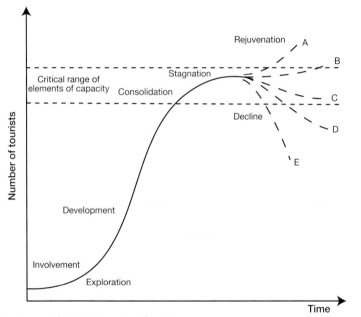

Figure 2.1 Butler's Tourist Area Life Cycle

Source: Redrawn from Butler 1980.

Basically, Butler described four stages that a destination (or place) goes through in terms of tourism development, plotting them on a bell curve. Initially, visitors arrive in small numbers and are supported by limited facilities, there is often poor access and restricted local knowledge of their needs. At this initial stage they are highly adventurous, looking for places that have not yet been 'ruined' by tourism. However, as other models demonstrate, visitors bring the seeds of change with them, and can be instrumental in actually creating the type of destination they despise. This is the great paradox of tourism mentioned at the beginning of the book, and one we will return to many times.

In the second stage, awareness of the destination is growing, as does the number of visitors and facilities. It is around this stage that the destination begins to increase its marketing, information dissemination and further facility provision. Its popularity grows rapidly and the destination moves into the third stage of the life cycle, which often becomes a form of mass tourism. Finally, as capacity levels are reached, the destination fails to cope with the social and environmental costs of mass tourism, and as a consequence the rate of increase in visitors declines until the destination fails.

However, as we know, millions of destinations around the world continue to support tourism. Butler recognises that there is a stage just before the decline where destinations can intervene and pursue a range of options to reinvigorate their tourism. For example, they may increase capacity, move to encourage a different market or different 'type' of tourism. However, these take political will and a strong theoretical (as well as practical) understanding of the complexities of tourism development and its relationship with the host community.

Butler notes that there is a need for tourism developers to understand this model – his words of warning from over 25 years ago still ring frighteningly true. Take these quotes as a case in point:

> The assumption that tourist areas will always remain tourist areas and be attractive to tourists appears to be implicit in tourism planning. Public, and private agencies alike, rarely, if ever, refer to the anticipated life span of a tourist area or its attractions. Rather, because tourism has shown an, as yet, unlimited potential for growth, despite economic recessions, it is taken for granted that numbers of visitors will continue to increase (Butler 1980, p. 10).

and

> These observations also suggest that a change of attitude is required on the part of those who are responsible for planning, developing, and managing tourist areas. Tourist attractions are not infinite and timeless but should be viewed and treated as finite

and possibly non-renewable resources. They could then be more carefully protected and preserved. The development of the tourist area could be kept within predetermined capacity limits, and its potential competitiveness maintained over a longer period (Butler 1980, p. 11).

Butler's model has been criticised as being too simplistic, but it forms a good basis from which further understanding can be developed. However, when we look at Butler's original paper, he acknowledges the complexity of what he is attempting to define, and recognises that testing will be needed to ascertain the accuracy of his model. There have been hundreds of academic papers and student dissertations either using or refuting the model, yet it remains a strong theory today as can be seen by two recent volumes based on his theory, which he has edited (Butler 2005).

Understanding the industry: Leiper's industrial tourism system

While Butler's model described what happens at a destination over a period of time, others were striving to explain the entire tourism system at any given time. They recognised that a tourist's journey is not only an integral part of the tourism experience, but also needs to be seen as part of the tourism industry, not simply the final destination. Neil Leiper developed a simple model based on the earlier work of other geographers to describe this system in terms of such tourist movements (Leiper 1995). While not the first to use the terms, Leiper refers to the Tourist Generating Region (TGR) and Tourist Destination Region (TDR) as well as considers what happens in-between in the Transit

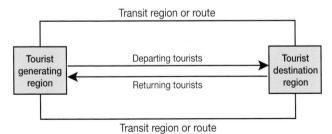

Figure 2.2 Leiper's industrial tourism system

Source: Leiper 1995.

Region (or route). These transit regions can also perform the role of a secondary destination – however, they are reliant on the fortunes of the primary destinations and may need to work closely with them.

For example, if a family is travelling from one major urban centre (city) to another by car, they will be driving through a number of other destinations on the way, such as small towns, larger towns, rural areas, national parks and so on. They may choose to stop at any of these places out of necessity (to purchase fuel or food, or for a toilet break) or interest (to walk in a national park, to experience a theme park ride or to photograph a view). While these places may not have been part of the traveller's primary (and final) destination, they provide services and experiences that enhance or detract from the overall tourism experience. In fact, it may be the attraction of the journey that encouraged the family to travel by car in the first instance.

It is important for a community to understand where it is in this model in terms of understanding its position with its visitor markets and relationship with other destinations in the model. If it is a stopover transit destination, certain businesses will be supported (such as restaurants and motels) while others may not (such as theme parks). A classic example of misunderstanding this role can be seen in Neil Leiper's account of the Big Banana in Australia (see Leiper 2002).

The industry as a market: Hall's tourism market system

Colin Michael Hall developed a model based on the work of Murphy (1985) and Hall and McArthur (1993; 1996) that forms the basis of his tourism discourse in his detailed introductory text (Hall 2003a). The model represents Hall's description of tourism as a complex system by incorporating the demand and supply elements of tourism into its behavioural and social context.

Simply put, Hall sees the tourism *experience* as central to tourism, which places the tourist or 'market' at the focal point of the entire system. Having the tourist experience as central may appear to be an obvious approach; remember that these theoretical models are not designed to be obscure, but to make even clearer how things exist and operate today. Hall maintains that the 'experience' is the result of both the tourist's needs and desires (demand) and the actual product provided (supply). This encourages us to think of the tourist experience in far broader terms than simply as the product that is supplied, which is how many may initially view tourism.

Hall also acknowledges that it is the tourism experience that creates impacts which in turn affect both the supply and demand elements.

While this is a good model in as far as it goes (and is part of an introductory text to tourism), Hall does not go far enough. He does not include the host community in this model, which is a significant omission, and one that needs to be considered by all players (or 'actors') in the system. Hall takes primarily a market-oriented approach, not a community approach. It is interesting that he claims to have based his work on Murphy's 1985 publication, *Tourism, A Community Approach* (cited in Hall 2003a, pp. 17, 20, 25). In light of this omission and its connection to community tourism, Murphy's model from that publication is outlined later in this chapter.

Human motivation: Maslow's hierarchy of human needs

While not initially developed with tourism in mind, Maslow's Hierarchy of Needs (see Maslow 1954) is used extensively in the tourism literature to describe the needs and experiences of travellers and their host communities. Developed in 1954 to describe post World War II culture, Maslow purported that there was a particular range of personal needs that had to be met in order for people to live and prosper. He presented this as a hierarchical pyramid, maintaining that the lower level needs had to be met before a person (or society) could 'progress' to the higher levels. At its base are the basic Physiological Needs of food, water, air and shelter, followed by the Safety and Security Needs of protection, order and stability on the next level. Once these two levels are met, people need to fill certain Social Needs that include affection, friendship and belonging.

Maslow identified two 'higher order' needs, namely Ego Needs that include the desire for prestige, success and self-respect, while at the apex of the pyramid are those seeking self-actualisation or self-fulfilment.

In the 1950s it may have been considered frivolous to apply Maslow's hierarchy to tourism, yet it can relate not only to the ways that certain people travel, but can also provide some insight into their motivations and behaviour. For example, travelling often entails the traveller not having his/her primary needs of shelter and safety immediately met. By arriving at a destination with nowhere to stay and little understanding of safety structures, a traveller may feel stressed and upset, requiring those needs to be filled immediately. Once accommodation, food and safety are met, the traveller can now consider socialising and ultimately move to the other levels.

Some have criticised the model, claiming that not all of one level needs to be met for a person to be at another level; that is, each level is not mutually exclusive. However, when considered in terms of travel and tourism, such a hierarchy does explain, to some extent, the continued success of guided tours and all-inclusive travel such as cruises.

Tourist motivation: Push and pull factors

As more people developed an interest in understanding tourism, researchers began to move from simply considering the numbers of people and the dollars they brought, to trying to understand why they come, why they return and why they do not (see Dann 1977 and Crompton 1979). Tourist motivation remains the most complex, fascinating and at times misunderstood area of tourism.

In one of the most-applied, developed and debated of the early tourism motivational theories, Dann (1977) attempted to explain not only why people travel, but also what drives their destination choice, arguing that earlier motivational research failed to address the question 'What *makes* people travel?' He considered a range of socio-psychological motives that drive a person to take a holiday, such as the need for a break due to high levels of stress or to escape routine (boredom), referring to these as 'push' factors. These are the factors that motivate us to consider taking a holiday. Dann identified a range of basic push motivations as being a reaction to anomie (a feeling of social alienation) or ego-enhancement (providing psychological boosts supported by a desire for fantasy). He then looked at the actual decision-making process of where to go, which tended to reside with the promotional activities of the tourism industry and destination, calling these 'pull' factors. Pull motivations consisted of the appealing attributes of a destination that the individual is seeking, such as the weather, beaches, cleanliness, recreation facilities, cultural attractions, natural scenery or even shopping (Dann 1977; Crompton 1979).

Crompton (1979) is also attributed as supporting and developing this 'push–pull' tourism dichotomy, referring to it in terms of a socio-psychological continuum. He considered the desire to escape (push motivations) as relating to the desire for prestige, fitness, to spend time with family. Crompton (1979, p. 145) notes that '… the essence of "break from routine" was, in most cases, either locating in a different place, or changing the social context from the work, usually to that of the family group…'. Crompton identified seven motives that provide more detail and relate broadly to Dann's push elements of anomie and ego-enhancement (Hall 2003a). The seven motives are noted below with Dann's categories in italics.

1   Escape from a perceived mundane environment *(anomie)*
2   Exploration and evaluation of self *(ego-enhancement)*
3   Relaxation *(anomie)*
4   Prestige *(ego-enhancement)*
5   Less constrained behaviour *(ego-enhancement)*
6   Enhancement of kinship relations *(anomie)*
7   Facilitation of social interaction *(anomie).*

Crompton (1979) identified two additional motives that fall into a cultural category: novelty and education. While they do not directly relate to Dann's categories, they can still be considered push factors.

In marketing terms, the 'push–pull' strategy takes on a slightly different meaning. Basically, a 'push' marketing strategy pushes the tourism product (experience) through to the consumer via the distribution channels (intermediaries such as travel agents, booking services, consolidators and so on). A 'pull' marketing strategy focuses on the end-user to induce them to purchase the travel product/experience, consequently 'pulling' the product through the distribution system.

Tourist motivation: Iso-Ahola's travel motivational model

In the 1980s, Iso-Ahola brought together many of the motivational factors discussed above, proposing that there are two sets of motivational forces driving individuals in all aspects of their life, namely the individual's desire to escape personal or interpersonal (for example, work) environment and the search for intrinsic rewards (Iso-Ahola 1982). He maintains that tourism simultaneously meets both of these forces, providing an outlet for avoiding something (such as work, family responsibilities) while seeking something (such as enjoyment, learning, relaxation) at the same time.

Iso-Ahola argues that it is futile to attempt to separate the reasons for travelling (motivations) from the benefits gained, as often they can be one and the same. For example, a reason for travelling such as exploring new places can also be a benefit, while a benefit of escaping from routine can also be a reason for travel (Iso-Ahola 1980).

This model of seeking and escaping resonates with many in the tourism industry linking in with Dann's push–pull theory and has received much critical support.

Refining tourist motivation: Plog's psychographic segmentation

Further refinements of the push–pull, escape-seeking dichotomies can be developed by considering them in terms of specific market segments or niches (Plog 1974). Early segmentation models were based almost exclusively on demographic data, such as country of residence, age, education level and income, and remains central to many of the first-run, basic segmentation groups we talk about in tourism (such as the 'baby boomers', 'generation X' and so on). However, it became clear that simple demographics did not explain everything.

It was a practitioner who was among the first to develop and make public a segmentation of groups of tourists by their psychological preferences and behaviour, namely Stanley Plog (1974). Plog divided tourists into two basic personality groups based on their interests, needs and behaviour. He suggested that tourists with different personality traits seek different travel experiences, selecting different forms of travel and types of destination. Understanding that a person does not always belong to a simple, cut and dried personality group, Plog placed them on a continuum, from one extreme to the other. He called these two profiles psychocentric and allocentric tourists. Simply put, Psychocentric tourists tend to be anxious, self-inhibited, non-adventuresome and concerned with 'little problems', while Allocentric travellers are self-confident, curious, adventurous and outgoing.

The astute reader will have noticed the use of the words 'tourist' and 'traveller' in the last sentence of the preceding paragraph. During the 1980s, the term 'tourist' came to represent the Psychocentric or mass tourist. In an attempt to differentiate their style of travelling, those Plog identified as Allocentric tourists preferred to consider themselves as travellers. However, as we moved into the 21st century, the term 'tourist' has been reclaimed by the industry and many of those (former) 'travellers' as an acknowledgement that they are outsiders visiting a place regardless of their Allo- or Psychocentric persuasion. While some may see this particular discussion as 'academic', it does reflect developments in the general travelling public's understanding of who and what they are. Also, tourists are no longer maligned in the media as ignorant, arrogant types – primarily due to the exponential growth of travel-based programs. This has occurred mainly because tourism has been recognised as an industry in its own right (along with the explosion of travel documentaries), and is in no small way due to the work done by the theorists and researchers.

Resident–visitor relations: Doxey's 'Irridex'

Apart from Butler's TALC, the theories and models discussed so far have focused primarily on the tourist. However, over time it became clear that without the support of all stakeholders, tourism would not be successful in the long term. This is particularly pertinent to the communities who host the visitors – the focus of this book. In 1975 Doxey proposed a simple set of stages describing a host community's response to and relationship with an increasing number of visitors. He proposed that local tolerance thresholds and the hosts' resistance to increasing tourism development were based on a fear of losing community identity, and that these host communities went through a series of stages, not unlike a 'hierarchy'. Doxey's model describes the community's responses to the cumulative effect of tourism development on social interrelations in the host community (Doxey 1975).

In the early stages of tourism, the community is euphoric, welcoming the potential economic and social benefits tourism may bring. This then moves to a state of apathy as the early promises are not realised by all members, moving on to annoyance with the inconveniences of the increased numbers of visitors, such as limited parking spaces and crowding. According to Doxey's model, if the crowding increases, residents begin to show antagonism towards the visitors, which may ultimately be expressed through violence. The final stage that Doxey

Table 2.2 Doxey's Irridex Model of Host Irritation

	Social relationships	Power relationships
Euphoria	Visitors and investors welcome	Little planning or formalised control
		Greater potential for influence to be exerted by locals (not often taken)
Apathy	Visitors taken for granted	Marketing is the prime focus of plans
	More formal relationships between hosts and guests	Tourism industry lobby grows in power
Annoyance	Resident misgivings about tourism	Planners attempt to control by increasing infrastructure rather than limiting growth
	Range of saturation points approached	Local protest groups develop to challenge institutionalised tourism power
Antagonism	Irritations openly expressed	Remedial planning fighting against pressures of increased promotion to offset declining reputation of destination
	Residents perceive tourists as the cause of the problems	Power struggle between interest groups

Source: Doxey 1975.

described is that of resignation, with many residents becoming resigned to the effects of tourism, possibly altering their behaviour or simply avoiding visitors.

Doxey referred to this model as an 'Irridex' and, while it is extremely simple, it has remained one that is often referred to by community planners when considering the potential negative aspects of tourism. However, not all relations between tourists and the host community are as simple or inevitable, which Doxey also acknowledges. Table 2.2 outlines the social and power relationships in Doxey's model. For now, we are primarily focusing on the social relationships. In Chapter 4, the concept of different levels and types of power in a community are covered in more detail.

This Irridex can be considered in conjunction with Butler's TALC, where the exploratory phase on the life cycle correlates with Doxey's euphoria and moves up along the curve to antagonism when carrying capacity is exceeded. By combining the two, we now have a model that considers what's happening from the tourists' and host community's aspect as the destination life cycle progresses.

Resident–visitor relations: Acculturation and social exchange theory

Where Doxey considered the cumulative effects of tourism on a community and their response in general, the theory of Social Exchange is more concerned with the interactions between hosts and guests. The theory assumes that such interactions can flow one-way from host to guest or vice versa or in varying degrees of two-way exchanges (Nunez 1977).

Basically, when two cultures come into contact for a period of time, an exchange of ideas will occur. The model describes an initiation of the exchange, followed by either an exchange of information or no exchange. Where the exchange has occurred, there is an evaluation of that exchange by all parties. If the evaluation is positive and seen as equitable between the two parties, both will continue with the relationship; if the evaluation is negative, one or both parties may attempt to withdraw from the process. This theory is primarily behaviourally focused, concentrating on the social process of reciprocity, not on the psychological motivations of the actors (participants).

It is the nature of the exchange in terms of the various power relations between the parties that is of particular interest. The exchange may be unequal with one culture dominating the other in terms of the type of contact, socio-economic characteristics of the members or size of population. This is particularly evident in tourism to less developed nations, marginal and indigenous communities where the visitor tends to have higher education and income levels than the communities they are visiting. Such inequalities can be used in a constructive way to develop a community, which is the premise of this publication. However, without sufficient understanding or planning it is unlikely, as the group with the greater power tends to dominate, be that consciously or unconsciously. This may result in what is known as 'acculturation' (Nunez 1977).

'Acculturation' is related to social exchange. This can occur when one culture (the less dominant) starts to take on elements of the other culture as a result of their exchange. Related to this also is the 'demonstration effect' where locals desire to possess the accoutrements of modern Western society (the primary source of tourists) as witnessed when they deal with (undertake social exchange with) these tourists.

The level and type of acculturation depends on the type of contact, the socio-economic characteristics of the members and the size of the population and may be a positive process, even though it is usually presented in negative terms. Acculturation may not always affect the day-to-day lives of residents, particularly where tourism and tourists are isolated from the main community, but even learning to speak the language of the tourist may begin the process (a concern often expressed by those who come from the cautionary platform discussed in Chapter 1). The results of acculturation are particularly evident in less developed nations and indigenous communities, but acculturation occurs to some extent in virtually all communities that have some form of visitation or migration. The worst case is where a culture becomes completely subsumed by the dominant one, losing what it was that people came to experience in the first place. (There's that paradox again ...)

Some sociologists who believe that retaining one's culture is paramount have dismissed tourism as being too socially disruptive and destructive. However, travel and tourism are not going to cease, so it is important to acknowledge the potential issues that may arise, such as acculturation. Nevertheless, as I have inferred in the previous paragraph, not all change is bad and some is inevitable (and desirable) in any living community, so it is important not to view all of the so-called negative aspects of tourism as such. As Hall notes:

> Despite concerns over undesirable social impacts, Australian governments have long held out hope that tourism might be a mechanism for the economic development of Aboriginal communities, particularly with respect to reducing Aboriginal unemployment (Hall 2003a, p. 285).

Acculturation and social exchange are intricately intertwined with power and power relations in a community and those who influence it (tourists, commercial enterprises, governments and so on). We re-visit these elements in Chapter 4.

Tourism as a living system: Chaos-complexity theory

Faulkner and Russell argue that tourism is a living system that needs to be treated as a dynamic entity. They cite Wardrop, who refers to living systems transcending matter not so much because they 'are animated by some vital essence outside the laws of physics and chemistry, but because a population of small things following simple rules of interaction can behave in eternally surprising ways' (1992 in Faulkner and Russell 1997, p. 97). They argue that the essence of complex, lifelike systems such as tourism lies not in viewing them in a top-down manner, but from the bottom up, where individuals driven by simple rules are the basis of these complex (or chaotic) systems.

Another element of this theory is what has become known as the 'butterfly effect' (Gleick 1987) where a small change can precipitate a chain reaction that culminates in a dramatic event or fundamental shift. Gleick shows how a butterfly flapping its wings in Beijing is capable of setting off a series of events that results in a cyclone in Florida. Further, Faulkner and Russell introduce Waldrop's (1992) 'edge of chaos' phenomenon, where a system is in a state of tenuous equilibrium on the verge of moving into a rapidly changing state, such as an ecosystem that is stable, yet continually perched on the precipice of collapse – a change in any additional element (crowding, pollution) may send the system into chaos. However, if one change is able to be offset by another, then the system remains stable, in equilibrium.

In order to illustrate the concepts of chaos-complexity theory in terms of tourism, Faulkner and Russell take Butler's TALC and rein-terpret it in this framework. They envisage the phases of the Butler cycle (exploration, involvement, development, consolidation, stagnation and decline or rejuvenation) as being driven by events that are essentially random. For example, at the exploration stage the random encounters between travellers and local residents induce a few residents to provide commercial services, which in turn opens up the opportunity for others to do so. Eventually there is a complex web of tourism service providers which results in more people coming to visit and so on throughout the cycle. Each stage of the cycle represents a period of instability where there are fundamental shifts in the relationships between the various groups (Faulkner and Russell 1997).

This alternative perspective presented by Faulkner and Russell has been well received by many eminent researchers in the tourism field, and is one of the theoretical elements, perspectives or frameworks that can be used to understand how tourism can be used (or not) to develop specific communities. Faulkner and Russell conclude that

… an approach to scientific investigation involving the adoption of paradigms according to their utility in specific situations is more pragmatic and potentially productive. Thus, rather than assuming that the alternative paradigms are mutually exclusive, each should be applied to certain domains of the phenomenon within a field, depending on where they prove to be more or less useful (Faulkner and Russell 1997, p. 100).

Basic business theory

As can be seen from many of the so-called 'tourism' theories introduced above, most of them have their genesis in other disciplines, such as psychology, geography, sociology and marketing. As tourism is a business, it is also important to consider some of the basic business theories that underpin current business thinking.

There is a plethora of information on business management, some of which can be applied to tourism and community development. The following theories have been selected as pertinent examples of business management as viewed through the lens of the main subject of this book – community development through tourism. As with the tourism theories outlined earlier, this section is not a comprehensive discussion of tourism business management, but an attempt to present some of the relevant theories that can be applied in the field. Leiper supports this effort when he says that '[m]anaging is about imposing and maintaining order of some kind in purposeful human organisations, appropriate to its aims' (Leiper 2003, p. 116). By imposing a few of the major business theories that underpin the work presented in this book on you, the reader, I hope to bring some order to the topic.

Over the past 20 years there has been a shift in business behaviour from pure competition through to cooperation, customer focus and the current knowledge-based focus, however, competition theories remain pertinent to business management in the 21st century. By looking briefly at the theories espoused by some of the major business commentators and researchers including Porter (1998), Lampel and Mintzberg (1996) and Drucker *et al.* (1997) we can trace such development.

Porter, often considered as the father of modern business management, identified three broad categories for developing business strategies: cost leadership, differentiation and focus. While he was referring to single businesses, much of this concept can be considered in terms of a community, particularly if it is competing with other community groups for tourists or other resources.

Organisations following a cost leadership strategy aim to produce their services (or goods) at a lower cost than their competition so that they can reduce their prices in a price-sensitive market, or maintain the original price, but net a higher profit. For those who follow the price reduction path, economies of scale are needed in order to maintain a reasonable profit margin, and this in tourism is seen as 'mass tourism'.

Those who take the differentiation approach aim to convince their customers that there is a unique element of the product (service or even community) for which they are prepared to pay a premium. In tourism, where sheer numbers of visitors is an issue both environmentally and socially, often fewer visitors paying a higher price is seen as desirable. This requires a high level of understanding the market, which comes from in-depth and ongoing research and development, but is often a key to differentiating certain communities (or places).

The final strategy proposed by Porter is one directed towards a specific market need or niche, which is the focus of much tourism interest. However, once again this requires a high level of knowledge and research.

In direct relationship to a 'community', many tourism business operate in business clusters, which Porter defines as '... a critical mass of companies in a particular location (a country, state, region or even a city)' (Porter 1998, p. 7). This challenges the traditional notion of competing businesses working in direct competition with each other, and once again relates directly to tourism in communities. In order for tourism to be successful, the individual operators need to work together in order to create an environment that visitors wish to experience – very few individual businesses can do this alone as the basis of the tourism industry is the small to medium-sized enterprise. It is this clustering that often creates or supports the community and its development. This has been referred to as 'coopetition' (see Ritchie and Crouch 2003). Classic examples of tourism clusters can be seen in rural and regional communities such as the country town of Maldon in central Victoria, Australia, where the entire town has been classified by the National Trust and the businesses rely on their heritage and small town community assets. Urban examples include the rejuvenation of Hollywood Boulevard and ethnic communities such as the Chinatown precincts in many Western cities.

While I referred to the McDonaldization of business and culture, I also noted that one reaction to that is a desire to return to 'community'. Related to this, there has been a shift towards various levels of customisation. Lampel and Mintzberg (1996) believe that businesses operate along a continuum from pure standardisation through to various levels of customisation: segmented, customised, tailored and pure. This is similar to Porter's niche strategies. Lampel and Mintzberg note that there is a relationship here with tourism, where it '... has been common in transportation [and] leisure ... where firms often respond to the needs of individual customers despite the ceaseless drive toward greater economies of scale' (Lampel and Mintzberg 1996, p. 23).

Drucker *et al.* (1997) acknowledge the development of what is known as the knowledge-based economy of the late 20th century, where competitive advantages are less linked with money and technology and more with knowledge. They note that knowledge '... constantly makes itself obsolete, with the result that today's advanced knowledge is tomorrow's ignorance' (Drucker *et al.* 1997, p. 20). This in turn impacts on *who* is taking a holiday along with *where* and *what* they want to experience, as the developed and emerging countries are coming closer together through the development of their knowledge (Beeton 2004b). We are now seeing many emerging nations in terms of tourist generating regions resulting in a fluid move between hosts and guests in many communities.

As a service industry, tourism operations and communities must primarily focus on providing the customers they wish to attract with what they want. Consequently, communities must decide who their customers are (or will be) through undertaking marketing research as well as using existing marketing information from sources such as government agencies, marketing publications and academic institutions.

How these theories relate to communities as well as tourism

Tourism operates in communities, whether they be spatially defined such as countries, cities and towns, or in terms of human interest and activity. Therefore, all of the theories outlined above relate in some way to developing certain communities through tourism. However, few theorists considered tourism in terms of community until Peter Murphy began to look at this in the 1980s. While his work is widely cited, it has not been until the later part of the 20th century that the notion of community development through tourism (and its inherent problems) really comes to the fore. As I postulate in Chapter 1, I see this particularly as a reaction to some of the elements of globalisation and internationalisation.

While it is tempting to synthesise the theories outlined here into one 'mega theory' or model of tourism in communities, this would create a complex yet prescriptive model that would actually negate any benefit the theories can provide. There is no grand narrative or 'theory of everything' – however, as noted in the chaos-complexity discussion, we can apply what is relevant. That said, many researchers and practitioners have combined two theories in order to gain a more complete picture (especially when considering the supply and demand sides), such as Doxey's Irridex and Butler's TALC as indicated at the end of the section on the Irridex. Others have taken the Irridex model and empirically tested it (in the real world), often amending or adding to it from their own findings, which in turn can develop new models. Such is the case with Sofield's Adaptindex described below.

From irritation to adaptation: Sofield's Adaptindex

Sofield has over 20 years' experience in working with and studying indigenous communities in the Asia-Pacific region. His work with these communities, ranging from the macro world regional level to national and micro local levels, has provided him with one of the most comprehensive and in-depth understandings of community development and tourism's role in it. In his seminal work, *Empowerment for Sustainable Tourism Development*, published in 2003, Sofield demonstrates how he has moved through various theoretical paradigms as part of his own journey (Sofield 2003). He accurately summarises some of the more sociological paradigms that I have not gone into here, including post World War II development theory, modernisation theory, colonialism, dependency and underdevelopment theory through to sustainable development and community empowerment (see Sofield 2003, Chapter 2). These last two are considered in some detail in this book and underpin much of the current work in community development and tourism, particularly community empowerment, which is introduced in Chapter 4.

Sofield contributes to many areas of tourism theory and as noted above, one of the tourism theories that Sofield considered in his work is Doxey's Irridex. Sofield argues that the process from euphoria to antagonism is not linear and that '… in many instances the reality of tourism within the social space of a community will result in adaptancy over time with a degree of power sharing denied by Doxey's original hypothesis' (Sofield 2003, p. 327). As an example, he cites one of his case studies where the residential community put tourism to work for them rather than them working for tourism and moved from euphoria straight into sustained acceptance through a continual process of adaptancy.

Sofield has relabelled Doxey's 'stages' (which indicates a linear progression) as 'states of affairs' (where the community can move to, between, return to or completely skip), and sees the entire process as one of adaptancy. Consequently, Sofield has named his model the 'Adaptindex'.

The community's role in the tourism system: Murphy's ecological model of tourism planning

Murphy is acknowledged as one of the early proponents of the position and role of communities in tourism. His seminal 1985 work remains one of the most cited sources and is a good starting point for anyone looking at the role of communities in tourism as well as providing a general introduction to tourism (Murphy 1985). That said, it is some years since it was first published, and Murphy along with other researchers have built on this early work, many of whom are referred to throughout this book.

Murphy primarily takes a geographic approach when he considers communities, defining them in terms of their physical footprint on the earth; yet he also considers temporal elements (that is, the place over time). In addition, he is primarily concerned here with *destination* communities, not communities of travellers or their origin.

He proposed that tourism should be viewed as 'part of a destination community's ecosystem … where an ecosystem is "any area of nature that includes living organisms and non-living substances interacting to produce an exchange of materials between the living and non-living parts"…' (Murphy 1985 and Odum 1970, cited Murphy 1985, p. 166).

Part of the strength in applying the ecosystem concept is its inherent nature of reciprocity. Murphy also argues that by taking this approach it is sufficiently flexible to apply it to any scale of destination community.

Murphy presents two models, the first one being a general hierarchical model, with the second demonstrating how it may be applied to a specific situation (ecological model). For the sake of this discussion, we are simply going to consider the hierarchical model and include examples from the ecological model as required.

In this model, Murphy has three concentric circles, coming from the centre which contains local decisions (such as resident participation and site capabilities), while the next circle out refers to regional objectives (such as ecological models) and the outer circle relates to national goals (economic and social policies). Four primary considerations are presented as spokes of the wheel emanating out from the local area through the regional to national level: environmental, social, economic and business. Each spoke has a negative and positive aspect for each of the primary considerations. For example, business considerations relate directly to the positive element of having satisfied visitors, but if visitors have been treated as 'prey' by the local, regional and national groups, this will have a direct negative aspect.

While this model is (as Murphy acknowledges) quite simple and unable to measure the extent of the positive and negative elements of each consideration, it does demonstrate the intricate interrelationships between all elements.

One of the main legacies of this relatively early work of Murphy's is to stress the importance of including local communities in every stage of tourism planning. He emphasises that as the scale of planning decreases (from the outer national circle to the inner local one) 'more public participation should be expected and encouraged' (Murphy 1985, p. 171). This call for participatory planning did not start with Murphy, nor has it stopped – as any community development professional knows, such planning is difficult and time-consuming, therefore often it can be neglected in favour of a top-down planning approach.

This issue is one that is continually raised throughout this publication, particularly in Chapter 4 when the area of 'community empowerment' is discussed. There is no easy answer to ensuring effective community involvement in tourism development. However, we aim to present some realistic approaches, particularly in the case studies such as the one at the end of this chapter.

Community based tourism

By this stage – if you have read this book through from the beginning – you can be forgiven for sighing at the thought of yet another term to describe tourism that occurs in a community. However, there has been a proliferation of research and literature around the concept of 'Community Based Tourism' (CBT) to warrant its mention here. I did not introduce it earlier, as the concepts underpinning it relate closely to those we have been discussing, making this part of the book the best place to consider the notion of CBT. And, of course, we now have 'Community Based Ecotourism' (Jones 2004), which I will not discuss independently as I believe the aspects of ecotourism, tourism and communities have been well covered and can be incorporated into this discussion.

CBT aims to create a more sustainable tourism industry, focusing on the host community in terms of planning and maintaining tourism development. This concept was coming to the fore by the 1990s, with Pearce (1992) suggesting that CBT presents a way to provide an equitable flow of benefits to all affected by tourism through consensus-based decision-making and local control of development. This theory is close to the elements discussed in this book, yet as is illustrated in many of the case studies and other examples, real consensus and true local control is not always possible, practical or even desired by some of the communities we work with.

There have been numerous criticisms of CBT which, in many ways, has now moved out of today's community tourism lexicon. As presented in the 1990s, CBT differs from general community development theory and process in that it does not have the transformative intent of community development and does not focus on community empow-erment. In addition, local communities are presented as homogenous entities for whom 'consensus' is rare; and finally proponents of CBT failed to ignore the external (power-based) constraints to local control (Blackstock 2005). This brings us to the vexed issue of power relations and empowerment (as discussed in Chapter 4), which must be understood and addressed in all community-inclusive processes. CBT was a good start, but we have moved on towards more inclusive and effective community based tourism planning and development. However, issues and difficulties remain, as illustrated in the case studies in many of these chapters, particularly the one at the end of Chapter 4.

From theory to practice: The case of the irritated host

The small rural village of Goathland in the United Kingdom has witnessed not only several tourist area life cycles as described by Butler, but also is a classic case supporting Doxey's Irridex – a theory often cited by opponents of overdevelopment of tourism in communities. Whether the community ultimately suffers or benefits from the tourism it receives is not the focus of this case – we leave the reader to decide.

For many years, Goathland, a village of approximately 300 residents in the middle of a national park, was a base for people wishing to go tramping (hiking or walking) on the surrounding moors of North Yorkshire. The village had a strong, thriving (if specialised) tourism industry supporting these primarily middle-class nature-lovers, with many B&Bs and small hotels supporting the annual visitor population of 200 000.

In 1992 a television series began filming in the village, based on the 'Constable' books by Yorkshire resident, Nicholas Shea. It follows the fortunes of a small community in the 1960s, revolving around the local police force. The series is still being shown on TV stations around the world and much of it is still filmed on site. It was not anticipated that the series would continue to the present day, so the effect of long-term filming and tourist interest in the village was not considered. In fact, most of the village, apart from one resident who registered several early complaints, welcomed the filming and subsequent notoriety of the series. The popular series is known as *Heartbeat*, with Goathland standing in as the fictional village of Aidensfield.

Information provided by the North Yorkshire Moors National Park Authority (NYMNPA) presents an interesting timeline of

Table 2.3 Doxey's Irridex Model of Host Irritation and Goathland Community

	Social relationships	Power relationships	
Euphoria	Visitors and investors welcome	Little planning or formalised control Greater potential for influence to be exerted by locals (not often taken)	
By October 1993, visitation was up to 480 000 per annum.			
Apathy	Visitors taken for granted More formal relationships between hosts and guests	Marketing is the prime focus of plans Tourism industry lobby grows in power	
Annoyance	Resident misgivings about tourism Range of saturation points approached	Planners attempt to control by increasing infrastructure rather than limiting growth Local protest groups develop to challenge institutionalised tourism power	
By December 1995, visitation was up to 1.19 million annual visitors.			
Antagonism	Irritations openly expressed Residents perceive tourists as the cause of the problems	Remedial planning fighting against pressures of increased promotion to offset declining reputation of destination Power struggle between interest groups	

Source: Adapted from Beeton 2005a.

Goathland		
Timing	Theme	Community response
First two years (1992–93)	Finding problems – Seeking solutions	NYMNPA asked to take action: Attended Parish Council meeting – concern over possible visitor pressure leads to additional meeting. Park looks at range of options: – extension of existing car park – one-way system – additional car park. Open meeting planned by NYMNPA: – to take the form of community-led ideas being expressed and discussed by the community. Over 60 villagers turn up. NYMNPA proposed 4 coach bays as part of car park improvements. New signposts more in keeping with the village ambience.

1994	Pragmatism: recognition of limitation of resources and powers	YTV asked for financial assistance to alleviate traffic problems. Reports of positive economic and employment impacts to counter negative stories.
1995	Community tries to regain control	Objections to coach parking plans and yellow lines. Residents association formed on the 'no coach park and yellow lines' platform. Parking restriction proposals agreed by Parish Council, Duchy, NYMNPA, police and Highways.

1996	Back to basics? Opposition groups re-form	One resident questions re the 'legality' of filming in the village without sanction from NYMNPA. NYMNPA responds that it is legal. Residents claim their freedom of movement is curtailed when filming is taking place. Tensions heighten between village and YTV with concern expressed over their use of the car park. Some residents oppose parking restrictions as a blot on the village and drive traditional visitors away – campaign launched.

community attitudes towards the tourists that began to come to Goathland in search of the *Heartbeat* sites and small village experience, especially when considered in terms of Doxey's Irridex.

As explained in Chapter 1, when presenting empirical, real-world cases, they rarely fit absolutely into the theoretical area they have been used to illustrate. However, it can be seen from Table 2.3 that the Goathland community has moved from overall welcome through to a form of passive resistance and even antagonism. Some community members have reacted more strongly than others, with some of them actually changing the way they live in their homes due to the intrusion of visitors invading their privacy (Mordue 1999, 2001; Beeton 2005a). For example, some have moved their living areas to the back of their homes so that tourists cannot peer in to their daily lives and impose on their privacy. This is a form of adaptancy, and as such we can also look at this in terms of Sofield's (2003) Adaptindex. However, for the sake of this illustration we will remain with Doxey, as the model is still effective in assisting our understanding of the Goathland community.

We can also see some elements here of Gleick's (1987) 'butterfly effect' and a community teetering on the verge of collapse (or chaos). Back in the early 1990s when the series was being developed and sites chosen, the producers had no idea that it would be so popular and have such effects on the Goathland community. In actual fact, they only believed it would last for one series, so had paid little thought to any ongoing chain of events (Beeton 2005a).

What has also occurred at Goathland is that there are now two quite separate, and at times conflicting, tourism segments visiting the town, that of the earlier, predominantly middle-class visitor to the national park and now the primarily working-class day tripper into the village (Beeton 2005a). They not only compete for resources and services, but at times one group alters the very resource the other desires (for example, peace and quiet). Beeton notes that:

> Goathland attracts both classes and type of visitor, however the friction is evident, even to a casual observer. Ironically, it is the rural idyll presented in *Heartbeat* that is now

encouraging the new, lower class tourist to the region, who may in turn squeeze out the traditional, middle class nature tourist (Beeton 2005a, p. 104).

These conflicting differences can also be illustrated through applying Butler's TALC to each different market segment as it can be argued they are looking for a completely different tourism product at the destination, which are at different stages on the life cycle. For example, the level of nature-based visitors who tramp over the moors does not appear to be affecting the capacity of the environment (with a few exceptions of overuse of some paths) or the village community, putting it at a mature level that would have been consolidating or even stagnating. The film-induced visitors coming to the village do not impact at all on the natural environment of the moors as they either arrive by road or train, park in the village (or alight at the station) and spend most of their time in the village. This has put high pressure on the environment of the village, its services and community. However, it is not declining. Ultimately, this visitor may replace the nature-based visitor due to their appropriation of the village services and frustration of the community.

This raises an important question: Can two different tourism products with two distinctly different markets survive in a small community? If this situation is left to 'run its course', there is a strong possibility that both forms of tourism move into decline. If such decline brings them both to a sustainable level, then such equilibrium may be desirable.

However, as we all know, small communities are not entities entirely to themselves and, according to Murphy's model, may be central but are surrounded by regional and national influences and concerns. In the case of Goathland, the North Yorkshire Moors Tourist Authority is actively promoting further filming of movies and TV series in the region. So, the saga continues ...

3

Strategic tourism planning for communities

All organisations (companies, communities, destinations and so on) experience three 'states of being' in terms of their approach to planning and managing. The first state is 'reactive management', where all the organisation's time and effort seems to be taken up responding to problems as they arise – in other words, reacting to a situation. Of course, things do happen that cannot be specifically planned for (I am writing this chapter with the shadows of Hurricane Katrina and more bombings in Bali), but simply reacting and not planning can be disastrous as we have seen in some of the events I've just mentioned. The second state is where many tourism businesses and communities tend to be, which is at the level of 'compliance management' where systems have been established and plans implemented to comply with legislation and regulation. The 'big stick' approach of some governing bodies does have some effect. However, this is still not the ideal state to be in, as compliance can occur in a negative and powerless environment – 'We have no choice, we must just do this'. Such attitudes do not create a positive, responsible and responsive business or community.

The final state of being (which any half-awake reader will realise is the preferred state!) is where businesses are managed proactively and communities are permitted to plan for their future as well (see the 'Empowerment' section in the next chapter). From a business perspective, the organisation attempts to foresee hazards and even future regulations, and works systematically to minimise their effects on the environment and community as well as on their business concerns. The elements of strategic planning and management come into this final stage.

The term 'strategic' comes from the military and relates to battle planning. Theorists have taken this term into the world of business, equating 'battle' with 'competitiveness', which may be true in some instances, but in terms of tourism and community development we need to refine our use of this term in a less combative framework. As Leiper (2002, p. 1818) cogently argues, tourism businesses 'are about achieving the purpose of each organisation, which is not beating the competitors but satisfying the customers'. This often requires working with so-called competitors, not battling against them. As noted in earlier chapters, the tourism industry revolves around coopetition, with examples of such cooperation evident in airline alliances, cooperative regional marketing exercises, private–public partnerships, philanthropic relationships and industry associations. Consequently, the term 'strategic' now reflects the notion of *flexible* planning rather than outright competition.

This chapter focuses primarily on the areas of strategic planning and management, moving from a discussion of them in commercial enterprises to applying them in community development and tourism. Some 'strategic' tools that have been effectively used in a community tourism perspective are outlined, particularly the often-cited notions of triple bottom line, benchmarks and indicators. Social Representation Theory is introduced as a way to understand a community's attitudes towards tourism development, with a case study that demonstrates how this can be done. The related areas of community empowerment and the complex nature of power relations in a community are discussed in Chapter 4.

Strategic planning

Strategies need to be planned and communicated to others, so they are usually written down in some form or other. In the past, many strategic plans were so physically impressive that they made very good doorstops but were useful for little else. There has been a move towards presenting these plans in simpler formats that are easy to read and understand, and can be quickly updated as circumstances change (something that must be central to all tourism planning today with the political and environmental uncertainty around the world). Many are now presented electronically, which makes them easier to change, and not even printed out – which may save on trees! Strategic plans should not be confused with operational or tactical (the military rhetoric remains) plans which are more short term (one to two years), outlining how the strategies from the strategic plan will be applied. Table 3.1 outlines the basic differences between strategic and tactical (operational) planning in terms of length of time, who is responsible, what information is needed and the degree of detail in the plan. Strategic plans tend to be bigger-picture, longer-term plans for three to five years containing the overall goals of an organisation (community or destination).

Simply put, there are three primary steps involved in strategic planning and management: strategy formulation, strategy implementation (tactical area) and evaluation (Murphy & Murphy 2004), which are all considered in more detail below. The evaluation area also relates to maintaining some sort of control over the process by developing reasonable tools to measure the degree of success of the strategies. This is extremely important when we consider communities and tourism as many of the goals are not easy to measure. This is covered later in the chapter, where we look at some ways of measuring the effects of tourism in communities.

Table 3.1 Comparison of strategic and tactical planning

	Strategic planning	Tactical planning
Duration	Long term (>3 years)	Short term (<3 years)
Done by	Senior management; community leaders	Middle management; individual businesses and organisations
Necessary information	Primarily external information – regional, national, international	Primarily information from within the organisation/ community
Degree of detail	Broad in nature; subjectively based	Detailed information and analysis; objectively based

Source: Adapted from Beeton 2004b.

Strategic community tourism management and planning

Much of the literature on strategic management revolves around large commercial enterprises, with all of their concomitant reporting and information structures, handled by numerous (presumably trained) managers. However, strategic planning and management are also important for amorphous groups such as 'communities'. By establishing a (shared) vision, aims and goals for the future of a community, members can work towards realising their desired outcomes individually and collectively.

As noted previously, strategy formulation, implementation and evaluation are the main procedural steps to be undertaken when strategically managing an enterprise, destination or community. In terms of tourism to and within communities, the first step of strategy formulation includes a series of decisions taken to determine the mission or vision of the community (usually a destination) and the specific objectives and policies required to realise that vision. To give a somewhat simplistic example, a destination community may agree that its overall vision is to be a vibrant, exciting community that retains its young people in meaningful employment and regards its older members as valuable participants. The objectives and policies that flow from such a vision may include encouraging tourists to visit, training young people to open up tourism service businesses and using the historical knowledge of the older members to interpret the place for visitors.

Once the objectives and so on are established, the proposed ways to achieve them need to be implemented. Often the process stops here as the community believes they have completed the planning and management processes. However, the strategies must be tested in order to ascertain the levels of success and/or identify problematic areas. This is a reiterative process that continually feeds back to itself, over a period determined in the strategy itself.

Central to developing successful strategies is understanding what members think and feel about any changes to or development in their community. Many methods can be applied to acquire some such understanding, and the one that I have found to be the most illuminating is based on Social Representation Theory, which is outlined below, along with my reasons for making such a statement.

Social representation theory and community planning

As established in the first chapter of this book, communities are complex entities comprising many different groups or stakeholders. These groups can have different values, attitudes and perspectives and some may have a stronger voice that can mask the disenfranchised, disadvantaged, weaker and less articulate community members (Ife 1995). However, many community based studies have tended to treat the 'community' as a single entity with a homogenous attitude towards tourism development issues. This has resulted in misunderstandings that are reflected in unsuccessful development or dissatisfied community groups who resent the changes, particularly in relation to tourism and tourists, going down the path of Doxey's Irridex as outlined in Chapter 2. Ultimately, some communities may even break down entirely.

In order to prevent such a situation, we need to understand the more internal, complex and in-depth community relationships regarding tourism in and to these communities. In their publication, *Tourism Community Relationships*, Pearce, Moscardo and Ross (1996) build on earlier broad-based community tourism work by introducing the concept of social representation as a means to achieve this. They maintain that the more commonly used approaches to studying people's attitudes, from both the psychological and sociological aspects, do not take into consideration where such interrelationships and attitudes come from (Pearce *et al.* 1996). They have applied Social Representation Theory (SRT) as developed by Moscovici in the early 1970s to their own tourism community research, demonstrating its significance as a means for understanding what is going on in a particular community (Pearce *et al.* 1996; Moscardo and Pearce 2003).

The central premise of SRT is that there are groupings of individuals in a community who will have similar values or attitudes (social representations), but it does not presume to know what elements make up these groups nor what their attitudes may be. In other words, individual attitudes are sought and identified, then they are described according to whatever similarities the members with those attitudes may have. As this is driven by the subjects being studied, SRT is an emic form of study, providing each person with the opportunity to drive the research, rather than the researcher prescribing the path. This is the key to understanding how a particular community may operate, yet is often missed by those working with communities due to them taking a more prescriptive approach when looking for attitudes and also in segmenting the community. The most common approach has been to look at the groups and issues that other researchers have found to be prevalent in communities, assume they are common to their community and try to make them fit. This often occurs due to time and resource constraints, but is not always successful and, at its worst, can be destructive and borders on stereotyping all communities. As Moscardo and Pearce (2003, p. 265) explain,

> [s]ocial representations are complex meta systems of everyday knowledge and include values, beliefs attitudes and explanations... [and] are not deterministic or static. They vary along many dimensions including the level of consensus about them, their level of detail and how they are communicated. Individuals can and do influence, create and change social representations.

SRT occurs in a socially determined context and emphasises more of the social influences and interactions of the community and society, not just personal interpretations of events. Pearce *et al.* (1996) outline a three-step process to help establish and identify social representations, the first being to identify the individual concerns and secondly establish their intensity. The third step is to then establish a list of priorities and levels of performance.

For example, some studies suggest that increased crowding is an important issue for all members of a community – yet there may be those who enjoy the liveliness that extra people may bring to a community and not consider crowding to be an issue. The two different groups of people may in the past have been differentiated by their age (for example), but now there are other elements that differentiate them. However, as other studies have grouped 'age' and 'concern of crowding' together, they continue to do so. If research is done from an SRT perspective, the participants are simply asked to list what the issues are that concern them. If 'crowding' comes up as an answer more than a few times, then those people who have responded that way are clustered together and studied to find what personal attributes they have in common. Instead of age, we may find that this group has lived in the area for a similar amount of time, may have come from another place to settle here, may have similar levels of education, similar types of employment, attitudes to development, and so on. Once these similarities have been ascertained, this now becomes a particular group with a certain social representation (or attitude).

By using this process, the people being surveyed are telling us (the researchers) what concerns them and who they are. This is one of the most important elements of community development, particularly in terms of individual and community empowerment, as discussed in the next chapter. It provides a more contextual, interrelated study of the human community condition, offering a framework that assists in explaining how groups of people understand and react to certain phenomena (Beeton 2005a). The case study at the end of the chapter is a real-life empirical example of how SRT can be used to help our understanding of tourism and community development and can be utilised to assist in the strategic planning of many of our communities.

Measuring communities and tourism

In order to understand and communicate to others where a community is placed in terms of its progress and development, measures that can be reported on need to be established. This in turn can also reflect the relationship between elements of that community and tourism in the area. While there are many ways in which to measure such aspects, those that are considered most relevant and successful in our field is the notion of the Triple Bottom Line (TBL). While not developed specifically for tourism, the elements of this concept are closely linked to local communities and can be applied to tourism. An outline of TBL and its relationship to the theme of this book is set out below, followed by a relevant tourism example of benchmarking.

Triple bottom line – a strategic approach to indicators of success

While for many of us, it may seem like the term, Triple Bottom Line, has been around for decades, in fact it was coined by John Elkington in 1997. He considered there to be three prongs of business that should inform all corporate strategies: social, environmental and financial. Many of today's business plans are (in theory at least) developed around those three prongs, and is particularly pertinent to the field of tourism.

For example, Tourism Victoria's strategy for the tourism industry, while not using the term 'triple bottom line' includes references to the three prongs, with statements throughout much of their strategy such as:

> The message will resonate strongly from the industry that tourism is a key economic driver directly creating more jobs for Victoria than the education, agriculture, government administration, defence or mining sectors. It is also a significant contributor to social cohesion and environmental sustainability.

> The social, environmental and economic contribution of tourism will be a major benefit to regional Victoria as the State's marketing programs expand to encompass specific regional destinations and attractions … The theme of this plan **Advantage Victoria!** signifies the economic, social and environmental advantages to Victoria from a strong, vibrant and growing tourism industry (Tourism Victoria 2005: www.tourismvictoria.com.au/strategicplan/ plan2002_2006/1_introduction/executive_summary.htm)

But what does TBL really address? It is directly linked with the concept and goal of sustainable development and is underpinned by the belief that a long-term view of any business (destination or community) is central to a successful outcome. In addition, the application of a TBL perspective provides information to enable others to assess the level of sustainability of an organisation's or community's operations. However, it is rare to find a long-term perspective adopted by governments, particularly in Western democracies where regular elections may 'keep them honest', but does little to encourage a long-term vision or responsibility. Unfortunately, it can also be difficult to maintain the enthusiasm and commitment required by communities.

However, many community development professionals (who are primarily employed by government) are committed to applying such a concept due to its clear and obvious significance to community development. In addition, tourism can be introduced into this framework and directly contribute to the development of a healthy, sustainable community.

The process of integrating TBL accounting and reporting into a community preferably requires all three measures to be incorporated into a single, all-encompassing measurement. An example of such a measurement is the Index of Sustainable Economic Welfare, which adjusts the normal levels of welfare by subtracting costs associated with unemployment, commuting, auto accidents and environmental pollution (Daly and Cobb 1989). The obvious challenge here is to identify and then quantify such 'costs'.

There is no single currency into which value-adding or destruction in any of the dimensions can be assessed, so most efforts aim for a convergence, recognising that different indicators need to be assessed in different ways. However, researchers are working on ways to improve these measurements, and it is a high priority in tourism research. The concept of measuring 'yield' in terms of the costs noted above is a major research priority for groups such as the Sustainable Tourism Cooperative Research Centre (ST CRC) in Australia. While initially economics driven, the group has taken the concept further and is working to understand the costs, benefits and yield of non-monetary items. A brief description of the project is shown in Table 3.2 which reinforces the notion of TBL reporting in tourism.

Table 3.2 ST CRC project on concepts and measurement of tourism yield

Summary of project
Achieving long term sustainable and profitable tourism products would secure a competitive advantage for Australia as a desirable tourist destination with benefits to all tourism stakeholders. Increasingly, tourism firms and destinations are attempting to maximise the yield from tourism. However, the concept of yield is often ill-defined. The industry, at its different levels, needs clarification, however, as to what yield is and how can tourism yield be measured and improved. Increasingly, tourism operators want tourism to improve their performance economically, environmentally and socially. Tourists are also demanding evidence that profitability is based on long-term sustainability. This project discusses the various meanings of 'yield'. It also explores the TBL approach as a framework for measuring and reporting yield. This project will develop tools for measuring and maximising the yield from tourism at different levels (operator, regional, national). The major aim of the project is, within the context of sustainability reporting, to extend the concept of yield from accounting profit for tourism firms to a consideration of broad economic, environmental and social effects of tourism. An outcome of the study will be enhanced capacity for tourism decision makers to enact policies to enhance destination long-term competitiveness.

Source: ST CRC, http://www.crctourism.com.au.

Returning to the discussion of TBL, we need to identify a limited set of key performance indicators for each bottom line. Due to the amorphous nature of some of the elements that constitute some of these areas, as noted above, the indicators may be qualitative (or descriptive) as well as quantitative. The concept of indicators is discussed below following the discussion of TBL auditing.

Triple bottom line audit of a community

At the risk of becoming repetitive, it is important to reiterate that communities that focus merely on economic development with no regard for the need to sustain people and their environment are **not** sustainable. In order to ascertain the stage or state of a community, it is advisable to undertake an audit, which is more than simply a stock-take of assets and liabilities. A community audit examines and measures performance against internally and externally established principles and policies (Rogers 2001).

A community TBL audit brings insight into how different aspects of the socio-economic and environmental systems interact, and can highlight areas of dependency, vulnerability and strength. In addition, it encourages the community to consider their long-term attitudes towards the environment as well as social and economic development, which is a major aim of the whole notion of TBL planning.

Benchmarks and indicators

In the current business lexicon, we often hear reference to 'benchmarks' and 'indicators' – almost as often as we hear the term 'community'. But what is really meant by these terms and what is their relevance to community development and tourism? As has been noted throughout this book, governments in most Western-based democracies have been moving towards devolving many of their responsibilities upon the regional (local/community) level. In order to do this successfully, at the very least, requires that there are adequate arrangements for reporting and accounting for the outcomes of the various programs and respon-sibilities that are taken on at the local level. In addition, these programs need to be monitored and assessed for their effectiveness. This requires the development of sustainability indicators that can be used at the regional/local scale.

So, what are 'indicators'? Simply put, an indicator is a significant variable (physical, biological, social or economic) that can be measured. For example, the number of landholders participating in Landcare groups may be one indicator of the level of success of educational programs promoting environmental management in a region.

At the national level, we find indicators such as the Gross Domestic Product (GDP), which is seen to indicate a level of our standard of living. Other indicators may include State of the Environment Reports and Quality of Life Indices that can be presented at local as well as national levels.

One example of this is what has become known as 'Genuine Progress Indicators'. These indicators are developed by taking financial trans-actions from the GDP that are relevant to the concept of 'wellbeing'. These transactions are adjusted for aspects of the economy the GDP ignores – such as adding the value of time spent on household work, parenting or volunteer work, while subtracting the expenditure needed to defend quality of life such as burglar-proofing homes, social costs such as divorce and depreciation of environmental assets and natural resources. This represents a significant shift in the development of indicators that go beyond simple economic data. However, much data is only available at national or state level, and is expensive and time-consuming to gather.

This brings us to considering the issues that need to be taken into account when trying to develop (or use existing) indicators. For example, how do government targets translate to a target at a regional level, and can agreed benchmarks be set for each indicator? A benchmark is the level set for a particular indicator against which performance is measured (such as 80 per cent of landholders participating in Landcare programs). However, when we want to look at multiple outcomes in complex communities, we also need to consider whether existing benchmarks need to be modified to allow for the tensions that exist.

Basically, when we consider establishing (or choosing) indicators, the primary rule would be to consider the common desired outcomes of our community. These would be in terms of the main areas of activity, such as increased economic growth, sustainable use of the region's land and water resources and an improved quality of life or social wellbeing. Such aims are highly commendable, but most are costly to measure and often present those involved with a large amount of information to be collated and distributed. Sometimes the sheer amount of data can become so daunting that community groups and managers simply put the information aside. In order to prevent this, the data must be useful to many agencies and groups and for multiple purposes, such as policy development, strategic planning, prioritising of resources and reporting.

Each indicator should be reliable, consistent, tailored to objectives, able to detect trends, be scientifically credible, meaningful and understandable to the average person, as well as being cost effective.

Some suggested indicators

Many indicators can be found in existing data. For example, in economic terms we have population change, property values and numbers of building/planning permits issued over a certain period of time. And while the Gross Domestic Product may be too broad to be applied effectively at a local level, there have been developments in establishing Gross Regional Products that are more locally described (Beeton and Pinge 2003).

Environmentally, a spatial comparison of land use and management can be an effective indicator of the health or status of the local environment, and such information can be found in many local government or agricultural departments. Associated with land use is measuring the area that may be affected by pest plants, considering water quality and stream or ground water condition as well as water use. The condition of the soil and the amount and placement of remnant vegetation are also significant indicators of the health of the environment.

From a social perspective, indicators that measure the so-called 'quality of life' are important, and often combine elements of those discussed above. In addition, education facilities, crime rates, age profiles of residents and the mobility of residents in and out of the region are also social indicators. Many of these form part of the Index of Sustainable Economic Welfare noted in the earlier discussion of the TBL.

In order to measure the importance of these indicators, benchmarks or 'minimum standards' need to be developed. When we consider this in terms of community development, these standards should be agreed upon by that community. An approach that is holistic in its purpose and has some similarities with the concept of the TBL is the work that has been done in Australia to develop benchmarks for a community based management model known as the Tourism Optimisation Management Model (TOMM). In response to residents' concerns over uncontrolled tourism development at a popular island off the south coast of Australia (Kangaroo Island), a Sustainable Tourism Development Strategy was developed by the community based island's Development Board, which included a tourism strategy. However, instead of simply developing a standard strategy that would primarily consider limiting the current and future tourism impacts, it was decided to look towards optimising the tourism potential of the island in a sustainable manner for the local community as well as environmentally. The residents had to agree which core data and monitoring programs ought to be set up – which ones were important for them and how they could be measured (what indicators are appropriate) – followed by the establishment of benchmarks to actually monitor and measure these key areas (Manidis Roberts Consultants 1997).

Indicators and benchmarks were established in the areas of economic, market opportunity, environmental, experiential, infrastructure/development and socio-cultural. Rather than setting a firm benchmark (for example, the preferred number of visitors per night is 200), they developed an acceptable range as their benchmark (between 180 and 220 visitors per night), setting optimal conditions (TOMM 1999, 2000). Table 3.3 gives an example of Key Performance Indicators (KPI) and benchmark/acceptable range in each of the key areas. (Each area had more than one issue/indicator.)

This model is not so much about setting limits, but identifying the best conditions for tourism to occur, as seen by the host community. This is done by identifying a range of scenarios for tourism in terms of increasing or decreasing its scale and outlining the costs and benefits of each scenario to key community stakeholders. Once the optimal conditions have been specified, the acceptable ranges for achieving those conditions are agreed upon.

However, simply establishing these indicators and benchmarks is only the beginning, and data need to be gathered in order to monitor any changes. This can be time-consuming and costly, yet without such information gathering, the model remains simply that – a model. So, when

Table 3.3 Key performance indicators

Desired situation	Key performance indicator	Acceptable range (benchmark)
Economic indicators		
Visitors stay longer than 2 nights	Annual average number of nights	2–7 nights
Market opportunity indicators		
Growth in proportion of visitors form the cultural/environmental sector	% of visitors matching the cultural/environmental profile % growth of the number of visitors by that segment	60–80% of all visitors match the profile 0–7% annual growth
Environmental indicators		
Majority of visits to natural areas occurs in visitor service zones	Proportion of visitors to natural areas who visit managed sites/areas	85–100% of all visitors go to specifically managed sites
Experiential indicators		
Visitors have a memorable experience	Proportion of visitors that identify a 'tourist experience'	85–100% of all visitors
Infrastructure/development indicators		
Visitors are satisfied with accommodation	Proportion of visitors satisfied with type and quality of accommodation	85–100% of all visitors
Socio-cultural indicators		
Growth of local employment is consistent	% increase in number of people who derive all or some of their income from tourism	Any increase from previous data

Source: Adapted from TOMM Annual Report 2000.

monitoring is done and any of the ranges are exceeded, the causes need to be identified and potential effects considered, along with considering how any desired corrections can be made. For example, management activities may bring the indicators back into an acceptable range, or the marketing communications need to be adjusted.

The benefits of this type of management model compared with many others is that it is holistic in its approach, giving weight to the many dimensions of tourism and the community in which it occurs. We do consider the importance of including multiple stakeholders in other areas in this book, but this is certainly one of the TOMM's strengths.

However, developing such a comprehensive model takes time, money and a high level of ongoing commitment from the local community, local government and the tourism industry. One of the repeated calls by those charged with implementing TOMM on Kangaroo Island has been for guaranteed funding in order to coordinate not only the process, but also to maintain the community's interest and (good)will (see Jack 2000; TOMM 1999, 2000).

The TOMM example is an excellent case of relatively successful ongoing community and tourism planning. However, it has not been without its difficulties and critics. There is no simple answer to strategically planning for tourism in communities, nor is there only one way to measure or understand our communities. The case shown below demonstrates how the theory of social representation outlined earlier can be used to discover some of the underlying issues in a community as well as identifying those who may hold similar views and attitudes. By understanding who believes what, strategies can then be developed to address any issues and increase the positive attitudes that members have.

From theory to practice: Using social representation theory in order to understand a community

An Australian television series, *Sea Change*, was shown in 1999 and 2000, becoming the most popular television drama series for both years. The story-line was based around a jaded female corporate lawyer whose husband was imprisoned for fraud. She moved with her two children to the only place where she recalled having an idyllic time with her family – a small seaside community known as 'Pearl Bay' – to work as the local magistrate. The series traces the quirky characters in this small community and her attempts to find her place in it. The popular series was primarily filmed in the small seaside town of Barwon Heads on the Victorian coast.

Barwon Heads was predominantly a fishing village with a high seasonal influx of family holiday-makers during the summer months who either camped in the caravan park (where the series was based) or rented houses. While the region itself (the Bellarine Peninsula) was well known to the Melbourne market (less than

90 minutes away), Barwon Heads had been bypassed by the trend for seaside developments. The popularity of the series and the growing fascination with film-induced tourism put the small town 'on the map' and has been credited with, at least in part, increasing the land values and altering the services provided in the town (Beeton 2001a, 2005a).

As part of a larger study into the phenomenon of film-induced tourism (see Beeton 2005a), I undertook a four-year study of the effects of the series on the community. However, while I wanted to find out what the community's attitudes were, I was not happy with using the work of others who had previously identified issues of community attitudes towards tourism such as Doxey and others (see Chapter 2). There were a number of reasons for my reticence. The main one was that much of the work based on Doxey's Irridex simply followed what he had proposed without adequately testing its accuracy or relevance to the specific case. This was a very specific case as there had been very little (in fact, not even one) in-depth study into the relationship between television series, tourism and the host communities. In addition, there could be cultural differences – most of the accepted theories on communities and tourism come out of North America, Europe and some developing areas – Australians are different in their outlook and attitude which may affect the results if not taken into account.

By looking into other methodological approaches from other fields of research, the relevance of using Social Representation Theory (SRT) became apparent. As SRT does not nominate that there are certain discrete groups and then tries to find out their attitudes, it allows the community members to tell the researcher (me) what they believe without being prompted. The emic approach of SRT assumes nothing – we start with a 'blank canvas' and see what appears.

So, in this stage of the study of Barwon Heads I wanted to find out what attitudes and representations the community had towards film-induced tourism and then see what similarities those with similar representations had. In that way I hoped to identify groups and attitudes specifically relevant to *this* community that may have otherwise been overlooked using a more traditional segmentation method.

A questionnaire was developed that contained a series of open-ended questions in terms of the participants' attitudes and feelings towards *Sea Change*, Barwon Heads and tourism, with no prompting. A list of recurring themes came out of this, which is outlined in Table 3.4. I found that the variables of age, gender, average length of residency in the town, whether they initially lived in a city or not, their home ownership status and whether tourism featured in their top three preferred industries for the town were found to actually define the groups within a range of representations.

Another benefit of SRT is that it allows the same person to hold what may at times be contradictory social representations. For example, a parent who has invested in a holiday house at Barwon Heads (considered as part of the community in my study) may see the increased profile of the town as a positive thing from an investment perspective, but as detrimental to the future aspirations of their own children who want to purchase their own property in the town. By allowing people to nominate the good and bad things about tourism and explain their reasons, SRT can accommodate this.

The groups that I was particularly interested in were those that were in some way different from the entire sample (the last section on Table 3.4) as they demonstrated that they were more likely to be holding a certain representation or attitude in relation to the effect of *Sea Change* on Barwon Heads. So, the patterns noted in the table allowed us to identify nine groupings with similar social representations and concurring aspects. I have labelled them in relation to their most significant stance, namely:

- 'Good for Traders' (economic benefits)
- 'Good for Tourism'
- 'Raises Profile and Pride'
- 'Good for Property Sales'
- 'Bad for Property Purchase'

Table 3.4 Film-induced tourism aspects affecting residents of Barwon Heads

Comment/representation	Age	Gender	Length of residency	Ex-city resident	Own home	Tourism in top 3 preferred industries	Total
	% of opinion group						% of total sample
Positive							
Economic benefits – local business, upgrading of shops, employment	18-39 34 40-59 34 60+ 32	M 33 F 66	<5 yr 53 6+ yr 47	61	79	60	48
Increased tourism	18-39 33 40-59 40 60+ 27	M 29 F 71	<5 66 6+ 34	51	78	73	40
Raises profile of the town – put Barwon Heads on the map	18-39 28 40-59 35 60+ 37	M 27 F 73	<5 51 6+ 49	61	85	78	36
Increase property values (positive)	18-39 24 40-59 36 60+ 40	M 38 F 62	<5 46 6+ 54	70	85	64	18
Neutral							
Great place as it is – retain 'village by the sea'	18-39 32 40-59 32 60+ 36	M 25 F 75	<5 57 6+ 43	62	82	59	34
Negative							
Fiction vs Reality: Barwon Heads is not Pearl Bay	18-39 32 40-59 42 60+ 24	M 37 F 63	<5 48 6+ 52	68	86	58	34
Crowding/congestion/traffic	18-39 35 40-59 37 60+ 28	M 35 F 65	<5 55 6+ 45	50	84	65	31
Increased property values – rental etc. (negative)	18-39 28 40-59 45 60+ 27	M 19 F 81	<5 39 6+ 61	44	78	47	10
Future issues (not necessarily film-induced)							
Planning – development must be managed, including tourism	18-39 37 40-59 35 60+ 28	M 27 F 73	<5 58 6+ 42	58	80	60	59
Maintaining infrastructure and services	18-39 30 40-59 34 60+ 36	M 33 F 67	<5 41 6+ 59	70	89	63	15

A common vision							
Village atmosphere and careful planning	18-39 33 40-59 37 60+ 30	M 28 F 72	<5 56 6+ 44	59	81	60	54
Entire sample							
	18-39 30 40-59 33 60+ 37	M 34 F 66	<5 52 6+ 48	58	83	58	100

- 'Flash in the Pan' (fiction – Barwon Heads is not Pearl Bay, so will not last)
- 'Don't Crowd Me'
- 'Steady as She Goes!' (the need for careful planning)
- 'Retain Village Atmosphere'.

Their main points of similarity in each representation were their average length of residency, ex-city dweller and listing tourism as a top three preferred industry. The model in Figure 3.1 has taken these stances and placed these social representations on a three-dimensional axis of the main variables that differentiated them from the entire sample and population. I was also interested in seeing if there were any representations that could be clustered around these variables.

The following discussion does not cover all the information that this model reveals, but is a brief summary of some of the points. A more in-depth discussion can be found in Beeton (2005a). The model shows that there are two groups of representations, A and B, clustered in a common region on all three axes. The groups are quite close to each other and could have been missed using other research methods, but they do exist and are quite separate in their representations or attitudes. More importantly, they can and do influence the nature of the Barwon Heads community. They also show us that groups (and individuals) can hold so-called conflicting views – such as in Cluster A where we see one positive and one negative attitude, suggesting that while this group recognises some benefits from *Sea Change*

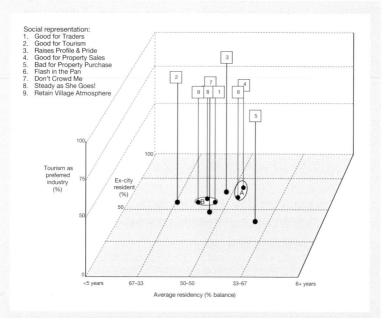

Figure 3.1 Social representations regarding film-induced tourism within clusters of the Barwon Heads residential community

Source: Beeton 2005a, p. 126.

in terms of property prices, they are limited, short term and temporary (a 'flash in the pan').

Cluster B is a little more complex, with three representations in this group, indicating that they see tourism as important (at least for the traders), yet desire to retain the town's village atmosphere. Around 60 per cent of this cluster come from a major city and are slightly shorter-term residents. As it is common to find new residents with some knowledge about a place before moving there, this group may have first come across Barwon Heads as a visitor, so they also recognise the role that traders play in the community.

While the other representations are not clustered, they also need to be considered. However, as this is being presented as an example, I will not go into detail here, except to discuss one of them – the group that is concerned about crowding and congestion in the town (Number 7). This group has slightly more recent residents in it, and more than half have moved from a rural or small town environment. Even though they are concerned about crowds, they still prefer tourism to many other industries, demonstrating another group with contradictory attitudes.

So, what do these representations 'mean' in terms of the community's role in planning for tourism and the development of their community? The results discussed above actually identified some representations that may not have been clear in the early stages of development, which can result in a fragmented, hostile community.

In Chapter 4, which looks more closely at community tourism planning in particular, it is stressed that identifying a common vision that is held by all (or most) of the community is key to any development or planning. Two of the representations identified in this study (Numbers 8 and 9) point us towards a strong view held by many in the town. When combined, they make up over half of the entire sample, which is significant in this type of study. So, a common vision relating to the need to retain the village atmosphere and plan carefully can be gleaned from these findings.

4

Community-inclusive tourism strategies

In the previous chapter, we looked at issues and elements related to applying strategic planning and management to tourism and communities and establishing community based measures that can be used to indicate the progress of any strategy. In this chapter we follow on with the strategic theme by looking at the complex areas of empowering individuals and communities along with the vexed area of power relations. Understanding these elements is critical to an understanding of how to best develop our communities through tourism, which we look at here in terms of 'Community Based Tourism' before outlining the process (and pitfalls) in a real-life case of community development through tourism exercise.

Community wellbeing

Before we even consider community development and empowerment and tourism, we need to understand what is actually meant by 'community wellbeing' and why it is important. As with so many of the terms used in the community development field, community wellbeing is intrinsically understood by many. However, for our purposes it is worthwhile to provide some sort of definition or explanation of its meaning and use within the context of this publication. Simply expressed, community wellbeing refers to the quality of life and level of sustainability as seen by the members of that community. In effect, 'it is shaped by a range of social, psychological, cultural, economic and environmental factors that shape the way that people think and act in their daily lives ... as well as how they relate to others in their community' (Dredge, 2003). Once again we come across an area that is subjective in its interpretation and not easy to measure, as with so many areas of community development and tourism. What works for one community may be seen as a negative aspect in another – for instance, more people may create a lively, vibrant environment in the eyes of one community, but the same level may simply be perceived as adding to crowding and carrying capacity issues for another.

Community wellbeing is not defined solely in simple (measurable) economic terms, but is shaped by the (harder to quantify) complex relationships between the physical, psychological and environmental factors faced by all communities regardless of their type (Dredge 2003).

So, if this is so difficult, why bother? As well as being important in terms of community development, wellbeing is also a tourism asset that can be used to further enhance community outcomes and wellbeing, if managed. Community members who are happy to be there create a positive environment that tourists sense and respond to. While this may not be a tangible asset, visitors soon sense if a place is one where they are welcome and one they wish to spend time in or not. If they do not feel comfortable, they will move on to the next community where they do feel welcome.

This is not about forcing people to smile and say 'G'day' to visitors, but something that inherently flows out from a healthy community. And most visitors are quick to pick the difference! Healthy communities with a strong sense of their own wellbeing are well along the path of self-determination and empowerment, even though they may still need some assistance in these areas to truly benefit. These points are detailed in the following section.

Community development and empowerment

By advancing the notion of empowerment and its associated power and powerlessness, I aim to demonstrate its usefulness (and necessity) in understanding tourism development at the community level, as well as community development from a tourism perspective. There are also many issues that complicate its application which are outlined here and in the case study at the end of this chapter.

Power relations

No discussion about empowerment can overlook the concept of power, being an integral element of the term itself. And no discussion on power can ignore the significant contribution of Foucault (1975) who emphasises the importance of local manifestations of power and the process of legitimising power relationships through knowledge. Foucault maintains that knowledge defines power, not hierarchy nor status alone.

In the context of the theme of this book (community development through tourism), the power that I am particularly interested in is the relationship between social and political power – particularly the shifting relationship between those with various levels of power. As Sofield puts it, 'empowerment of and by communities cannot occur without social forces at some point in time combining with political forces of the state to arrive at a new balance of power relations' (Sofield 2003, p. 69).

Power can exist in a hierarchical manner. This is often imposed power, such as in village governance in terms of leaders, elders, councils and so on, or organisationally in terms of local council, state government, national government and so on, which is often seen as *political power*. Power can also exist in a non-hierarchical manner among communities and groups (which has often been conferred by the community members), often considered to be *social power*. One of the most widely accepted definitions of power comes from Weber who states that power is 'the probability that one actor within a social relationship will be in a position to carry out his own will despite resistance' (cited Sofield 2003, p. 70).

Power itself governs the way in which our communities develop and whether tourism will be a part of that development and if so, what 'type' of tourism will be encouraged (resort development, ecotourism, educational tourism, adventure tourism, golf tourism and so on...). Understanding how the power relations work and what they are in any community is crucial to developing a sustainable tourism industry within a sustained community.

Political power

Hall (2003b) argues that politics and power are so intricately related that one cannot be studied without the other. Political power does not solely reside with those who have the appropriate title (mayor, tourism minister etc.) but usually results from the power-playing and positioning of all parties with a vested interest. It involves the actions, values and ideologies of individuals, interest groups, public and private organisations as actors in the 'game' of politics. These actors may or may not be members of the tourism host community, depending on how that community is defined.

In a paper on community tourism in Southern Africa, the author addresses the question of what can governments do when it should be up to the communities to decide if they wish to develop tourism by responding:

> Governments have a crucial role to play. What communities do in tourism depends on the **opportunities and power** they have, the incentives and prices they face, and their access to skills, training, capital and markets. All of these are shaped by government policies, regulation and taxes. (Gomera c.1999, p. 1) [own emphasis].

The paper goes on to explain that even economic linkages (the most easily recognised by those unfamiliar with tourism) cannot be assumed, but need to be encouraged by those with the political power (that is, governments, whether local, state or federal). Public–private partnerships are also stressed as effective ways to develop tourism in communities (Gomera c.1999). If these areas are not encouraged by those with the political power, many communities will not be able to move towards self-determination and empowerment.

Hall reminds us that '[p]olitics denotes the struggle over scarce resources, the domination of one group over another and the potential exercise of state control' (Hall 2003b, p. 101). However, Gomera also stresses that 'there are two extremes to be avoided: one is to ignore community tourism ... The other is for government to try to do everything and do it now, without allowing time for local people to develop their ideas and skills' (Gomera c.1999, p. 6).

One issue that is evident in the political power structure in Australia is the overriding role that government can have in the community decision-making process which, if we subscribe to the community development credo, must respect the community's decisions (as long as there has been 'true' inclusive public participation). The whole notion of community based planning infers that there is at least a partnership in the planning and implementation process, and ideally community control of the process (Hall 2003b). There are many instances where a community has refused to agree to a certain development (one of the options of community planning for tourism) that has been overridden by the government 'authorities'. In addition, the notion of 'public participation' has, in many instances, been primarily notional, with little true effort to include and consider all of the various community perspectives, particularly where the political power is perceived to be predominant.

One case where the political power of a government organisation was usurped was in the planning proposals for one of Victoria's most high-profile national parks, Wilsons Promontory National Park. This park has a high level of natural environment and is a mecca for nature-based adventure tourists and day trippers from surrounding areas. In 1996 the state's public land management agency proposed to develop certain areas of the park. They intended to provide a higher level of on-site accommodation (instead of restricted camping and a few cabins) in the form of a hotel and lodge as well as open up opportunities for visitors to fly into remote areas, stay and then walk out on hardened, upgraded tracks. The agency requested public submissions, and instead of receiving the usual amount (less than 100), they received thousands of submissions condemning the proposals. What the agency had forgotten was that the 'community' involved in such a national iconic park consisted of many people outside the region in which it existed. In addition, many Australians may have not been there for many years, yet they retained a strong affinity with and sense of ownership of the place. This is a classic case where the 'community' is far more than the local residents.

Also, many of these people (stakeholders) had their own political power and were able to mobilise the media into reporting extensively on some extremely graphic demonstrations. For example, the state's daily newspapers ran front-page stories on a protest where thousands gathered on a beach with their bodies spelling out the words 'Save Our Prom'. Suddenly, the government funded and supported management agency had little power as the voting public exercised their own political power!

The campaign was far more complex than described above, but suffice to say that the proposed developments were scrapped. In effect, in this instance social power had superseded political power.

Social power

Sofield (2003) identifies five main models of social power from the social sciences literature: reputational model, positional approach, decision-making model, control model and the resources model. The *reputational* model assumes that power is distributed among those with the reputation for influence and power, and is related to the *positional* approach that considers power to be in the hands of those in formal leadership positions. Social power that is seen in terms of the ability to make decisions and get them implemented, regardless of other people's wishes, is known as the *decision-making* model, while the *control* model primarily considers power in organisational as opposed to personal terms, which primarily focuses on vertical power relations. The final model, the *resources* model, considers power in terms of the actor's access to resources, and is used by many from the political sciences, economics and market research fields.

These are all useful indicators of the characteristics of power, but each is incomplete and lacking in some way or other, particularly when we consider communities, or social collectives. A more satisfactory way to consider power relations in communities and tourism is to do so in terms of the presentation of power through contested issues, which are those that are important to both (or all) sides and there is disagreement (Jacobsen & Cohen, 1986). If there is no disagreement or if the issue is unimportant to one side, there is no need to exert power.

Embedded in the whole notion of power and powerlessness is 'resistance' or conflict as an integral element of power and power relations, not only in terms of political power. Often in our efforts to avoid confrontation all that occurs is a shift in the power balance – one that is usually not positive. Hall reminds us that 'tourism continually redefines social and political realities at that community level ... the very notion of serving tourists affects notions of belonging, place and community no matter where in the world tourism is occurring' (Hall 2003b, p. 110).

Powerlessness

The actor who wins a contested issue is the one with power resources, while the other actor in this instance is seen as powerless. Those who are powerless in a community are alienated or marginalised, such as the residents in 'slum' areas that have been marked for 'redevelopment' such as the New Cities movement discussed in Chapter 1. The residents themselves had no say over this change – it was imposed from above. Such powerlessness also presents itself in relation to certain approaches to increased tourism and tourism development. To return to the seaside town of Barwon Heads (Chapter 3): the increase in numbers of visitors to the town on the back of the TV series *Sea Change* actually forced the poorer low-budget holiday-makers out of their caravan park sites to make way for serviced cabins that they could never afford (Beeton 2001a). These families had been holidaying in the town for up to five generations and considered themselves part of the local community, but were powerless to influence this development on public land. They were given other camping sites, but they were no longer the prime sites they had previously, marginalising this group. This scenario is outlined below in the four future scenarios for Barwon Heads.

An example of the differing power relations and levels of empowerment–powerlessness can be demonstrated in looking at the Barwon Heads–*Sea Change* case which was introduced as the case study in Chapter 3. Once the social representations had been identified and clustered, four future scenarios were proposed, each with differing power relations. A brief outline of each with their various power relations is presented below from Beeton (2005a).

Scenario One – Positive growth
- More visitors in off-peak times, evening out the high seasonal peaks and troughs;

- Increased accommodation range caters for all types of visitor, from the high-yield visitor through to the family budget holiday-maker;

- Economic opportunities increase for all members of the community;

- Barwon Heads receives increased support and recognition from the City of Greater Geelong;

- Services and facilities improved and maintained by the City of Greater Geelong;

- Major tourist precincts upgraded;

- Development is sympathetic to the fishing village ambience and nature;

- Heritage sites are retained and restored; and

- Increase in the general population base, supporting local amenities such as schools, medical services, police etc.

At first, the power in Scenario One may seem to be evenly spread amongst the local community and regular visitors, with the desires of all parties taken into account. However, in terms of political and power-relations practice, this is an unlikely scenario.

Scenario Two – Business as usual

- No further development;

- Accommodation and facilities continue to support the family budget holiday-makers;

- Everyone happy with the minor fillip to the town;

- Visitors pass through, staying in other towns able to handle the added influx, limiting the impact on the tranquillity of the area;

- Housing and rental prices remain stable; and

- Traditional family holiday market continues to be welcome and catered for.

The above scenario sees the power residing with those in the community who like it as it is and the long-term regular visitors. The research identified these are the shorter-term residents, many of whom had moved to the village after visiting as holiday-makers and tourists. This group is powerful due to their political understanding and are resistant to change.

Scenario Three – Back to the drawing board

- New businesses cannot be supported by numbers of residents and visitors outside the peak season;
- Shops become run-down, deserted and vacant;
- Council funds diverted to other, more lucrative tourist towns such as Queenscliff;
- Housing prices fall and rental market opens up;
- Niche accommodation for the high-yield markets not supported, forcing closures or re-structure;
- Traditional family holiday market welcome, but may move due to the perceived downturn after the excitement of *Sea Change*.

In the third scenario, the strong anti-development groups have the power and have sabotaged any efforts of consultation and development. As with Scenario Two, this group tends to be dominated by the newer residents, with a strong representation of urban dwellers, often referred to as 'urban refugees' looking for their own private sea change.

Scenario Four – Losing the Pearl Bay feeling

- Regular budget holiday-makers forced out due to increased demand, prices and/or loss of amenity;
- Shops and services developed to cater for visitors – overpriced and unappealing to local residents;
- Barwon Heads moves from family holiday village to a day visitor attraction;
- Outside entrepreneurs not based in the region take over local business operations;
- Locals begin to resent the intrusion of thousands of visitors;
- Crowding severely impacts on local services;
- More Council funds required to maintain basic services used by visitors and residents;

- Housing purchase and rental prices skyrocket; and
- Pressure placed on natural environment – coastal and wetland areas.

In this final scenario, the regular visitors have no power and have been forced out of the region due to the power coalition of pro-development business and economic development supporters, which may include local government. The power group is also made up of some of the long-term residents who are looking for an economic 'future' for their children. (Beeton 2005a, pp. 149–151)

Powerlessness is a crucial aspect of tourism in communities as so often much of the tourism comes from outside that community. This not only includes the tourists themselves (who wield significant power in terms of economic resources in particular), but also the transport companies bringing the tourists, the developers and investors who may be outside the community, and even some of the government agencies that are not embedded in the community. It has been extremely easy to override the 'power' of many communities, particularly the already marginalised indigenous communities in Western cultures (Indigenous Australians, North American Indians, Celts, Innuit and so on). Other remote, resource-poor communities can also easily be rendered powerless by tourism. In order to correct the imbalance between power and powerlessness, we need to empower the powerless.

Empowerment

As with the term 'community', empowerment has entered the popular vernacular as a generic term relating to the capacity of individuals or groups to determine their own affairs. The term comes from political science, usually in discussions involving the re-assigning of power to a community whose power has been taken away by force. It certainly has much wider application today and is relevant to many situations and fields of endeavour, which has not helped us formulate a clear definition. Central to this discussion of empowerment is self-determination, and in many ways this is the key to defining and understanding 'empowerment'.

Minority groups such as the Black Power movement, Gay Rights movement and ethnic minorities have advocated empowerment to counter discrimination and advance their rights. In the health sector, both nurses and patients are being 'empowered' to make decisions that were previously the domain of the specialist doctors. Business management uses empowerment in terms of devolving authority and decision-making power from the top management to the workers, and it can be relevant to many areas of tourism such as hotel management (Sofield 2003).

Many forms of empowerment are seen as conferring power to groups that have never experienced real authority. This is problematic in that many of these groups do not have the personal resources ('habitus') or capacity to help themselves. Many 'empowered' tourism and community development initiatives have failed due to the communities not being able to maintain the initiative, particularly those who have been disempowered for a long time. The case study at the end of this chapter looks at a rural tourism community project in Australia where the members were not considered to be powerless, yet they resisted efforts to empower them. Were they merely lazy, or did they not have the personal resources and capacity to be truly empowered and self-determining? Often a community's capacity for empowerment needs to be developed before any true empowerment can take place, but this step is far too often overlooked.

Capacity building

The central element for building capacity is primarily in the education and training realm, but is expanding to include other forms of development, particularly in relation to community development. There are four different kinds of capacity:

1 organisational capacity
2 technical capacity to deliver specific services
3 infrastructure capacity, and
4 community capacity.

Many local government organisations are investing resources in developing their community's capacity for learning, innovation and knowledge (Dredge 2003). By developing communities and tourism they build the capacity of community to achieve their own or greater objectives, such as to take part in local development partnerships and schemes funded by local government and other public sources. This can be used in other related sectors, such as building the capacity of local authority officers to engage with local communities or building the capacity of local community members to serve the interests/needs of tourists.

In terms of tourism, the focus is on capacity building and training to assist all stakeholders (including governments, indigenous and local communities) to analyse and interpret baseline information, undertake impact assessments and evaluations and be adaptive managers. This capacity building is useful too in areas such as the development or strengthening of mechanisms for impact assessment with all stakeholders. Including local community members can be important in terms of approving the approach, content and scope of impact assessment.

In order for capacity development to be effective, logical solutions that work locally and meet local requirements and conditions need to be created. For example, in weak, fragmented communities, working towards joint action will increase the capacity of that community. Building partnerships/bridges towards achieving collective capacity is a main focus in many communities, which is concerned with entrepreneurial as well as participatory activities.

However, as with all elements related to empowerment and self-determination, there are limitations to the success of capacity-building exercises, which are primarily dependent on the current make-up of the community as well as its history in terms of past developments and capacity-building attempts. One example is an attempt to build capacity for community based entrepreneurs in Uganda (Victurine 2000). Victurine found that the community resisted some of the empowerment strategies, requiring training to be embedded into institutionalised programs. He also acknowledged that progress is slow, recommending that sponsors or donors need to have a longer-term view before they pronounce something as a 'failure'. This notion of failure and its impact on further community participation is crucial – in many instances, we need to reconsider our time frames relating to success and failure, particularly in this crucial capacity-building phase.

While capacity development is an element of empowerment and self-determination, support from higher-level policy areas and the public is needed. In determining what areas need attention in terms of increasing the capacity, it is crucial to understand the level of *social capital* in the community. Simply put, social capital refers to a community's social assets such as the extent and quality of members' involvement with others in their community. Engagement and trust between community members are essential ingredients of social capital. The connectedness of social networks, particularly where the members of these networks share social norms, trust and reciprocity, is valuable in fostering cooperation to achieve common goals (Jones 2005).

There are two elements of social capital – the structural and cognitive aspects. The structural aspect includes networks, roles, rules and precedents, while the cognitive aspect incorporates the norms, values, attitudes and beliefs of those in a community (Jones 2005). The former relates to what people do and how they do it, while the latter is more about perceptions of reciprocity and trust – what they feel.

Of course, simply having the structural elements does not create social capital – the processes are there, but the value that the cognitive aspects provide must also be present. Social capital is a value-laden term, and while it may be difficult to measure, it is the key to many healthy communities.

While it is easy to accept the notion expressed by some that tourism development that is primarily economic-based will reduce social capital, the opposite can also be true. More wealth can create more group activity as members move up Maslow's Hierarchy of Needs (see Chapter 2) and become interested in social and self-actualisation aspects. In other words, development can create or destroy social capital – yet another paradox! According to Mansuri and Rao (2004, cited Jones 2005, p. 307), 'social capital [is] part of the power relations within a system and embedded within its cultural and political context'.

So-called grassroots community groups are where the process of building social capital starts in a community. These groups come from the community, bottom up, and are not imposed in top-down process, demonstrating democratic processes by giving community members the opportunity to take an active role in local issues, events and activities. A community's sense of responsibility can be heightened by increasing the awareness of members about social issues and providing a medium through which their sense of social responsibility can be translated into action.

In the tourism industry there are various types of tourism that are considered to have positive effects on communities. However, all tourism should subscribe to sustaining and developing the communities in which they operate. The discussion on ecotourism below is one example of tourism that can aid in community capacity development, but should not be relegated just to the niche of ecotourism.

Ecotourism, empowerment and community development
Ecotourism is often referred to in community capacity development fields, especially in developing countries such as Costa Rica. The term 'ecotourism' is contested and at times has been used simply as a marketing tool. Basically, ecotourism is nature based, educative and managed in a sustainable fashion (Beeton 1998). Sustainable management refers to the community as well as the natural environment: it requires operators to support the local community through employment, products, education and in other ways. Ecotourism also incorporates aspects of TBL sustainability including generating financial support for protection and management of natural areas, benefits for residents and resident support for conservation. However, without proper planning and integration, projects work in isolation, failing to influence conservation, development or policy.

Community based ecotourism are enterprises owned and managed by the community. This implies that the community is taking care of its resources through conservation, business enterprise and community development, but is not always the case. Empowerment issues such as who participates come to the fore – often the disadvantaged (those who need it most) are left out of the process and women are restricted to low-paying service roles (cooks, cleaners).

The Appendix has the text of a keynote presentation on rural ecotourism and communities from a conference held in regional, outback Australia that reinforces many of the points made in this book.

Planning tourism for a community

One of the major difficulties in undertaking planning from a community perspective, which is exacerbated with tourism planning, is the political nature of the planning process as discussed above. The whole notion of community planning implies a high level of community involvement and participation, yet often the community does not have the control that is implicit in such a notion. As noted earlier, this is not always possible in certain political environments and structures. However, this does not mean we should not try. As Sofield (2003) notes, many of the benefits of community based tourism planning lie in the process, not simply the outcome. By taking the journey down the community engagement and empowerment path, problematic areas, power imbalances, lack of social capacity and capital can be highlighted, which can then work in our favour. This really is a case of 'Rome wasn't built in a day'. Personally, I have learnt so much about myself and the communities I live, work, study and play in through the numerous community development processes I have been involved in. This enables a far more constructive attitude to everything I now approach – and the journey continues!

Many good manuals have been developed to guide community groups through the strategic planning process, particularly in North America, with one of the most effective, yet easy to follow summarised below (see Community Tourism Handbook, http://extension.usu.edu/wrdc/ctah for full details).

As well as resulting in capacity building and empowering the community members, one of the strengths of engaging the community in its own development process is also one of its weaknesses. Volunteers from the community, not paid outsiders, handle the majority of the community based work. However, recruiting and maintaining an enthusiastic, committed volunteer group is problematic, particularly in small communities and those used to a hierarchical, top-down power structure. In the first instance (small community), responsibility for many of the community based projects can fall to the same few people, which negates the notion of empowerment and capacity building and may also result in burnout of those involved. The second issue can be even more problematic, where the community is used to being told what to do by a person in a position of power. Even if the person genuinely desires to empower the members, they will tend to resist any move of responsibility to them – this is the contradiction inherent in community development, much like the contradiction of tourism (carrying with it the seeds of its destruction). Effecting the change required to empower such communities and relieve the load on the few takes time and requires an ongoing commitment.

The first phase is to conduct an audit and assessment of the assets and capacity of the community. The audit needs to be broad ranging as there are many elements that may not be thought of as tourism assets, yet can be exactly what tourists are looking for. This stage requires time and commitment and should not be rushed. Information should be gathered on aspects such as community organisation, visitor profiles, resident attitudes, visioning, product inventory, marketing and project identification and scoping, impact analysis and a post assessment phase, which are outlined below.

Community organisation
The first step is to establish an Assessment Committee that has an overview of the project. This requires a long-term commitment, so it is important to identify and recruit a group of volunteers dedicated to improving their community. Also, it is preferable to bring together a (small) group that is representative of the community and a facilitator who can make sure that all members have the opportunity to contribute. This facilitator may be a paid outsider or a local person, depending on the needs and structure of the community and its current levels of empowerment and social capital.

Current visitor and economic profiles
The first project of the Assessment Committee will be to find out what the current situation is in terms of tourism and the community. Existing data can be compiled to capture a picture of the current impact of tourism and other sectors on local economy. Visitor travel patterns and characteristics need to be analysed. The extent of this will depend upon the availability of existing data, much of which can be obtained from government tourism bodies, annual census figures and other sources.

However, in a small community, there may be little data that focuses purely on that area and decisions need to be made about its relevance.

One solution is to engage local education institutions, particularly tertiary ones, to undertake projects that may provide data for the community at a relatively low cost. However, this will take time and if there is no money for consulting fees, it will often be a student project that may not be totally reliable.

Resident attitudes, visioning and product inventory

Research also needs to be conducted to assess how tourism 'stacks up' in the minds of residents. It is important that the Assessment Committee does not assume that they understand all the views of the community. The case study in the previous chapter demonstrates one method for obtaining the views of the community, while at the same time illustrates the complexities of actually obtaining a true representation of views.

One method that can help in this early stage is to conduct formal or informal focus groups with a range of community members, allowing them to discuss their hopes and fears for the future. These groups need to be efficiently facilitated so that the more vocal, power-dominant members do not overpower the less powerful.

At this stage, it is appropriate to bring the community together to develop a *Vision* of where they would like to see their community in the future and how tourism fits into that vision. Such an undertaking enables all community members or the Assessment Committee to decide among the various alternatives for their community in terms of what the actors want.

This is central to all planning and absolutely crucial when developing communities via tourism projects. The challenge here is to initially get participation from all areas of the community (not just those with the power) and to gain consensus. The case study at the end of this chapter is an excellent example of this process in action (or inaction!).

There are some methods that can assist in getting the community together and encouraging them to participate, such as combining the exercise with a social event or local celebration. The facilitator can personally invite individuals to participate, and arrange transport so that local people can attend without having to make special efforts.

So, once the group is gathered, a *Vision Statement* is required that identifies what is really valued and desired for the community. Underpinning the statement will be a set of goals that need to be articulated and agreed upon, such as the number of jobs, for whom, at what pay scales, for what seasons, or to encourage new residents, retain young members of the community and so on. While agreeing on this is important, there also needs to be a commitment from the community to work to achieve the vision.

Now that the community knows who is visiting them and what they want for their future, they must understand what they actually have in their community by undertaking a *Product Inventory*. This is primarily a list of all existing attractions and tourism-related facilities that is then rated on their value to the tourists and their competitive advantage.

In addition, the community's infrastructure needs to be assessed so that the capacity to support an expanding tourism industry can be determined. Of particular concern are water, sewerage, waste disposal and transportation systems.

Tourism marketing and markets
At this point some decisions on the markets that the community wishes to attract can be made. If the current market is suitable and desirable, strategies to continue to support and develop them can be developed. However, if the community wishes to broaden or even change the type of visitor, they need to understand the nature of different market segments and niches. The marketing basics of supply and demand have to be taken into account – there is no point in trying to attract a certain type of visitor if you cannot provide what they want.

There are many ways to segment visitor markets, from simple demographic segmentation (by age, income and so on – such as the Baby Boomers, Generation X etc.) or by their behaviour and psychological needs (looking to rest and relax, to be challenged, meet others and so on). Understanding market segmentations is a continual process, but some of the more common segments that many communities are interested in attracting include:

- *Nature or eco travellers*
  Focus on learning, experiential activities and efforts that

support conservation

- *Outdoor enthusiasts*

  Active holiday-makers

  Natural, healthy food

- *Heritage travellers*

  Want to understand the culture and history of an area

Further information on market niches and marketing for communities and tourism is in the next chapter.

Project identification, scoping, impact analysis, assessment

Once the community's assets (supply) and the potential tourist's interests and needs (demand) are established, short and long-term projects can be identified and prioritised according to their value to the community, value to the tourist and their advantage over competing communities. Then the highest priority projects can be outlined along the lines of projected revenues and costs (construction, operation, maintenance), employment (local and imported) and the infrastructure needs (*Project Scoping*). These needs can then be assessed in terms of the costs by undertaking an *Impact Analysis* that establishes the economic, social and environmental costs and benefits of each scoped project. Such measures may require the establishment of key indicators and benchmarks as discussed in the previous chapter. This enables the community to see who or what may be adversely impacted and decide on which, if any, projects should proceed. In this *Assessment Phase* the community may decide that tourism is no longer a development strategy they wish to pursue and choose to turn to other community development strategies. Or they may still desire to pursue tourism, but have not identified any acceptable projects, so go back and consider projects not assessed in the first round.

Once the community decides on a project from a number of projects they move on to the *Post Assessment Phase*. This includes project development, marketing, implementation and management and monitoring and evaluation of the projects.

The case study below does not exactly follow the process outlined above, yet contains many of the aspects and looks at them in terms of a real-life case.

From theory to practice: Trying to empower – the case of the country towns project

While the concept of individual and community empowerment is clearly a preferred way to develop communities, and tourism can clearly be a contributor to this process, in reality, it is not always simple to empower people. This is particularly the case where the power balance in a community may be skewed towards certain groups or individuals who, by either their very nature or desire, operate in a top-down fashion. A community whose members are used to being 'told what to do', instead of welcoming the bottom-up approach associated with empowerment, may resent the responsibility it entails and actively work to subvert such a goal. While many readers may be thinking of indigenous and other marginalised communities while reading this, this situation exists in many (if not all) communities to one extent or another. The experience of working on a project referred to here as The Country Towns Project (CTP) in regional 'mainstream' Australia (that is, not indigenous or remote communities) is one such example.

Six small-town taskforces have been working together with a regional university research centre and the Community Employment Council (CEC), a Regional Management Team, on a holistic community development project. The original goal of the project was:

To establish continuing community and business building processes which will empower selected towns to implement practical and achievable employment and economic development actions.

The desired outcomes for the project included the:
- Formation of Community Business Builder Taskforces and teams in eight towns;
- Research profiles in each town;
- Empowerment of enthusiastic community and business builders;
- An implementation program of tangible actions for job creation and economic development initiative in each town;

- Empowerment of teams of enthusiastic community taskforces;
- Implementation of tangible projects and activities that generate actions for job creation and economic development and strengthening of communities across the region; and
- Successful attainment of funds to support the implementation, undertaking and management of community supported projects and activities.

The main objective of the project was to empower the communities and develop structures to take them into the future. It was acknowledged from the outset that such structures must be community driven and owned, not imposed from without, reflecting an attempt to move from individual leadership, which faces problems of burnout and the leader leaving the community.

Tourism workshops

I facilitated two tourism workshops for the project, the first one being very loosely defined and described, and was more about getting the actors comfortable with each other and myself as an outsider. My main concern and aim was for the participants to develop a regional vision for tourism, which could then be taken back to each town to guide their development which would have some overall cohesive image that could then be promoted effectively. However, due to the need to develop rapport and relationships, this could not even be considered until the second workshop.

Tourism workshop no. 2

The stated objective of the second Tourism Workshop was to identify, investigate and discuss strategies to attract visitors to the towns; to provide a valued and memorable experience for visitors (to encourage return visits); to attract and/or enhance business opportunities in tourism related sectors. This in turn would generate local employment. However, this was presented as a top-down 'directive' from the power-brokers of the project and related communities, so before such objectives could be met, a vision that the entire group could support and embrace had to be found.

The main aim therefore was to develop a united vision for tourism among the project towns, rather than a specific discussion of individual needs. The purpose of developing a vision that is owned by all towns is to assist each town and individual to assess and rank their various tourism opportunities in a cooperative manner. It has been long understood that clustering (or working together) in any small business arena provides individual businesses with greater promotional and resource opportunities, resulting in more successful operations. As the facilitator, this was the first message I had to impart to the participants, which had to be seen to come from them.

After many hours of discussion, we left the workshop with three sentences that covered the main aspects for the future of their communities that resonated with the group. We were able to develop a vision that was strong, focused and owned by all partners. The vision was:

To access our community's culture of welcome to help our visitors experience, celebrate and enjoy our local colonial, indigenous and natural heritages and environment, as well as participate in our vibrant cultures.

This vision tied in well with the vision of the regional tourism organisation, which was an ideal outcome but one that I had not referred to earlier as I wanted the group to be as free as they could be from the constraints of a 'powerful member' such as the tourism organisation, particularly being presented by a 'powerful outsider' (myself as the facilitator). I was very aware of my position of power in the group and worked to let them speak freely without coercion – this was the aim behind the first workshop. The regional tourism organisation's tourism goal was about:

Offering the highest quality colonial heritage experience in the nation ... augmented by excellence in accommodation, food and wine, arts and crafts, and service standards.

By linking the towns' vision with the regional tourism organisation's vision, even greater synergy and success could be achieved, particularly as the group had worked their vision up independently.

A list of desired outcomes was developed and then prioritised into various levels to reflect the group's vision and goals. The first level included:

- creating wealth
- developing a culture of welcome
- creating jobs (for whom? – youth, residents, new residents with new expertise...)
- valuing and preservation of assets.

While the second level consisted of:
- encouraging new residents
- visitor education
- vitality
- diversity
- accessibility.

In addition, I included in my report to the group some further comments and suggestions that might assist in addressing some of these issues. I stressed that they were only suggestions and were not the only solutions, but some had been shown to be helpful. I explained that in the end, it was up to them – no-one could do it for them. But I also gave them information as to where they could access help for the asking from other organisations in the Arts and Heritage fields as well as tourism. While this may be seen as a powerful outsider (myself) directing the community members, such guidance was crucial as there had been a great deal of resistance to actually taking on any responsibilities for the process and its outcomes – initially a surprising response from a group that, as I came to know them better, was not empowered and had difficulty in taking on these opportunities. This was a classic example of a relatively unempowered community resisting attempts to empower them – at times I felt that they preferred this situation as they could always blame someone else if it did not work.

I also felt compelled to express some of the issues of carrying capacity, as many members in this group could not see beyond their immediate needs (wants) of increasing their visitor numbers, and some of the areas we were talking about are highly environmentally fragile (let alone the communities themselves!). The following extract includes the additional information I provided the group in my final report from the Workshop.

Popularity of tourism and carrying capacity
Tourism can destroy the very things it celebrates if we are not clear on what line we are taking, especially in relation to authenticity. Desired visitor behaviour and attitudes need to be incorporated in the marketing plan, at both individual and group levels. For example, if we are celebrating friendliness and relaxation, we need to consider how and where people may travel through the area – an example may be to encourage cycle tours so as to reduce noise and pollution from vehicles.

Advancing individuals, not community tourism
This is a difficult issue to overcome, but if the vision is strong and widely publicised and used, others will come into line as they recognise the benefits.

Infrastructure and service needs
This relates directly to issues of popularity and needs to be continually monitored. It is not wise to go ahead with a project until there is the appropriate supporting infrastructure. Local councils and their Economic Development Units need to be kept in the loop here.

Risk
Assistance from industry groups who have risk management experience and insurance schemes would be one option here. Many accreditation programs also provide information on risk management.

Funding – lack of skills and time
University graduates are experienced in writing projects, many of which are similar to funding applications. The tourism awards submission also leads you through most of the material that you

will need for a funding submission – there are many similarities. A business plan is essential before you even attempt any submission process. Small Business Victoria and local educational institutions often run workshops on business planning.

Also, if funding is being applied for from a voluntary group, set up a process that ensures the knowledge of the person putting the submission together is retained and accessible to others.

Burnout and rustout of staff and volunteers
Sharing workload, varying tasks and responsibilities and developing a culture of sharing, as opposed to individual ownership of community projects, will assist. Always plan for succession on committees.

Townspeople not accepting the vision
This requires some creative promotion and support to encourage others to feel part of the 'welcome'. Getting schools involved and enthused can often filter up to their parents and others. Another point is to make sure that the vision is not perceived to be one person's territory – it cannot be seen to be forced down from the 'top'.

So, what's the next step?
Now that we have a vision and some understanding of the issues, you can:

1 Identify and rank specific projects and concepts in the knowledge that they tie in with the broader view of the towns and region

2 Conduct a cost-benefit analysis on the highest ranking projects

3 Decide whether to proceed with them in light of the analysis.

Thank you for your input and contribution to this workshop.

Issues

As inferred and noted throughout this case study, a number of issues arose over the two years of my involvement in the project, with the major ones shown below.

- Difficult to develop and maintain an overall vision of the project within each taskforce. Each town more concerned with their own vision and at times may compete with the others.

- Each town is at a different stage of development.

- Changing membership of the taskforces often requires 'going over old ground' which frustrates others and dislocates the group.

- Not all taskforce members attend each meeting.

- Members looking for immediate, tangible results, which in the process of developing community structures does not occur.

- Inconsistent expectations.

- Lack of young people involved in the project.

- Communication was at the very best piecemeal and haphazard, resulting in many participants and community members being unaware of what was happening.

Of major concern was that, prior to any real strategic thought relating to tourism's role in community development, each town had developed a number of priority projects, the majority of them being tourism related. This caused me some concern as tourism cannot survive on its own (or only in a few 'tourist towns'). It needs people, and many of these towns were not attracting visitors and had a limited amount of transit visitors.

A personal note on letting go
One of the hardest things to do is facilitate introductory workshops such as these, then hand the outcomes over to the communities to run with them. Especially when they want someone to do it for them ...

At the time of writing (some five years after my first workshop) the project with these towns is being 'completed'. I wait with fascination to see what has been achieved over that time. I feel confident that, while many will not know the origins of the tourism vision for these communities, it remains very much as it was developed by the members.

5

Marketing community tourism

While there are many good books on tourism marketing, it is rare that they include any discussion of the host communities, not only in terms of how to market them to the potential visitor, but also how to 'market' tourism to the community. Presenting the potential visitor and/or a proposed tourism development or activity to the community as a positive occurrence is crucial. In effect, in relation to tourism and community development, we have three 'customers' – the tourist, the community and the tourism industry itself.

We begin this discussion by outlining what marketing is and what it is not. What follows is very much an introductory note for those not familiar with marketing as it stands today. While you, the reader, may feel that you are knowledgeable about marketing, by reading this brief introduction you will understand the principles I have based this chapter on.

Following the general introduction to marketing is a brief discussion of the differences between product and services marketing – in essence, the core of tourism and communities are intangible experiences/interactions which have more in common with the notion of a service rather than a product. The key to marketing and to community development centres on understanding our markets **and** our people. Understanding who they are, what they want, why they want it and what we can provide requires a certain amount of research, and some of the basic elements of market research are introduced.

Once these introductions are out of the way we look at community based marketing in terms of destination promotion and networking or cooperative marketing between and within industry sectors. The need to promote tourism within our communities is then discussed, followed by the essence of this chapter (and book), promoting communities through tourism. This leads us into a discussion on the ethics of marketing and the growth of 'ethical marketing'.

While much of what we consider to be 'marketing' is based around a strategic, conscious plan (outlined next), there are also other activities that affect the marketing of a place or community, which I have called 'accidental marketing'. We look at this in terms of fiction media in literature, art, film and music, with a focus on movies and television series. The main part of the chapter finishes with some thoughts and a strategy on what to do when we become too successful, ending up with too many visitors. The case study at the end of the chapter returns to an important element of this chapter by outlining how a not-for-profit moving event promotes itself to the many communities through which it travels.

Marketing and management are intricately linked – the marketing strategy or plan is part of the business strategy or plan, yet most reference books tend to look at business management or marketing, not both together. As Drucker notes, marketing 'encompasses the entire business. It is the whole business seen from the point of view of the final result, that is from the customer's point of view' (Drucker 1950, p. 30). In this chapter, I move between using the terms 'marketing' and 'management' where necessary, as these elements of operating a business or developing a community are so closely intertwined that in many cases the marketing activities affect the management activities and vice versa.

Marketing and services marketing

Over the years, the term 'marketing' has come to mean many different things to different people. Marketing is 'the process of planning and executing the conception, pricing, promotion and distribution of ideas, goods and services to create exchanges that satisfy individual and organizational objectives' (American Marketing Association 1985, cited Dann & Dann 2004, p. 6). Marketing involves research, planning and implementation; it is not simply 'selling' or a 'quick fix' to any problem an organisation may face. Marketing does not have the power to make people buy anything regardless of their needs and wants (Dann & Dann 2004).

Marketing is primarily customer focused as opposed to production focused, asking *What does the customer want?* not *What can we produce?* After finding out what the customer wants or needs, the product (or service) is developed to satisfy those needs and then it is promoted at prices mutually acceptable to both producer and consumer.

There are various genres or fields that marketing is involved in, all of which take a different approach. These include direct marketing where individual customers are contacted personally, public sector marketing (political parties are the clear leaders in this area of marketing, but other public sector agencies run marketing programs to promote their services), relationship marketing (building loyalty such as through frequent flyer programs), social marketing (including educational programs such as the 'drink drive' programs where an attempt is made to alter behaviour) and destination marketing (getting people to visit places, keeping them there and getting them to come back again).

A core component of the modern economy is that of service provision. Services are *intangible* in that they cannot be tested without using them being *inseparable* from the provider/producer and they have a strong people presence in any transaction. Being intangible, services cannot be seen, tasted, felt, heard or smelled before they are purchased, so we need to provide some type of tangible evidence or representation (such as brochures). In order for a service to be delivered, the provider and customer must both be present, making them inseparable. Tourism and many aspects of communities are intangible and inseparable services.

Apart from intangibility and inseparability, services are also *variable* and *perishable*. The quality of the service depends on who provides the services, what mood that person is in, what state of mind the customer is in and where they are provided, making each service provision a new and different transaction. Because of all these points, a service cannot be stored to be sold later – once the aircraft has taken off, that particular (empty) seat on that flight cannot be sold. It is perishable (Kotler *et al.* 2003).

These points are important, as tourism and tourists' encounters with communities are essentially service-based experiences. The elements that visitors most recall are not the physical things they saw, but the emotions they experienced through the interactions they had with community members, their tour hosts or others. This does not necessarily mean that every visitor wants a deep and meaningful encounter with every community member – some may simply want to have some peace and quiet and be left alone. Recognising the level of encounters desired at any time by a visitor is an integral element of your 'product' (service).

Anyone who has done the smallest amount of marketing study will have come across the four *Ps* that make up the marketing mix: product, price, placement and promotion. Added to this from the services sector is a fifth P: people. This is about the people who are the service as well as the customer, who also becomes part of the service encounter, which is based on notions of reciprocity. This is the essence of inseparability and intangibility.

In order to market such experiences, they need to be tangibilised in some way in order to provide the potential visitor with some idea of what they can expect. In tourism, the most common way is through the use of promotional material such as brochures, videos, advertisements (print and television) and the Internet as well as souvenirs and gifts. An extremely important thing to consider is: what message does the staff uniforms or dress codes send to the customer as to what they may expect in terms of service and style? The physical environment of the service company can be another way to tangibilise the service, and correlates to the environment in which the community lives, which in many cases is the physical appearance of the town, village, suburb or centre of that community. The beauty here is that if the community also desires an 'attractive' streetscape or other such environment, developing (tangibilising) this for the visitor will have flow-on positive effects for the community as a whole. Of course, if the community does not agree with the changes (such as putting street names in another language), the community will resent tourists and tourism and may even move away.

If we consider communities to be a service 'business' (or a combination/amalgamation of many service businesses), then there are a number of management strategies and issues that need to be addressed. These issues also influence the marketing strategies (remember the 'product' is part of the marketing mix and needs to be developed and, when it is a service, continually managed). Employees need to be managed positively as they are a crucial part of the marketing mix. This can include paid staff working in the community or for the community (such as local government), voluntary staff (many of whom work at visitor information centres, welcome centres, festivals, museums and art galleries – all tourist attractions in their own right), as well as members of the general community (who often do not see themselves as being involved in tourism). Understanding and managing these elements is the key to a successful tourism industry based on a community.

Perceived risk also needs to be managed as customers may feel that purchasing an intangible product that cannot be tested is risky. Consequently, a satisfied customer will be more loyal in a service environment than when purchasing a tangible product as it is risky to change, and potential customers tend to rely on word of mouth recommendations. These are key elements to remember in terms of marketing and delivering that service. Perceptions are powerful, and regardless of whether they are right or wrong, can be difficult to change.

Balancing the capacity of your community to support tourism and the demand of tourists to visit and experience the range of services you offer can be problematic, particularly at peak times. Tourism tends to be seasonal, both over one year and during one week (where weekends generally tend to be busier), or even at specific moments such as during an annual festival or event. This has marketing implications – decisions have to be made as to how much to promote your community during its peak times and how much to encourage people to visit at other times. Over-promotion can result in crowding, and it has been found that for many service operations customer complaints increase when capacity is over 80 per cent (Dann & Dann 2004).

In order to understand many of these management and promotion issues, reliable information is needed. Research provides management/community leaders with relevant, up-to-date information about their community, their visitors and their service performance. One issue in working with a community is finding a person or, preferably, a group of people to analyse and interpret the data and provide recommendations to the relevant groups based on the information, not merely their 'gut feelings'. That said, often research will reinforce a 'gut feeling' that someone had – however, it is better to confirm this rather than assume we have it right. Undertaking market research can be time consuming and costly for a community, but there are simple ways to gather some of the data, and these are discussed below.

Market research attempts to answer questions such as:

- Who is the customer/visitor? (This can be done in terms of country of origin, demographics, reasons for travel, means of transport, expenditure, length of stay and so on.)
- Why do they purchase the tourism product or leisure activity? What motivates them to do this?

As I said earlier, there are many ways to locate such information, or data sources, including primary and secondary research. Secondary research (or desk research) reviews data which already exists, such as that from government departments and organisations (especially tourism organisations, but other government departments will also have relevant information, such as the Department of Arts, Bureau of Statistics, or Immigration and so on). Industry based associations, such as the Pacific Asia Tourist Association, World Tourism Organisation and so on also provide their members with relevant research data, and do make some available to non-members. Conferences also are great sources of research data. Finally, many university researchers publish the findings of their research in academic and non-academic journals. These tend to be focused on certain elements and go into more depth, nevertheless much of the data can be used. There are numerous tourism and marketing journals held at university libraries. Some people are daunted by the thought of reading academic journal articles, however, all you really need to do is read the abstract and conclusion to decide if the rest is worth persevering with!

Undertaking secondary research avoids the costs associated with collecting, sorting and analysing data, saves time and also prevents you from already doing work that someone else has done, saving personal energy as well. But there are some limitations to the value of this secondary data, such as it may not answer your specific problem and may be out of date. The research methodology may be flawed, which is not always easy to examine, or the results biased. Often it is easy to see which of Jafari's (1989; 2002) platforms (advocacy, cautionary, adaptancy or knowledge-based as introduced in Chapter 1) the researcher/writer is coming from, which may help you decide how best to use the data – usually with care!

Primary research is research undertaken in the field and is data that you (your community or organisation) collect in order to answer a specific question or questions. In marketing terms, this usually revolves around understanding current and potential customers, your competitors and your own resources. In community based tourism we also research the host community, who are a resource, but also so much more.

There are various ways that this can be approached, including using face-to-face interviews, a self-administered survey (often mailed back to the organisation), a household survey, focus groups, observation, or even simply asking your frontline staff/volunteers and customers for feedback. Each of these can be done using qualitative or quantitative methods, or a combination of both. The choice of the method you use depends on what you want to know as well as practical limitations such as time, money and skills. In addition, particularly when dealing with your community, there may be some ethical and privacy issues in terms of what you ask them, how you do it and how you report your results.

I have found that one of the most useful and powerful forms of research in tourism and community situations is observation. However, this should be done by experienced people and tempered with some other data so that there is limited personal bias in the observations. There are obvious ethical issues here as well – tracking and filming visitors may not be appropriate, ethical or legal, which is why experienced, responsible leaders are needed for this approach. But it is important to recognise that all research that is done by people about people is biased to some extent. There are many references on ethnographic studies that explain many ways that observational research can be done (for example, see Jennings 2001 for an introduction and direction to other references).

One of the main outcomes from marketing research is the identification of possible market segments that can allow you to isolate exactly who your most likely customers are and why they are purchasing. The market is divided into portions and then you target the most appropriate portion or segment.

Before undertaking data collection, the questions shown below need to be addressed.

- What do you want to find out through the primary research?
- How will the data be used?
- What survey method will you use?
- Can the survey be repeated using this method?
- What costs are involved?
- Will the benefits outweigh the cost? (Dann & Dann, 2004)

For example, if I wanted to find out the economic contribution of people visiting Melbourne, I would be asking questions such as how many visitors come to the city, how much are they spending and how long are they staying for. This is quantitative research and usually entails the use of 'closed' questions that require a definitive 'tick the box' response. If I was interested in why they were visiting, I would be asking more open-ended, qualitative questions that are designed to get inside the customer's head.

In conclusion, marketing is not possible without market research, and successful marketing is not possible without the appropriate market research. We must understand our customer, which is even more crucial in service industries due to the inseparability of the customer from the product.

Community based marketing

In the previous section we looked at some of the basic marketing elements, with a particular focus on services marketing, acknowledging that a community and tourism are *services*. We take that premise further in this section, looking at marketing *communities* that are geographically or spatially based, such as towns, villages, cities, rural areas or national parks. I have taken this definition of community as it is the one we most associate with tourism, and is the primary type of community that we consider throughout this book (see Chapter 1). In other words, we are looking at marketing for destination communities. Nevertheless, much of the material covered here is applicable to other types of communities, such as communities of interest, as well as ethnic and indigenous communities.

Destination/place marketing/promotion and its relationship to communities that host tourism and tourists

Destinations (also referred to as 'places') are geographically based, usually referring to a region or town. They are complex, with a large range of different types of attractions, communities and supporting infrastructure. These various elements of a destination interact to create the particular nature of a place that is more than simply the sum of its components. This needs to be understood by anyone who is charged with marketing that destination. In addition, whereas communities are generally defined by their own members, a tourist destination may be defined by the tourists themselves, which can result in a place meaning different things to different people, regardless of any marketing effort.

Destinations are often viewed in a hierarchical manner, from an individual enterprise (such as a theme park) to a town or city (such as Surfers Paradise), region (the Gold Coast), state (Queensland), national (Australia) and supranational (Asia-Pacific) levels. Each level incorporates the level below it. In spite of all the talk (in this book and elsewhere) about empowerment, cultural capital and so on, destination marketing itself is often seen as a top-down process. This tends to come from government or (tourism) industry funded Destination Marketing Organisations (DMOs) that provide the basic destination marketing and imaging strategies, often based on a hierarchical approach. Marketing an entire destination can be a costly exercise that benefits an entire range of community members, so it has been argued that public organisations such as governments should undertake this role. However, there is still scope for individual communities to become involved, particularly at the enterprise, city and regional levels.

A major issue in destination marketing (and with communities) is that many of the elements within it compete with each other, particularly the tourism businesses, and it is a challenge to get them to understand that they need to work together to get people to the destination. Only then can they compete for the visitor's business. Another related issue is that some businesses that benefit from tourism do not see themselves as part of tourism, particularly some providers such as electricians, plumbers, mechanics and other tradespeople. As they rarely actually serve tourists, they are unaware that their work may well be paid for by the money those tourists are bringing in to another business. The most successful destinations have a community that recognises this, with the businesses and community all contributing in some way to the marketing of the destination, whether they are direct or indirect beneficiaries.

For similar reasons to those outlined above for individuals, destinations may compete with each other, but at the same time have to work together, depending on their target market. For example, if a town wants to attract international visitors, it is more effective if it teams up with the larger destination groupings such as a state or country to attract them.

Related to the marketing issue of attracting international visitors above is the potential visitor's geographical frame of reference, which plays a major role in selecting the places they wish to visit. The visitor is looking for a destination that is different to what he/she perceives to be its neighbours. So, a domestic day visitor will want to know how one destination differs from the others nearby (such as between Surfers Paradise and Coolangatta), whereas interstate visitors will want to know more about the differences between particular regions (the Gold Coast and the Sunshine Coast), and visitors from overseas need the entire country differentiated from its neighbours (Australia and New Zealand). Consequently, it is important to know whom you are targeting in your marketing strategy – it may need to be different for each group.

In terms of this balance between cooperation and competition we need to understand what makes a destination 'competitive' and how this relates to our community. Ritchie and Crouch (2003, p. 2) explain this as the destination's '... ability to increase tourism expenditure, to increasingly attract visitors while providing them with satisfying, memorable experiences, and to do so in a profitable way, while enhancing the wellbeing of destination residents and preserving the natural capital of the destination for future generations.'

In addition, even at the simplest level, destinations are growing, complex entities in a constant state of change. As a destination matures in terms of tourism its character may change, as illustrated by Butler's TALC discussed in Chapter 2. This means that destination marketing organisations need to keep pace and adapt, which requires constant monitoring reviewing. External factors outside the direct control of the destination include the political situation (particularly in terms of regional stability), the changing fashion and tastes of the market and even the influence of the media.

Destination marketing organisations (DMOs)

Insofar as our communities are destinations, we need to understand what the organisations are who market and manage our destination, commonly known as Destination Marketing Organisations (DMOs). At each level of a destination there are organisations responsible for marketing and management and to develop and maintain cooperative relationships with the other levels. A recent problem has been the increase in organisations (DMOs or otherwise) who are involved in marketing a destination (or community), which has led to a blurring of roles. In order to help you sort through the jargon here are the common terms for destination marketing organisations at various levels in Australia, which has similar counterparts throughout the world:

- NTOs (National Tourism Organisation/Office), such as Tourism Australia
- State and Territory marketing organisations (eight in Victoria), such as Tourism NSW, NT Tourist Commission
- RTOs (Regional Tourism Organisation) (75 in Victoria), such as Geelong-Otway Tourism, Goldfields Tourism
- Local tourist or visitor bureaux (countless!), such as Shipwreck Coast Tourism, Bendigo Tourism, Ballarat Tourism.

In addition to the 'formal' DMOs, there are other government departments that have an interest in promoting a destination, including immigration and business development departments, tourism departments (often different from their marketing arms), local governments and export trade missions run at the local, state, national and supranational levels.

With all of these different groups involved in destination marketing, there is no single structure for a DMO. At the higher levels there tends to be a more corporate structure with representative Boards of Management, which (ideally) should include representatives from the government, industry and host community. However, as with our discussion on power relations in a community in Chapter 4, this is a top-down approach that tends to favour those with political power. In reality, the community is rarely included on a DMO board, and is more of a token gesture when it does occur. Even so, representation on a board does not always guarantee an appropriate share of the power. The major industry 'contributors' may get a greater say, but not all regions/industry sectors can be represented and/or the government may simply choose to ignore the industry. Therefore benefits may not be fairly distributed, which may be a real or perceived inequity and in any case can lead to crisis of representation.

That is not to say that there are no exceptions to this, but we must be aware of the overriding majority of these organisations in order to better work with them.

One of the elements relating to the power relations in a DMO is where and how it receives its funding. I have already mentioned the power some individual tourism businesses may wield, which can be a direct influence of their funding contributions. In Australia, most of the DMOs are at least partly government funded, but there can be funding from the industry in the form of membership fees, levies and licences. In some cases there may be funding from tourists themselves, but this is rare in Australia, with the Northern Territory being an exception. From 1987 to 2000 the Territory imposed a 'bed tax' on those staying overnight (Northern Territory Treasury 2000). This tax was used exclusively to fund the region's destination marketing programs. However, it was politically unpalatable and actively resisted by the industry due to the inequitable distribution of the costs of such a tax, so it was ultimately abandoned.

While marketing is the primary role of DMOs, they do have a multitude of functions and roles, with some undertaking more functions than others. This is dependent on a number of factors, including funding and political support, support from industry and existing industry based structures, as well as the reciprocal support from (and for) the community. Many of these roles rely on the various person-alities and skills of the staff and the community, as well as the aforemen-tioned power roles. However, the roles of DMOs can be summarised as marketing, particularly in terms of undertaking and gathering research data, and management, such as facilitation and coordination.

Up to this point, the astute reader may be wondering how on earth the community can get a look in to this significant area that can have such an effect on them. Fortunately, more and more DMOs are moving towards facilitating and assisting community involvement in tourism, rather than simply taking a top-down management approach. This is due in no small way to their own diminishing funding. Politics and power are now working in a different, more positive way for the community. This facilitation role includes activities such as:

- managing the flow of data/intelligence
- representing the destination overseas
- participating in and facilitating workshops
- coordinating familiarisation trips for travel buyers and the media
- supporting the production and distribution of promotional literature
- developing joint marketing initiatives with the industry and community
- providing information and reservation systems
- providing general advice to individual operators and community members.

The case study in Chapter 4 on the Small Towns Project was supported and actively contributed to by the local and regional DMOs. As noted earlier, destinations often need to work together, as do individual businesses and community members. There are numerous examples of the success of such cooperative relationships, which is considered in more detail below.

Cooperative tourism marketing/networking

Networking is a range of cooperative behaviour between otherwise competing organisations that are linked through economic and social relationships and transactions. This can include vertical (cross-sectoral) or horizontal networks and has great significance for community based tourism (and destination) marketing. Porter also identifies such alliances as 'clustering', describing it as '... a critical mass of companies in a particular location (a country, state, region or even a city)' (Porter 1998, p. 7).

An example of a horizontal marketing network is the various airline alliances that have developed over the past few years. While the individual airlines compete for business, they also cooperate to increase their market reach. This primarily came from the need to gain further competitive advantages in a highly regulated and costly industry. One of the primary motivations for airlines to enter into alliances is to gain entry into markets that are difficult for them to enter alone, particularly in the domestic markets in countries other than the airlines' home. The range of benefits that such alliances can bring to an airline is outlined in Table 5.1, and many can relate to tourism destination communities.

Table 5.1 Airline alliance benefits

Alliance element	Benefit
Code sharing	Added revenue due to increased customer traffic
	Multiple listing of a single flight causes a crowding out effect on CRS display, encouraging reservations for those flights
	Greater combination of flights in various markets
Joint frequent flyer programs	More benefit alternatives for customers
	Larger network from which to collect frequent flyer miles
	Preferred use of allied airlines, increasing customers
Cross-border feeding	Seamless service through an international hub to large set of domestic destinations
Schedule coordination	Reduction of waiting times between connecting flights
Resource sharing	Elimination of staff duplication at airports
	Joint marketing
Airport access (terminal slots)	Access to congested international airways through sharing and exchange of slots and terminal facilities
Technical cooperation	Sharing of maintenance, emergency equipment and information systems
Travel agent commission overrides	Increased travel agent incentives to book alliance partners
Halo effect	Travel agents' (and others) tendency to book more on a carrier associated with a brand they know

Source: Beeton 2004b; Vander Kraats 2000; Gudmundsson 1999.

While these benefits are significant, there are some issues that concern the overall tourism industry, such as the effect these alliances may actually have on competition, particularly where the market may become dominated by a few 'mega carriers' as well as create barriers for emerging airlines. However, in terms of destinations, some of these issues do not arise due to their complex nature and multiple competitors.

Additional benefits that the tourism industry can gain from forming alliances with similar businesses in their region include increased effectiveness and efficiencies in marketing spend, giving them greater control over how their product is marketed.

In terms of tourism in destination communities, horizontal marketing can also occur between similar destinations, which is usually those geographically nearby. Instead of competing, neighbouring towns may decide to promote themselves cooperatively so that they can create a stronger appeal to potential visitors by providing them with more choice. Which destinations are seen as 'neighbouring' is very much in the eye of the visitor and where they are coming from, as discussed in the destination marketing section earlier.

Vertical partnerships (or networks) across different sectors can also be across the hierarchy of destinations, such as a local village networking its image and promotional activities in with the broader region, then up to the state and so on. This requires some common imaging and cooperation between the hierarchy – there is little point cooperating with a region when your own community's image and aims are not in line with that region. This was an important outcome of the Small Towns Project case outlined in Chapter 4 – unless the community had a similar vision to the region, there would be no point in working with the region. Many of the regional DMOs offer special cooperative deals to smaller destinations by subsidising some of the advertising in their promotional material, representing them as a group at trade and consumer shows and so on.

From 'marketing' to 'promotion'

Promotion is part of the marketing of a place/destination, community, product or service, and is one of the *Ps* of marketing briefly discussed early in this chapter. Many people consider promotion to be all that marketing does, but as you will now be aware (if you weren't earlier), there are many elements of marketing. At this stage in our discussion I want to focus on the so-called promotional aspect, which is more than simply promoting our community or destination to potential visitors.

Promoting tourism in communities

If we decide that tourism is a positive force for our community, then we need to promote/market the concept of tourism to all of the community members. This is not unlike 'internal marketing' in an organisation, with Dann and Dann (2003, p. 412) explaining that:

> [e]mployees [or community members] within the firm [or community] should be respected and treated as a client group in their own right and second, that unless employees fully support and understand the reasons behind a marketing strategy decision, implementation will be at best flawed.

They stress that this is particularly true in the services marketing aspect of community based tourism, where the community members are part of the actual product by interacting with visitors. Even if it is simply passing a tourist in the street, this is part of their entire experience, which can be ruined if they are sensitive to resentment from the general community. While this may not be openly articulated by a visitor, the number of times people actually comment on the welcoming nature or friendliness of a community they have visited denotes that it is not always present. After travelling widely internationally, I came to see that Australians are overall friendly and hospitable to our visitors, but then I visited New Zealand where, every time I go and every place I have visited, I am met with another (higher) level of hospitality. New Zealanders are truly interested in and incredibly generous towards their international visitors, even Australians!

In order to obtain a sense of community engagement and interest in tourism and tourists, a type of communications strategy may need to be developed, virtually treating your own community as a market with distinct market segments. If you apply methods such as SRT outlined in Chapter 2 you can identify these segments and their attitudes towards tourism and other forms of community development. Once that is understood, the community groups can be 'marketed' to, using any or all of a range of communication strategies. This needs to be an ongoing process – both the monitoring of opinions and attitudes and the communication approach. Music festivals such as the Port Fairy Folk Festival are good examples of how small coastal villages can promote a large festival to their community, successfully creating a genuine sense of welcome to those visiting the village and attending the festival. Its Board of Management spent much time not only promoting the general economic benefits of the festival, but actively sought the participation of local service clubs and charities in the event itself. This not only created additional opportunities for those involved, but also embedded the festival into the surrounding communities.

However, promoting an annual event to a community is relatively easy in that while it requires a concerted effort, it is contained. Promoting tourism throughout the year has longer-term challenges and opportunities. In many communities, one of the main challenges is convincing everyone that they are all involved in tourism in some way. A great example is that of a local bank manager who actually said that he did not gain from tourism in his community (that attracted hundreds of visitors each weekend). The tourism businesses (restaurants, motels, bed and breakfasts) stamped all their cheques and banking forms with 'paid for with tourism dollars' – the bank manager soon realised how much he gained from tourism, as did many others who felt the same (tradespeople in particular).

An important point here is that these issues do not go away after a once-off program to promote tourism to your community – it requires ongoing communication as new people come into the community. Also, as noted in earlier chapters, tourism can change a community, so different messages may need to be presented over time.

The aware reader will see that if a community is truly empowered and if there has been a concerted consultation and communication approach taken in the early stages of tourism and community development, internal marketing will already be a part of that community's overall structure. However, in practice, this ideal situation rarely exists, often due to the changing nature of communities and the associated power relations.

Promoting communities through tourism

In this section, the term 'promotion' signifies more than simply its marketing role. Promoting communities is really about using tourism to develop communities to meet their goals, which is the theme of this book. According to Kotler *et al.* (1993), destination marketing is more than simply getting tourists to an area – it is also about attracting new residents (who often start as visitors) and businesses as well as to increase their exports. Tourism can be a significant contributor but should not be seen as the only option. How promotion is approached depends on the vision the community has for its future. If the intention is to have more people living in the town, then one of the aims of tourism would be to create an environment that would encourage visitors or others to desire to live there. The promotion could start by encouraging the purchase of second homes, or 'weekenders'. However, such a move may not ultimately result in the goal of more full-time residents. If the locals envisage a community where their young people remain to live and work, then employment opportunities and training in tourism skills and management may be what they require. Consequently, it is crucial to understand where (and what) the community wishes to be in not only five years, but also in 10, 20 and 50 years.

Tourism itself is a powerful promotional tool, simply by increasing outsiders' knowledge of your community, where it is, what it does and who belongs to it. Tourism promotion is approached from a positive perspective, highlighting the (usually pleasant) elements of a community to attract visitors. This often includes aspects of friend-liness and welcome, relaxation and stress release, the opportunity to do something different in a safe environment (such as white water rafting, fossicking for gold, learning a language) and enjoying nature. For an urban environment it may include excitement, sophistication, shopping, entertainment and cosmopolitan food experiences.

Consequently, tourism can positively promote a community to potential investors and residents as well as visitors. However, not all tourist images attract the desired type of resident or even reflect the community's self-image. If the marketing organisation (usually the DMO) is focused solely on attracting visitors, they may simply end up promulgating outdated images and perceptions of that community. An example of this is the national tourism advertisements Australia has presented overseas. In 1999, a 'new image' was developed to market the country and community to various countries, including the United States. One of the advertisements used what many Australians considered to be a low level type of promotion that did not reflect their country or community – it was based on a nude beach with plenty of innuendo and schoolyard humour. Many Australians took umbrage at this image of Australians. However, the head of the Australian Tourist Commission argued that Australia could not compete with Europe in terms of sophistication, so we had to promote '… the diversity of Australia … with a uniquely Australian context. Which is relaxed, friendly and welcoming' (Smailes 1999). The Federal Tourism Minister, Jackie Kelly commented that 'at the end of the day, we're talking business decisions, and sex sells' (AAP 1999).

Once again, this comes back to having a community based development strategy with tourism as one possible tool that can achieve certain things, but is not the answer to everything. When looking at developing communities through tourism, one of the most important elements is that of the image of the community in its target markets. As illustrated above, this image can create certain expectations in visitors' minds and is the lens through which they will view and interpret what they see and experience in a community. This is a complex notion which we return to many times in this chapter, but it is important to acknowledge that if there is a conflict between the tourist's image and what they experience, they will most likely be dissatisfied. Such dissatisfaction will not lead to realising the community's vision and goals, unless it is to discourage visitors. However, there are more constructive approaches that can be adopted, such as those suggested in the section on demarketing.

Some of the issues noted above relate to how those who market the destination respond to the community's wants and needs as described by their vision. Some responses, particularly if incongruent with the community's desires, can be considered unethical. This conflict between promoting a place regardless of the cost to the community raises the notion of 'ethical marketing', which is discussed next.

Ethical marketing

The whole notion of marketing our community in an ethical manner is extremely important when considering that the goal is to develop the community by using tourism. It is not simply to develop tourism by using the community. Where community based tourism has failed, we see evidence of the latter occurring.

Marketing has long been criticised in terms of its impact on individuals in tourism destination communities; this can be in the form of increasing prices due to high distribution costs, advertising costs and excessive mark-ups. Price gouging our visitors is not ethical, nor is it appropriate or sustainable for community members who also have to pay those prices. Having differential pricing for tourists and locals also smacks of unethical pricing behaviour. In addition, deceptive practices in relation to pricing, promotion and packaging, where the customer is led to expect something else than what is offered is not only unethical but illegal in most parts of the world. In fact, holiday packages are highly regulated in terms of their providing what was promised in the promotional material, with the operator or agent often being prosecuted in the country where the package was purchased, not where it was consumed. Also, tourism marketing can be criticised for its negative impacts on society where it can be seen to produce false wants and too much materialism in a culture resulting in few social goods (Kotler & Armstrong 2004).

Many of these issues cannot be simply blamed on marketing and promotion alone, but as promotion is so pervasive, it is often seen as a primary contributor. Unethical marketing can also impact other businesses. This can be by creating barriers to entry through price wars that a new entrant may not be able to sustain, or through the aforementioned development of alliances that may exclude others.

As a response to such criticisms, many businesses have moved into what has become known as socially responsible marketing, or societal marketing. This is a relatively new concept and has as its basic premise that a product or service be presented in such a way that it '... maintains or improves the consumer's and society's wellbeing' (Kotler *et al.* 2003, p. 27). Such a premise resonates closely with what we have been discussing in terms of tourism as a tool for community development and is focused on the concept of ethics and ethical behaviour.

The notion of ethics as the moral basis of society and what is considered appropriate behaviour is based on societal norms, and can differ across countries and cultures. What is 'legal' may not necessarily be ethical and vice versa. Behaving ethically can be good for business, particularly in the tourism area where encounters with others are highly sought-after activities that carry with them many ethical elements. Ethics has become important to many consumers as is evidenced by the growth in 'ethical investment organisations'. For example, in Australia, there is an Ethical Investment Association that promotes the concept, practice and growth of ethically, socially and environmentally responsible investing in Australia (http://www.eia.org.au/).

The notion of ethics in tourism and communities as well as in marketing is considered in more detail in Chapter 8.

Marketing planning

While I have made a conscious effort not to present this chapter as a definitive introduction to marketing, many times I have referred to a marketing plan or strategy. Therefore, an outline of the basic elements of a marketing plan is needed in order to provide some cohesion. If you are unfamiliar with marketing, I strongly recommend you read some of the sources quoted in this chapter and talk with others who have some marketing experience. With regard to communities and tourism, the DMOs and some community members will be able to assist.

For the purposes of this book, a marketing plan consists of written statements of the community's marketing strategy, tactics, timetables, objectives and goals in relation to tourism. Such a plan enables the community to articulate its aims, and by doing this the community members are following closely the process introduced in Chapter 3 for community development strategic planning. In fact, the marketing plan forms part of that strategy. The plan also enables tourism to be developed and encouraged along the community's goals and provides a roadmap for the future, indicating where the community wants to be at certain times (Dann & Dann 2004).

While not all plans are exactly the same, there is a basic outline that is followed in some form or other. This includes an introductory section that sets the scene by describing the project for which the plan has been developed, followed by an analysis of the current community and tourism environment, with particular interest in the social, political and economic trends as well as the market trends in tourism. Then the target market segments are described in some detail, which may include demographics, psychographic, geographic, lifestyle, or whatever segmentation is appropriate. The rationale as to why these target markets have been selected follows, usually with a discussion as to the value or size of the market. At this stage it is important to introduce the marketing goals that have been agreed on for the community, showing how the target markets chosen will achieve them and how they will be measured.

Measurement is an important element of all planning, particularly in terms of marketing, where it is not always easy to measure the effectiveness of specific marketing or promotional campaigns. If the marketing objectives are expressed in measurable terms such as numbers of visitors, how much they spend, this is not too difficult. But when something such as the increase in community pride also has to be measured, this will require more thought. Chapter 3 outlines some ways to measure the more intangible goals.

Undertaking planning such as that outlined above is excellent, but the marketing plan must also include action plans with strategies and tactics that can be applied. This particularly relates to how the community will implement the marketing strategy in terms of the product, price, promotion, distribution (place), people (personnel), and other tactical variables. A key point to note here is that anyone should be able to pick up the action plan and implement it. This is particularly important with a community as the active members will change, so new participants need to be able to readily see and understand what the overall plan is, and be able to continue with it. Also, any potential problem areas with the implementation of the plan should be mentioned, along with suggestions on to avoid them.

At this point, the resources needed to support strategies and meet objectives should be articulated in as much detail as possible. This will, at the very least, include funds needed to implement the proposed marketing activities and range of expertise also required. A detailed budget should be developed that will include sales objectives, forecasts and quotas, expenditures against budget, and recommended periodic evaluation of all marketing objectives. This last point will lead in to presenting a marketing activity timetable.

One of the great benefits for a community that develops a marketing plan is that it is a growth tool that gives the community the opportunity to prepare for the future, as well as giving the leaders experience in actually setting objectives, timetables and the tactics to achieve them. However, the marketing planning process does not have to be onerous, nor does the plan need to be too complex or large. If it is too daunting, few people will read it and nothing will be achieved.

Accidental marketing – literature, art, film, music

As hinted in some of the material in this chapter, not all of the things that work to 'market' a destination or community are controlled by the community itself. I refer to these as 'accidental marketing', and as such they may be positive or problematic accidents. One pertinent area is the media, in all of its forms. We are all aware of the power of the news media to present and interpret 'current affairs' in ways that may or may not assist us in encouraging visitors to our place. The reporting of natural and man-made disasters and political unrest come immediately to mind. Dealing with disasters and crisis management requires more than just marketing, and is taken up in Chapter 7.

What I am looking at here is the area of fictional literature, art, film and music and how they can influence (or reflect) a community's self-perception and tourists' own perceptions and expectations and how that relates to marketing. The reason for this focus is the relationship between fictional media and image development of a destination or community. Elsewhere in this book and in other publications, I have talked about film and its role in community development, so I continue this discussion in the marketing terms of imaging, development and promotion.

Imaging

When planning for tourism, strategies are developed to create the 'appropriate' images of the place and then to cement them in the minds of potential visitors. Imaging processes are characterised by a combination of the actual facilities and/or attractions and development of leisure services as well as the results of the tourism development strategies (Hall *et al.* 2003). I have argued elsewhere that the powerful role of visual fictional media is an additional element of the imaging process (Beeton 2005a).

Tourism marketers have long acknowledged the importance of the role that the image of a destination plays in the travel decision-making process. Over 25 years ago, La Page and Cormmier (1977, p. 21) noted that, 'in many cases, it is probably the image more than the factual information that produces a tourist's decision on where to travel'. Most visitors already have some sort of overall image of a place (and its community) prior to any decision to strategically develop one. The best we can do is leverage the images that we want and attempt to limit the influence of those we do not. Each type of image (positive, weak, negative, mixed, contradictory or even overly picturesque) requires different strategies to either capitalise on or ameliorate the problems associated with the fit of the image with the target consumer groups.

Many community members, including destination marketers, believe that a beneficial image would increase the desire to visit a destination, whereas a negative image would deter visitation, consequently expressing concern when a movie or book with a negative story-line is set in their destination. However, this is not always the case, as 'beneficial' and 'negative' images are purely subjective. We return to this point later in the section.

Literary and art tourism

Before movies and television became today's most powerful media, readers of certain books yearned to travel to the places represented in their stories and poems, such as retracing the steps of early voyagers and travellers. As Seaton (1998, p. 16) acknowledges, 'the importance of the printed word to tourism development … cannot be over-estimated'. What is particularly interesting is that many literary tourists are also interested in tracing the writer's life and work or to visit a place that their reading has imbued with special meaning (Herbert 2001). Literary tourism is interested in the creator of the work, not simply the story or characters, as we can see in examples in the UK of regions such as 'Burns Country', 'Herriott Country' and so on.

The art and literature that has driven much of 20th century tourism has been closely linked to the Romantic movement of the 18th and 19th centuries, with writers such as Wordsworth, Keats and Byron stimulating an interest in nature, scenery and mountains, as a direct reaction to the Industrial Revolution (Lickorish & Jenkins 1997). With more people living in industrialised cities, the countryside became the desired place to visit, representing health, peace and goodness as reflected by the Romantic artists and writers of the day. Such movements occurred around the same period in Scotland, France, Germany and Switzerland as well as in England. This longing for 'unspoilt' or exotic landscapes still exists today, with many urban dwellers wishing to spend time in rural idyllic communities.

Literary tourism remains popular and has been around for many years, so its influence on image creation and reinforcement (or alteration) must be considered in terms of the affected communities. Philosopher Alain de Botton (2002) uses the work of writers including Baudelaire and Wordsworth and the art of Van Gogh, Hopper, Ruskin and others as his inspiration in his entertaining and inspirational work, *The Art of Travel*.

As with others who look at film-induced tourism, Hilty (1996) found that literary tourism needs to be managed, particularly in relation to preparing residents to deal with changes such tourism may bring and to determine social carrying capacity levels.

Closely aligned with Romanticism is the notion of 'picturesque' which was basically an ideology that envisaged the Romantic landscape in terms of pretty pictures to be enjoyed by the viewer, often devoid of any other meaning (Beeton 2005a). Such views were often presented in paintings that were also a key component of the tourist's gaze, with bucolic rural scenes and rugged landscapes equally perceived as picturesque, as represented in the work of artists such as Constable and Turner. Other elements of the rural idyll were expressed through art in beautiful youth and spring flowers, with Van Gogh's paintings of Provence inspiring many a traveller with his riotous use of colour. Without being consciously aware of the genesis of the picturesque, tourists often refer to a place in these terms ('pretty as a picture') when it correlates positively with such traditional notions.

However, in Australia (as in much of America), the land was not seen to be a benign softly lit landscape with hedgerows and contented stock, so a different expression of these places emerged – that of the land as the enemy, with the heroic pioneer battling against it. We see this image of the land as protagonist not so much in the art of the period (which was primarily softened to fit the picturesque), but in the Australian literature of Lawson and others. The popular media of the day, in the form of literature and poetry, played a major role in the formation and promotion of this harsh image of Australia. The city-based readers eagerly supported bush literature – albeit experiencing these themes through a Romanticised heroic lens, far removed from their place of daily routine (Beeton 2004a). This Australian image still resonates in certain communities and has been the basis of many successful Australian movies.

Film-induced tourism

By the beginning of this century, film (including movies and television series) has become so pervasive that its influence far outweighs that of literature. We have moved from the small, niche based personal literary tourist to the mass visitation of film sites. Film is to literary tourism what the jet engine was to mainstream tourism – a major boost for mass tourism. Where literary tourism is primarily interested in the creator of the work, film-induced tourism tends to ignore the author or scriptwriter and focus on the characters, places, actors and possibly the story-line.

Film and other incidental types of fictional tourism are subtle in their influence, as the viewer's initial motivation to see a movie is rarely linked to tourism. In other words, a movie set in a particular location may appeal to the audience as a place to visit, but the location was a secondary (or later) motivation for them to actually see the film. This makes the promotional process more subtle and akin to word of mouth, as opposed to direct destination advertising. It may be the exotic location, natural scenery, story-line or human relationships in the film that motivate people to visit certain places. However, the actual elements and what type of story-line works to attract visitors differ according to different market segments. In addition, motivations can relate to elements of escape, nostalgia, pilgrimage and celebrity worship.

Table 5.2 shows some of the types of image created through Australian films that have been credited with attracting tourists. These images from a selection of Australian movies and television programs appeal to both international and domestic tourists. They have all created a lasting image of Australia for their viewers. In some instances the

Table 5.2 Touristic imaging of Australian film

Movie/TV program	Location	Theme	Australian and international appeal/legibility
The Man from Snowy River	Alpine National Park, Victoria	Australian bush culture – the land as nurturer and protagonist Final frontier adventure Man and horse striving together	Reinforcement of an imagined bush heritage International appeal of final frontier in a 'safe' visitor destination
Crocodile Dundee	Kakadu National Park, Northern Territory	Australian bush culture – humour Laconic Australian identity	Supporting an imagined outback culture experienced by few Australians Appeal of final frontier in a destination that Americans can travel through safely
Neighbours	Melbourne, Victoria	Australian suburban culture Gender relations in the suburbs.	Appeals to a predominantly urban-based Australia as local, able to relate to International appeal of a clean, safe Australian culture
Home and Away	Northern Australian coast	Australian coastal lifestyle (sun, surf and sex) Youthful characters Small, caring community	Appeals to a predominantly coastal-based Australian culture as local, relatable Reinforces international image of sun, sand, surf and sex
Mad Max	Silverton, New South Wales	Futuristic, post-nuclear world Land as enemy Foreign, barren landscape	Landscape not perceived as Australian by either locals or internationals
Sea Change	Barwon Heads, Victoria	Change of lifestyle (competitive urban vs cooperative rural) Small, caring community	Appeals to Australian 'baby-boomers' longing for their own 'sea change' International reinforcement of a friendly, quirky Australia

Source: Beeton 2005a.

connection with tourism and the film is related directly to the scenery and in others the appeal has more to do with the story-line. Some of the strongest drivers appear to be films where the environment is a central aspect of the story-line – it virtually takes a starring role, such as in *The Man from Snowy River*.

However, in spite of the demonstrated effect of film on tourist visitation and expectations, destination communities that have worked to capitalise on the images portrayed in film have met with mixed results, not always positive. Community members generally have only limited input into the decision to film certain sites, and have limited control over the image presented, which can result in unrealistic and even negative images. However, if the image is desirable, tourism operators and destination marketers alike will take advantage of this so-called 'free' publicity, even to the point of re-imaging the destination to bring it into line with the film-generated imagery.

Not all films have equal levels of influence, with some television programs or movies having little impact, while others can be highly influential in terms of image generation. While the financial importance of a film depends on its popularity at the box office, the size of the production company and its distribution breadth also plays a role in reaching a wide audience – a Warner Bros production has far greater reach than the smaller, independent studios (Croy & Walker 2001). Also, global factors play a role in shaping a market's choice of film, such as in times of war when patriotic or even 'happy' films abound.

Literary maps and movie maps

Tourist Commissions and DMOs have long recognised the significance of literary tourism, to the extent that the British Tourist Authority (BTA) regularly publishes a Literary Map to Britain, which is now also available via the Internet (www.visitbritain.com). In the 1990s, the concept of movie maps developed, with many countries and regions developing their own maps and interactive websites. Today, the BTA produces an overall Movie Map of Britain, a Bollywood map for the Indian market, and a specific *Harry Potter* Movie Map, all of which are available online and in hard copy (Beeton 2005a). The United States has hundreds of such maps and good interactive websites (see the California site at www.gocalif.ca.gov.movies), while Hong Kong has a Movie Map that not only shows where certain scenes were filmed, but also where the stars shop, eat and stay.

The publication of movie and literature maps has become a significant marketing tool for many destinations around the world, from maps of entire countries down to specific regions and communities. The small town of Barwon Heads in Australia developed a walking guide of sites featured in the popular TV series *Sea Change*, which had to be reprinted many times over (Beeton 2005a).

As a form of promotional collateral and a way to 'tangibilise' the experience, such maps can be extremely effective, if the images are congruent with the community's vision.

Music tourism

I will not go into a great deal of detail on music tourism here, as it is primarily a niche form of tourism which is usually combined with other elements in terms of motivating visitors to come to a certain place. That said, there are places for which music is a major drawcard for fans, such as Vienna for classical music, Nashville for country music, New Orleans for jazz and Cuba for son and salsa. Also, there are music festivals that attract tourists to a destination community in their own right, many of which have become synonymous with the town itself. Few people would think of Tamworth in Australia without automatically linking this with the town's annual Tamworth Country Music Festival, and the fishing village of Port Fairy has become synonymous with folk music.

Port Fairy is a small fishing village in Victoria, Australia. One of the country's earliest settlements, the area was first settled in the 1830s with the establishment of an offshore whaling station in 1835. The first store opened on the mainland in 1839 and the village became primarily settled by Irish immigrants fleeing the potato famine. The town currently has a permanent population of approximately 2800, with the surrounding community consisting mainly of small rural service towns with a total regional population of 5000. Due to the influence on and relationship with local communities that successful music events have, I have included a brief outline of the Port Fairy Folk Festival, held in the seaside village of Port Fairy in Victoria, Australia, and known as one of the top folk festivals in the world.

The Port Fairy Folk Festival commenced in 1977 and is operated by a community based voluntary committee. The festival is presented 'with the assistance and hospitality of residents, businesses, the shire, many local community clubs and organisations and especially a large team of volunteers, the Friends of the Festival' (PFFF 2005). The aims of the Port Fairy Folk Festival Committee are to:

- present an excellent festival of significance in Australia and worldwide

- promote folk music, broadly defined as World Roots and Acoustic – music that is diverse, traditional, indigenous, multicultural, social, reflecting and enriching people's lives and culture

- provide support and benefits for the Port Fairy community (PFFF 2005).

The festival is a major international music event, winning many tourism awards, and is regarded as one of the world's top five folk music festivals. It welcomes over 60 000 visitors over the four-day festival (the tickets sell out within days of opening) and is predominantly self and community supported in terms of its funding. As noted earlier, one of the keys to this festival's success has been its relationship with the surrounding community, providing development funds and opportunities for many local service organisations, not-for-profit groups and charities to benefit from the festival. They also addressed issues of drunken youth outside the festival precinct by providing free, quality entertainment for them and the general community.

Apart from some work done in relation to festivals in general, at this stage music tourism is not an area that has been studied extensively. Even though I am myself a 'serious' music fan, travelling to various places purely because of the music (such as Memphis, New Orleans and Cuba), I have not (yet) investigated it seriously in terms of tourism and community development. For many travellers, music is the backdrop or soundtrack to their experiences and not the central, driving force. They may purchase music as a souvenir, but do not regard it as a primary reason to visit a place.

Nevertheless, music is important, and there are others who have looked more closely at the phenomenon, and may disagree with my comments. More on music and tourism can be found in *Music and Tourism: On the Road Again*, by Gibson and Connell (2005) who claim that 'music … has rapidly become a new rationale for travel…' (Gibson and Connell, 2005: 1). These authors may refute my statements about music tourism being a niche area.

What to do when it gets too much: Demarket!

In Chapter 2 I put forward the case study of Goathland and the problems they are facing with a high influx of film-induced tourists that at times has created serious crowding issues. However, it is not just film that increases tourist visitation beyond a place's carrying capacity. Many natural environments as well as cities are experiencing the problems of too many tourists or not the type of visitor that the community desires. Marketing is not simply about increasing numbers, and there are marketing strategies and tools that can be used to contain or change visitation. One such strategy is known as 'demarketing'.

Demarketing is a controversial and misunderstood concept, even within the professional marketing community. Coined by Kotler and Levy in 1971, it is defined as '… that aspect of marketing that deals with discouraging customers in general or a certain class of customers in particular on a temporary or permanent basis' (Kotler & Levy 1971, p. 75). The underlying rationale for this new term was that marketing, up to 1971, had been concerned with an ever-expanding market for which there was an unlimited supply of product (characterised as a buyers' market). Kotler and Levy recognised that there were periods of product shortages or scarcity (a shrinking market or one in which the sellers of product dominate) to which marketers (and managers) must respond. As such, the term 'demarketing' is not the opposite of marketing, but an intrinsic aspect of marketing management and part of the marketing mix.

Since the 1970s, demarketing elements have been applied in the public healthcare field, particularly to handle excessively high demand of 'free' services and to attempt to eradicate antisocial behaviour. Its effectiveness and the ethics surrounding some of the measures have been debated in many forums (see Borkowski 1994). While demarketing has not been extensively applied to tourism, there are cases where it has been consciously or even unconsciously applied (see Clements 1989; Benfield 2001; Beeton 2001c).

Demarketing in tourism and community development can be a powerful tool. By extending the range of demarketing instruments identified by Kotler to consider the potential of tourism strategies, we are able to take a management approach at the marketing stage of an operation, *before* people visit – the stage when images and expectations are created and decisions on destinations made. Tourism demarketing strategies range from pricing strategies and entry controls, to behavioural education and even a total reduction in marketing and promotion (Beeton 2001c; Benfield 2001). The range of tourism demarketing strategies is outlined below.

Benfield (2001) identifies eleven demarketing strategies that have been used variously by mass tourism attractions:

1   Increasing prices

2   Increasing advertising that warns of capacity limitations

3   Reducing sales and promotion expenditure

4   Reducing sales representatives' actual selling time

5   Curtailing advertising expenditure

6   Eliminating trade discounts

7   Reducing the number of distribution outlets

8   Separate management of large groups

9   Adding to the time and expense of the purchaser

10 Reducing product quality or content

11 Provision of a virtual tour.

As environmental tourism attractions also deal with issues of crowding and overfull demand, there are additional demarketing tools that can also be considered such as:

- Educating potential visitors regarding appropriate environmental behaviour at point of information gathering and within marketing and promotional literature

- Educating journalists and associated media regarding appropriate environmental behaviour
- Encouraging specific ('desirable') markets through the style and information provided in the promotional material
- Discouraging certain ('undesirable') markets through the style and information of promotional material
- Notifying visitors of banned activities at the point of information gathering and in promotional literature
- Publicising alternative sites for non-compatible or banned activities
- Limiting the activities permitted, either seasonally, due to local environmental conditions or entirely
- Warning visitors of environmental circumstances under which activities may be curtailed
- Permitting certain activities only under supervision of appropriately educated personnel (such as accredited commercial operators or park rangers)
- Re-imaging the destination to attract a certain type/demographic of visitor and deflect others
- Making access to fragile areas more difficult, simultaneously promoting less fragile options (Beeton 2003a).

It is important to understand that demarketing is part of the marketing process, not separate from it. Figure 5.1 illustrates where demarketing fits into the overall marketing process or cycle in relation to film-induced tourism.

Film is a powerful tourism inducer and image-maker, and while in theory filming should be incorporated into community planning, in reality this is rarely the case. It is doubtful that it ever will be possible to do so to any great extent, and even if this occurs there will be other unplanned-for elements that impact on the level and type of visitation. Too often communities are left to face the results of a too successful (or negative) image with limited resources and understanding. However, once a destination is aware of the nature of film-induced or other 'accidental' tourism, it is possible to incorporate appropriate

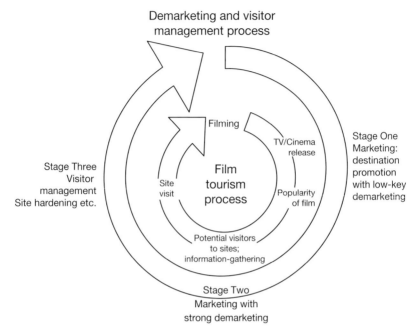

Figure 5.1 Demarketing and marketing model

Source: Beeton 2005a.

marketing and demarketing strategies into its own marketing planning processes. The tools that demarketing offers can be used to work towards re-imaging these communities, in turn empowering them and creating a more sustainable future.

Another marketing term that is used often in place of demarketing or in conjunction with it, is remarketing – often a place desires to alter their image and re-present themselves in a different light. This is not easy to achieve, as once an image is formed it is difficult to change, which is why I advocate doing as much as possible (even considering demarketing) at the early stages of marketing and image development.

The following case study is not about demarketing or remarketing, but about marketing to the various communities that are affected by a significant not-for-profit recreational tourism event.

From theory to practice: Bringing them out to play – the case of promoting the Great Victorian Bike Ride to many communities

Bicycle Victoria was founded in 1975 as a self-funded community association, owned by its members. Over the years, membership has grown to a staggering 40 000 in 2006, making it one of Australia's most powerful interest and recreational lobby groups.

Bicycle Victoria (BV) runs many cycling activities and events, with its most prominent being the Great Victorian Bike Ride, which attracts around 8000 cyclists. The nine-day event is not a competition, rather a fully supported cycling holiday travelling through various parts of the state. Over those nine days, participants travel through and stay at many small rural towns and communities. An influx of some 8000 people is significant for most of these communities, including the regional centres, and runs the risk of alienating the local people. Crowding, night-time noise, strain on infrastructure and services are just some of the potential areas for conflict. If such problems become associated with the Bike Ride, its success and future is in jeopardy.

BV has addressed these issues by developing and applying a strong marketing communications and public relations campaign in all of the regions the ride passes through, not simply the over-night stops. They work consistently over the year leading up to the event with these communities to make sure that all of their members are happy to welcome these visitors and that the community can gain from them. As BV is a not-for-profit organisation, they run the ride with a strong charity and fund-raising focus, encouraging participants to raise funds for their own charitable interests through sponsorship. Some of these interests relate directly to the communities the ride is travelling through, while others are more aligned to the participants' communities.

In addition, BV spends a great deal of time and effort working with the communities along the route of the ride, not only in organisational terms but also offering opportunities for community groups and businesses to capitalise on the influx of visitors. For example, they offer free listing for any local fundraising events in the Great Victorian Bike Ride Guide. They enlist local government and media to promote such opportunities to the wider community. According to an article in the *Camperdown Chronicle* (a regional community newspaper with a local circulation of 1500): 'The event is seen as a prime fundraising chance for the town and community groups have been urged to make the most of the opportunity' (*Camperdown Chronicle*, 29 September 2004, p.3). The article suggests a range of possible fundraising activities such as Internet cafés, mobile phone charging, barbeques, soup and scone stalls and heritage tours.

In the small rural town of Koroit in Western Victoria, over 25 community groups banded together to raise money during the ride for a community stadium. The head of one of their major charity groups (Apex Club) confirmed that the bike ride was 'inviting communities to showcase their towns to the riders' (*Warrnambool Standard*, 25 October 2004, p. 3). In the nearby seaside village of Port Fairy, the local community newspaper noted that each town visited during the ride should see some $200 000 in spending (*Moyne Gazette*, 11 November 2004).

BV does not only use the print media, but also holds many open community meetings during the planning stages. This gives the event a human face and reinforces BV's commitment to these communities.

By using the media and community leaders to spread the positive news about the bike ride, BV has been able not only to contribute to the communities the ride passes through, but also to create a sense of positive anticipation and festival atmosphere when the riders come into these communities. In this way the reputation of the ride itself is enhanced. These proactive marketing communications activities not only eliminate most of the friction (or irritation) locals may feel, but actually enhance their lives by creating a festival atmosphere, even if only for a few hours.

6

Rural tourism communities

This chapter takes a closer look at tourism based in rural areas and their associated communities. While many of the communities referred to throughout the book are in rural areas, such as small villages and the majority of indigenous communities, this chapter focuses more on those that specialise in rural tourism enterprises and activities. In addition, much of the previous discussion on community development and empowerment relate to this area, particularly in developing countries where multinational companies such as resort chains still drive much of the rural based tourism, not the local communities. Rural tourism occurs in almost every country. However, much of the focus in this chapter is on developed countries such as Australia, New Zealand, the United States and much of Europe, where rural tourism has a long tradition. This enables us to see how this particular type of tourism can develop, which in turn will assist those working in developing regions.

Following a discussion on what we actually mean by the term 'rural tourism' is a brief outline of the relevant changes in rural areas and agriculture over the past century that directly affect the delivery of rural tourism experiences and visitor satisfaction. Then a transcript is presented of a keynote address I gave in New Zealand at a Rural Tourism Conference on *Developing Rural Tourism Communities*, which reinforces much of what you are reading in this book in a less formal manner. After some concluding remarks on rural community tourism, the intricacies of tourism in rural areas are illustrated in the case study of a potentially successful rural tourism enterprise and its failure.

What is rural tourism?

Due to their complex nature, defining tourism concepts remains problematic, and rural tourism is no exception. There are a variety of terms used to describe tourism in rural areas, including farm tourism, agritourism, soft tourism and even ecotourism (Page & Getz 1997). Some groups, including Australia's Department of Tourism, have decided that rural tourism is 'a country experience' (DOT 1994, p. 1). However, not all tourism that occurs in country areas can be considered a rural experience, such as some of the resort-based tourism and theme parks that may only be in a rural area due to the cost and availability of land.

As rural areas are themselves in a constant state of change, rural tourism itself is a multi-faceted activity that can include nature-based recreational activities and community attractions as well as farm-related tourism. Butler and Hall (1998) see rural tourism as more than the sum of its parts, particularly as a policy response to the changing base of agriculture in a global economy, where many rural businesses have been forced to diversify in order to survive.

Consequently, definitions such as that provided by DOT are too broad to promote constructive and meaningful discussion and a true understanding of rural tourism today. While still quite broad in scope, Oppermann (1997) saw rural tourism as tourism that occurs in non-urban settings where human activity is present – a definition that allows for some differentiation between the limited human activity in national parks and that on farming land with its broad range of intrusive human activities (Beeton 2002c). Others see rural tourism as being located in rural areas, functionally rural, rural in scale and traditional in character (Page & Getz 1997), which tends to come from a European perspective. I lean towards Oppermann's definition of rural tourism, linking it with the aforementioned farm tourism and agritourism, that can incorporate a range of activities with adventure, industrial and educational aspects.

Figure 6.1 presents one way of viewing the complex nature of rural regions and communities and tourism's role (or place) by mapping the links between elements and issues. This 'map' was developed over seven years of researching, studying and teaching in the fields of community based and rural tourism, and as such is an organic map that has changed and developed in its complexity over that time. In order to contain it and make it legible, some generalisations have been made. Nevertheless, the map serves its purpose in illustrating the relationship between tourism, rural regions and their associated communities. The reader will notice that rural tourism is only one element in this map, and while it is situated at its centre, it is not the only way to approach resolving the issues identified, but one part of one of three overarching diversification approaches.

Unless marked otherwise, the direction of the linking lines flows down. However, this is not a flow chart, illustrating cause and effect, but a snapshot of a rural region at a particular point in time.

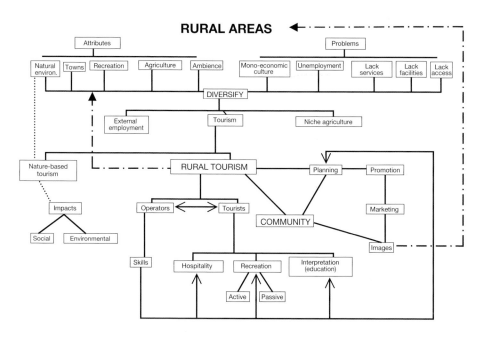

Figure 6.1 Rural tourism map

The overall environment in Figure 6.1 is the rural area or region that we are interested in, which has a series of attributes and problems associated with it, which in turn differ in terms of their importance region by region, but are generally recognised as important all around the world. The attributes can be broken down into the natural environment, town, recreation, agriculture and ambience; the problems are their reliance on a mono economy (such as wheat farming), high unemployment levels and limited opportunities, lack of facilities, services and access. A response to these issues and a way to use the attributes to do so is to diversify into external employment, niche agricultural enterprises or tourism, which can be rural and/or nature-based. This supports Butler and Hall's (1998) premise that rural tourism is a political response to the problems facing the countryside. Then we consider the elements and issues of rural tourism, which has a planning (promotion, marketing and imaging) element that ties intricately with the community. Tourism itself consists of demand and supply – the tourists who look for various levels of recreation (both active and passive) and interpretation, and the operators who require skills in those services. All of these elements link back to (and inform) the planning process, and ultimately the rural area.

The community is central to this process, and in many ways cannot be separated from any of the elements on the map. However, for ease of comprehension, I have placed it as a separate item on the map. The local community should be involved in and affected by rural tourism, overall planning of the region and establishing and marketing the image of that region.

While it may at first appear to be complex, the map outlined above provides an overview of how tourism fits with communities in the rural environment. There will be readers who find it easier to comprehend the notion of rural tourism communities in this way rather than the rather wordy (yet incomplete) definitions outlined earlier.

The rural idyll and rural development

The romantic concepts of rurality that are evident in much of the rural tourism discourse stem from the notion of the 'rural idyll' of the European Romantic period, particularly after the Industrial Revolution. At that time, European idealism was dominated by notions of Romantic pastoral images of a benign and welcoming rural idyll in direct opposition to the factory dominated, squalid city precincts of the time (Beeton 2004a). This was expressed in terms of softly lit green fields, spring flowers and beautiful youth, glowing with health, vigour and wellbeing. Even in Australia, where the reality of 'the bush' was quite different to this image of green fields and hedgerows, the artists of the mid-19th century, such as Von Guerard, Glover and Earle, deliberately softened it to present the accepted European notions of rural idyll (Beeton 2004a).

As discussed in Chapter 5, closely aligned with the idyll is the concept of 'picturesque', which remains important to rural tourism today, with tourists referring to a scene in such terms as 'pretty as a picture'. This is usually when it correlates with the traditional notions of the rural idyll of clear skies, beautiful sunsets, birds and flowers, domestic stock (in the distance), rustic cottages and winding, tree-lined laneways. This concept was promulgated in the 19th century Romantic era by poets such as Wordsworth, Shelley and Keats. Artists like Constable and Turner presented rurality as the ideal opposite to the corrupt, dirty factories of contemporary urban living. By the time of Wordsworth's death in 1850, with half the population of England living in cities, the notion of the need for regular travel through nature as an antidote to the evils of the city was 'seriously' accepted (de Botton 2002).

The rural idyll remains an important image and motivator for today's rural tourists. Rural tourism has continued to grow as a particular form of tourism. Alain de Botton, in his seminal work on travel: *The Art of Travel*, spends some time chasing the Wordsworth idyll, finding solace in nature, not only at the time, but also when back in the 'evil' city where he was caught in a traffic jam when

> These trees provided a ledge against which I could rest my
> thoughts, they protected me from the eddies of anxiety and, in a
> small way that afternoon, contributed a reason to be alive
> (de Botton 2002, p. 155).

This raises the more pragmatic questions of why and how rural tourism has retained its importance in times of rapid technological change and growth, along with the persistence of the rural idyll. While noted over 10 years ago by the OECD (1994), the key motivators they provided as being responsible for the worldwide growth in rural tourism still resonate today.

- Increased education levels that encourage interest in other places

- Interest in heritage, including tracing one's roots and genealogy

- Increased leisure time in the developed nations, who are the primary source of tourists

- Transport and communication bringing many previously remote places closer to their markets

- Health consciousness, with the fresh air of the countryside seen to be therapeutic and desirable

- 'Green' issues making people more interested in non-urban activities

- Interest in specialty foods, particularly those based on regional differences

- Ageing but active populations who are travelling further for longer, and looking for different (or new) experiences (OECD 1994).

At this point it is worth looking at how rural tourism in Europe (as well as North America and Australia) developed historically in terms of providing facilities for people to realise their idyllic dreams. In the past (and in many developing nations today), the bulk of the population was too busy with survival to consider recreation, and the leisure activities they had tended to mimic urban pastimes. Due to the lack of access, money and time, the only people able to participate in recreational activities in rural areas tended to be the landed gentry and some of the urban elite. Eventually, the properties of the landed gentry became uneconomical as working estates, so many turned to home hosting, providing rural facilities and activities for a growing urban middle class. These recreational activities tended to relate to the rural character of a place and the aforementioned romantic notions of the rural idyll, primarily being relaxing, passive, nostalgic, traditional, low technology, educational and mostly non-competitive (Page & Getz 1997; Sharpley & Sharpley 1997).

The transition of rural tourism to modern times and up-to-date farming practices has not always been smooth. In many cases tourist demand has resisted actual progress in rural enterprises, particularly where the visitor wishes to experience 'old time' farming activities and their own vision of a rural community (often informed by those quirky rural series seen on television). However, as people seek more and independent forms of travel and educated experiences, the appeal of rural destinations has been reinvigorated, opening new avenues for commercial opportunities (Roberts & Hall 2001). Over the past 30 years, additional activities have been added to this somewhat passive list that are active, competitive, individual, prestigious, highly techno-logical, modern and fast. Some of these new activities could not simply be added to existing rural facilities as in the past, requiring purpose-built facilities (Page & Getz 1997). Maximising such opportunities depends on understanding the nature and processes of the social construction of rural areas as well as the tensions they may induce, which we have considered in other chapters.

Rural change and restructure

Already in this chapter I have made many comments relating to rural areas and their associated farming enterprises being in a constant state of change, which makes the following discussion important in terms of contextualising rural tourism in rural communities. Prior to World War II, the rural systems of developed countries had a degree of homo-geneity and distinctiveness, where the distinctions between urban/city and country/rural were clear. Rural enterprises tended to be small, family owned and operated, with commercial agriculture growing, but retaining its rural nature. Post WWII the status quo was maintained through introducing protectionist subsidy systems for farmers that also allowed unprofitable, non-sustainable practices and production to continue (Roberts & Hall 2001). Such non-sustainable practices are particularly evident in parts of the United States and Australia where European farming practices were transplanted to environments totally unsuited to such processes and activities. In post-communist Central and Eastern Europe, as well as other developing countries in Asia and the Americas, these Western models and advice have been adopted, often due to the pressure of international (or global) corporations. This has often been in response to these transitional economies' aspirations for integration through EU membership.

With the industrialisation of the agriculture sector, change was inevitable, effectively reducing agricultural employment, with many European Union states losing between 40 per cent and 70 per cent of their agricultural workforce (Roberts & Hall 2001). Even so, industrialisation was only suited to certain areas and certain products, such as grain crops, and some smaller subsistence farms remain.

Such industrialisation seriously compromised the notion of the rural idyll, particularly in the United Kingdom, with the classic rural hedgerows and rustic walls being removed to create larger spaces that could facilitate the use of machinery in the fields. This was an important issue in terms of recreation and tourism as well as people's sense of all that is 'good' about the countryside, and is often referred to in relation to the loss of a 'true' rural environment. This alteration of the rural landscape has been criticised as negatively affecting rural tourism, as the countryside no longer fitted the Romantic pastoral rural image.

One of the primary concerns in rural areas is that of social exclusion, which comes from a combination of linked problems including unemployment, poor skills, low income, poor housing, high crime, bad health and family breakdown. These issues are often seen as occurring more in urban areas, particularly in inner-city neighbourhoods and urban public-housing, however they are prevalent in rural areas and are often compounded due to their low profile. They are not easy to identify in rural areas due to the spatial scattering of socially excluded households, distance, isolation and poor access to facilities. In addition, rural people's traditional attitudes of self-sufficiency can mask socially excluded groups or individuals (Roberts & Hall 2001).

On a more basic note, the global trend towards centralisation of government and commercial activities has contributed to the reduction and/or eventual elimination of service provision in rural settlements such as banks and other financial services, hospitals, medical specialists, agricultural departments, education and so on. Closer to major urban centres, the pressures of development have affected the urban-rural fringes in many countries. They are becoming places of friction and conflict between the newer residents and traditional farmers. These rural places are becoming attractive for many urbanites to live, with non-residential properties becoming available for new uses such as art and craft, tourism and spiritual or health retreats. These 'non-farming' populations, comprising retirees and commuters as well as those simply looking for life away from the urban sprawl, have driven massive social and demographic change in many rural areas.

While ex-urbanites may bring with them entrepreneurial skills, they also can carry a set of values and images of rural communities from the past (such as a rural idyll). People with these attitudes and expectations often oppose modern development, and can clash with the industrialised rural sector. This group also tends to be more familiar with political processes and can wield a high level of political power (see Chapter 4). The gentrification of rural areas may convert once productive farmland into mere extensions of urban living where 'dirty' farm practices are opposed, as well as losing cheap housing for residents who were forced to these urban-rural fringes for economic reasons (Roberts & Hall 2001).

Rural tourism can be a powerful tool that can be used to ameliorate social exclusion and some of the other issues outlined above. However, it needs to be approached in conjunction with other strategies and, of course, must include the local community.

Second homes – residents or visitors?

Another element of many rural communities is that of urban residents with 'weekenders' or second homes on farms or in country towns. Second home ownership can provide a significant economic benefit to rural areas, with many of these owners initially being tourists or visitors to those places. However, as with those living on the urban-rural fringe, there is often a clash of needs, not only between the longer-term residents, but also with the service expectations of recreationists and tourists. For example, a second-home owner may desire peace and quiet, whereas certain visitors (and other residents) may be looking for entertainment and ease of access. This is particularly the case in places that traditionally host a high level of summer holiday vacationers, such as the seaside, and was found to be an issue in the case of Barwon Heads (see Chapter 3).

Second-home owners are primarily absentee owners, who impact on rural communities in various ways, in a positive manner as well as potentially adverse. For example, additional spending in local shops will generate more economic benefits to the community. Visual amenity and the physical fabric of the community is improved by old or redundant buildings being given new lease of life through renovation or conversion into accommodation, and locals may gain temporary or permanent employment in building and service trades.

However, new development may in turn have adverse effects on the visual and environmental amenity of the place and community, not only by degrading the landscape, but also due to the prevalence of empty houses that are occupied only at weekends or even less regularly. The latter can seriously affect the safety and community environment of the neighbourhood. As already noted in the Barwon Heads case, increased housing prices may lock out locals, with the young people required to move away, increasing local resentment towards such affluent outsiders and the changes they have wrought.

Growth in rural recreation and tourism

As inferred in the previous discussion and noted by the OECD over 10 years ago, many of the changes to the countryside have coincided with a growth in (and change to) tourism and recreation needs and activities in rural areas. Some of the contributing factors include the desire of tourists for increased levels of participation in whatever activity they undertake, be it passive or active. Mass media images of rural areas and the success of fictional stories and television series based in small country communities have had enormous influence on people's desire to participate in such community experiences, also reinforcing the traditional rural idyll (see Chapter 5).

In terms of the newer recreational activities that require more sophisticated facilities and equipment, such as skiing and four-wheel driving, technological innovation that has created lower priced and user-friendly equipment is a major factor. In addition, the improved mobility and access of travellers has increased the potential of tourism in many previously inaccessible rural tourism areas.

Policy changes have also increased the supply of opportunities, particularly where previously restricted areas are now open, such as the use of water catchment areas and their associated reservoirs for sailing and fishing, and the increased management of public land for recreation as well as environmental purposes. Often the increased access to public land such as parks and reserves has come about due to the management agencies being required to fund much of their environmental programs from sources other than government funding. While not specifically related to rural tourism (according to my preferred definition), this increased access to public land flows on to tourist accommodation and service needs in rural areas.

While the above discussion is relatively brief, recognising the factors underlying rural change is central to understanding how rural tourism affects and is affected by rural developmental policies and the changing types of residents and visitors. It is also important for those living in rural areas who wish to develop rural tourism, particularly alongside existing rural practices such as agriculture.

Rural tourism and community solidarity

As noted by Huang and Stewart (1996, p. 26), 'close personal ties and solidarity are considered critical to the formation and maintenance of community', which are a product of a shared culture and lifestyle prevalent in rural communities. The make-up of many rural communities is more homogenous than in our ever-increasingly multicultural cities, in spite of efforts to encourage diverse migration to rural areas. Tourism, however, brings not only visitors from different cultural and socio-economic backgrounds but also new residents who operate the new tourism enterprises, and ultimately second-home owners. The original residents tend to resent this intrusion of outsiders, and it may take time for this new, more culturally pluralistic 'community' actually to develop its own sense of community.

When looking at a rural community in North America that has experienced such changes, Huang and Stewart (1996) found that by working on the community's image together (see Chapters 3 and 4), a new sense of community developed that the newcomers and original residents owned together, bonding this new group. Ideally such an image must relate to the everyday life of all residents, which is not a simple outcome to achieve. Nevertheless, as noted by Sofield (2003), it is often by going through the actual process itself that leads to further community bonding and a sense of shared solidarity.

Family businesses in rural tourism

Many rural businesses, be they in agriculture, services or tourism and recreation, are small, family based enterprises. It is estimated that 90 per cent of all business in rural areas are small businesses, and half of these are family owned or operated (Carlson & Getz 2001). The primary motivator for such groups to become involved in tourism is to diversify their existing farming or rural business, in an attempt to move away from a mono-economic base. This was one of the main issues identified in the Rural Tourism Map presented earlier in the chapter. The case study, while not focusing on an individual family business, outlines some of the issues that rural people face when trying to move into a service industry such as tourism.

While some are looking to diversify their existing business base, other family business operators dream of taking on tourism projects in their retirement. This often stems from false expectations and naivety – the demands of being involved in such an intensive enterprise as tourism have not been taken into account. Notions of meeting interesting people and socialising with them are often far removed from the reality of long working hours and impositions on the family's privacy (Oppermann 1997).

As with tourism and community development, these family operators need strong, strategic planning that not only considers the business, marketing and development aspects, but also links with the local community, who themselves are part of the rural tourism experience. Many of these issues are taken up in the following section, *Developing rural tourism communities*, which, as previously explained, is a keynote speech presented to a group of rural tourism professionals and public servants in New Zealand.

Developing rural tourism communities[1]

Communities are the destination of most travellers, not the physical attractions. Even at Uluru (Ayers Rock, Australia) tourists have always wanted to meet and deal with the local community, the Anangu – in the past, much to their detriment. So, it is in communities that tourism happens.

We could spend hours discussing definitions of 'rural tourism', but I consider it to be tourism that is reliant on the *rural environment and community* for its existence, such as farm tourism, community festivals and other related activities. This does not include those resorts, recreation and theme parks that are in the countryside purely because it is the only place they would physically fit. For example, Club Med resorts are the same around the world, operating in a totally constructed environment using their own currency and jargon (based on French) regardless of the country they are in. So, rural tourism is tourism in rural communities.

Over the past decade I have attended a broad range of conferences, and am told repeatedly that communities must be involved in tourism development. This is admirably supported by evidence from researchers showing us, for example, that those communities with the most positive attitudes towards tourism are those who have been involved in the development process (Craik 1991, p. 115). And of course I stress the importance of community involvement to my students [as well as in this publication!].

But, in my experience, tourism in rural (especially remote) areas develops in a slightly more ad-hoc manner, and I have my doubts as to how much we can really change, and wonder how much we really need to.

Government in Australia (as in most of today's democratic societies) has been removing itself from direct control over or intervention in most industries, particularly in the rural sector. Trade barriers have been lowered, supposedly providing us with a 'level playing field'. In tourism, government tourism agencies tend to focus on overall promotion and marketing, limiting their strategic planning to such aspects. In Victoria we have strategic regional tourism plans that make grand claims, but deliver little apart from increasing the expectations of visitors to our regions. It is left up to 'the industry' and local community to actually deliver on these government-funded recommendations, which include attracting that elusive 'high yield' visitor (pity about the family budget holiday market).

So, when we look at the rural tourism 'industry', what do we see? We usually find an operator (say, a farmer or vigneron) who has decided to expand or diversify into some tourism, such as selling produce at the farm gate or via cellar door sales, letting a room or hiring out horses. There is little discussion with the community (especially if they are operating on their own land), except maybe a few comments made at the local pub on Friday night.

The 'community' only really becomes involved when they notice more people in town, their roads deteriorating due to carrying increased vehicles, particularly heavy tour buses, when the local café goes 'gourmet', or when the tourists keep ending up at the wrong property (that's when they also ask for signage!). Unfortunately, it often takes negative aspects to motivate us, which can be too late as far as developing a positive rural tourism industry.

Community-driven vs operator-driven rural tourism

How has the local community developed tourism? – in the past it has been from the operator, rarely from the community. For example, the popular heritage town of Beechworth in NE Victoria was driven almost solely by a bakery that established itself as one of the best in Victoria and worked the tourism promotional aspect to its benefit. Prior to the Beechworth Bakery founding a local tourism association, encouraging antique and heritage businesses and taking out tourism awards, the town was best known for its mental hospital (Mayday Hills).

Without the motivation, drive and perseverance of the bakery owners, it is not difficult to see where Beechworth would be today. There are plenty of neighbouring towns with the same attributes, but no tourism, and unfortunately they are slowly fading away.

However, we are starting to see individual communities developing their own tourism strategies prior to any conscious operator/commercial involvement. They decide what 'type' of tourism they want, then develop the infrastructure and operations to meet these goals. I have seen some towns invent a tourism attraction through their community by developing festivals, local specialties or events based on a local tradition. A town in a gold mining region of Victoria has even made up its own legend, complete with gold mouse that is now featured on all promotional material and sold in numerous souvenir forms!

Generally, these communities are being driven by the belief that either:

- Tourism is the Great Saviour, bringing employment, economic and social gain; or

- Tourism is inevitable, and if unplanned will destroy them.

These two points remind me of a quote that is often used:

'Tourism is like fire. It can cook your meals or burn your house down.'

Apart from community support, community-driven tourism should also have true **local** government commitment, not merely tokenism. Local government has access to resources, experience and advice, and as such can be a great source of assistance apart from the obvious one of providing infrastructure and some funding. It is also local government that provides services and amenities such as streetscape development, road maintenance and rubbish collection. So, the community must involve local government in its discussions in the same way that local government must truly involve the community.

Community support for rural tourism

Community support is a major critical success factor in rural tourism. Our guests travel through and interact with our community, so it is important that the community is pleased to deal with the tourists. We need to identify the critical community groups by assessing who is impacted (both positively and negatively) by tourism, and who has the power in the community. For example, local traders will usually be affected positively by increased tourism, whereas retirees may find increased traffic an issue (and they have time on their hands to agitate!).

But, how do we reach the community and when should this be done? This is where things can get complicated. Putting an ad in the local paper announcing a public meeting to discuss a certain tourism issue may meet statute requirements (if you are a government body), but such a token gesture is not enough. To get truly representative support you may need to seek out the community leaders, which may include the clergy, publicans, teachers, store owners, historical societies, conservation groups and residents. Some towns will have an organised community structure with associations or clubs representing the interests of the groups, whereas others may require a little more sorting out. By personally inviting them to attend a general (possibly informal) meeting to discuss your plans and find out how they impact on each group will give you greater, more positive input from the community.

Some people fear that by making their plans public, someone else will 'steal' them. Well, this is certainly a possibility, but more often than not they will look for ways to build on what you are planning, which in turn assists in the development of an integrated tourism industry. Also, if you are operating on your own land, you may not need to divulge details of your plans, rather alert the community to the fact that there will be more people in the area looking for more facilities and activities because of your operation.

An important means for tourism operators and government employees to gain real community input and support for an enterprise is to become directly involved in the local community. This should be done strategically, utilising the particular skills you have to their benefit. For example, if you run a successful small business you may be able to speak at the local Chamber of Commerce meetings, local school groups about future careers, or even assist in developing a business plan for a local charity. By volunteering for positions on local boards and committees you are also demonstrating *your* commitment to the community. Now, of course much of this will be dependent on the amount of time you have to devote to such activities, but even speaking once or twice a year at events that are well publicised will earn you community standing.

Sponsoring local events is another means to involve yourself in the community. This can be done with direct financial contributions or through providing a prize or other service.

The community needs to be consulted at all stages of the development and implementation process – the more people feel that you are interested in what they have to say, the more supportive they will be, even if you don't take all their wishes on board. The community members themselves may well be able to come up with solutions that you had not considered to problems or issues. Such ownership can prove to be invaluable. Of course, it will not always be practical to do so, and there will be time constraints – a good dose of common sense needs to be applied here.

Community events and rural tourism

Ensuring community involvement is not all hard work, factionalism and doom and gloom, however. There are some other forms of rural tourism apart from the farmer or vigneron, with their cellar door sales or rooms to rent, and other community reactions apart from the locals objecting to general infrastructure damage and increased crowding and noise.

The most readily identified group are festivals, as they are usually community based and driven. A 'good' community based rural festival reflects rural community standards, priorities and imagery, usually in a positive manner, which is what tourists are looking for. Of course, it can also perpetuate incorrect images and negatively commodified products.

In a region of Victoria there is a Pumpkin Festival that incorporates pumpkin-seed spitting competitions, while another event that has captured the imagination of many Australian towns is simply called the 'Dog in Ute Parade'. Also, ABC TV has an excerpt from a beer barrel tossing competition at a small town festival as one of its station identifications. I'll leave it up to you to consider if they're reflecting the community or merely reinforcing outdated, marginal or inappropriate rural images.

Inherent pitfalls

There is a whole range of problems and barriers that rural tourism operators and communities around the world face, and unfortunately at this stage there are relatively few examples of successfully applied community based rural tourism schemes. This is partly due to the fact that the concept of community based tourism is relatively new and most schemes have not been operational long enough for us to adequately assess them. However, there appears to be a common set of issues that befall rural communities around the world, including the misunderstanding of pricing and distribution, economic imperatives, the need for private sector finance, lack of training and lack of interest from certain areas of the community.

Profitability and pricing of rural tourism

Let's get back to our farming family who want to rent out some rooms to tourists. Their traditional income source has been wool, which they sell at a fixed price to a wholesaler who then adds a mark-up to the product and so on along the chain. They also belong to a marketing cooperative that promotes New Zealand wool to the world.

Now, these rooms they want to rent require refurbishment to meet health and safety standards – no problem. Next, they must decide what to charge for a room. Generally, they'll look at what others are charging and usually decide to undercut them a little to get into the market (standard 'penetration pricing' strategy). They sell a few nights to people casually driving past, but soon realise that they need to do more than this. So they print up some brochures with their pricing schedule and proceed to distribute them around various tourism operations and information centres. They are then approached by a travel agent who wants 10 per cent commission and a wholesaler who wants at least 25 per cent! They have not incorporated this into their pricing structure as they are not used to paying commissions or distributing and selling a service as opposed to a product, and often have trouble recognising the benefits and necessity of working within the tourism system.

Our farmers may survive a few years in their tourism venture, but eventually they decide it is not worth the effort and close down. They not only close down, however, they also advise people not to get into tourism and generally spread negative information about the industry.

This is not their fault. In our rural areas we lack many of the support structures taken for granted in major cities, including education and business advice and support. Finding the time to leave the farm to learn about tourism is not easy. The situation could be improved by a stronger commitment from local government to work with its local community in tourism-related areas, particularly in education and training.

Another trap that we all fall into (and I'm finding this particularly so with government agencies not directly involved with tourism, such as the Department of Agriculture or even Regional Development) is that we've all been on some form of a holiday or even worked in a restaurant or pub, so we tend to assume that we understand the tourism industry. All of us here realise that tourism is a little more complicated than it appears – even the basic economic developmental argument that it can create local employment in marginal rural areas is fraught with assumptions and conditions that are not always met. Sure, some jobs may come from tourism, but many are part-time, seasonal and low paid, while the more highly specialised work goes to people from outside the region. Of course, if seasonal tourism work is at times when other seasonal work is low, there could be offset opportunities.

Economic imperatives

Due to their need to survive economically, we find that many people (including tourism operators) are dominated by their individual, short-term economic goals, which tend to be quite different to longer-term community objectives.

While we may intellectually recognise the value of long-term sustainability, there is a very human aspect that sees many operators tending to use certain resources 'before someone else does'. For the past 10 years I have heard comments such as: 'We wouldn't destroy that which earns our income' (especially in the case of the natural environment). In the real world, where we have to pay bills and feed our family, this is not the case. Privately, the operators are saying: 'Why should I make the effort and go to the expense of introducing minimal damage equipment and techniques when the others don't?'

Certainly, the advent of ecotourism has been of some help here, but it is a niche market with a relatively small customer base. However, the principles espoused by true ecotourism operators may eventually filter down to other operations as well. I know I and my colleagues work hard to instil positive community and environmental attitudes in our students – the next generation of tourism operators.

Another economic issue that can undermine local community control is the need for private sector finance. Additional infrastructure, environmental management initiatives and so on often need financial support from external funding sources. This not only reduces local control but can also see money in terms of wages, turnover and profits leaking out of the community, limiting the multiplier effect. However, what needs to be weighed up is whether some of the benefits of tourism are better than none and what level of negative aspects the community will be shouldering.

Lack of training

As a Board member of the Victorian Tourism Operators Association (VTOA), I spent a great deal of time representing the interests and needs of rural tourism operators to local, state and federal governments. As well as tackling some of the issues outlined here, I was particularly concerned with safety and risk management, especially within the horseback industry (which was my main field of operation at the time). Every time I investigated a mishap, the most common cause was a lack of staff or operator skills in accident prevention, observation ability and so on.

So, what could be done? Well, we could train these people with observation skills, risk management and safety, which I was able to instigate in my three years with VTOA. At each of our seminars, we asked people what were the main issues they faced and where did they need more training, and the most outstanding areas were marketing and business finance. Last year I surveyed our local region and the responses were the same, with a few areas that have now also become important in Australia, including service and health and safety.

Lack of interest from certain areas of the community

Getting back to our community, one of the main problems facing us is the fact that those not directly involved in or benefiting from tourism tend to only see the negative aspects of tourism, such as crowding and noise. Now, we all know that everyone in a community benefits from tourism – in most cases they can use the infrastructure for their own recreation, they benefit from greater variety in restaurants and entertainment as well as the flow-on economic effects. So, the challenge here is to educate the whole community! One way to do this would be through involving all those community groups mentioned earlier, but we need to do more to get concepts of tourism into the overall community psyche – one important means is to get the local media 'on side'. I don't have time here to go into the complexities of local media relations, but getting media representatives on your committees and boards would be a good start. Another important consideration is your local school – encourage teachers to access community based tourism activities and include the children.

Making it pay

With so many pitfalls, can we actually profit from rural tourism? The short answer is 'Yes', as long as you plan strategically, doing your homework.

Some tourism operators become involved in the industry, not to make money, but for lifestyle or even ethical reasons. Tourism enables them to maintain a rural living, with product decisions based on personal preferences rather than economics. However, without an eye on the bottom line, even those with the highest ideals will fail. Profit margins are tight and the industry can be fragmented due to the intensity of the work and remoteness of operators.

By working within the principles of tourism pricing and using the distribution network to your advantage, profitability can be achieved. In *Ecotourism, a guide for rural communities* (Beeton 1995) there is a chapter called 'Making it Pay' which outlines the benefits of using agents, inbound operators etc. and justifies the commissions they require. The book attempts to explain all this as simply as possible, stressing that businesses (and communities) must do their sums before setting their price.

Community based rural tourism – is it worth it?

Developing successful, long-term rural tourism with our community's support is not impossible, but too often in the past it has been improbable! We must face reality and work with what *is*, not what it *should be*. If the pub is the place most representative of your community, discussions over a few beers is totally legitimate and worthwhile. Just remember that you also need to speak to those you do not necessarily come across in your own day-to-day living, be that at the pub, church, local school or all three.

We must continue to work together through our associations and our own community groups. We need to consider these issues after we leave this conference as well as during it – rural tourism and our communities are intrinsically linked and require constant attention and consideration. Otherwise, the next media crew you see in your town could be the sensationalists from *A Current Affair*, not the friendly good-timers from *Getaway*.

Concluding rural (community) tourism

The above transcript from an address to a conference group in New Zealand is close to 10 years old, yet the comments and sentiments remain the same. It is an indictment of our understanding of tourism and its subsequent development that there has been so little positive change. One of the keys to this is the continued limited understanding of the relationship between tourism and communities, particularly in terms of community development. It is certainly hoped that this book will go some way to addressing this. One issue that continues to persist is that of matching demand and supply.

Supplying demand or demanding supply?

While there has been much written about the issues of too much demand impacting on communities and the environment, the other end of the scale is rarely discussed, yet is common to rural tourism. That is, supply actually exceeds demand on some rural areas. This is due to the ease of entry for farm-style accommodation, bed and breakfasts and so on, where the accommodation already exists in the form of a second house on a merged farming property, unused rooms in the main house or buildings that can be readily converted such as shearers' quarters.

There has been a general focus on rural tourism planning and development and not on understanding the market or the demand for the product. There are many rural areas that are not popular due to remoteness, limited access or other more attractive competitive areas. Also, the rural tourism market can be a budget market, and there has been a focus in many tourism areas on attracting the smaller high yield market, which may simply not be interested.

Also, many governments have seen rural tourism as an economic panacea, encouraging overdevelopment through grants and other forms of support. This can result not only in over-supply but also in propping up unprofitable and unprofessional businesses that should have collapsed some time ago.

These scenarios are not only detrimental to the region, but also to the communities that support them. The following case study considers a rural tourism enterprise that failed, partly due to a lack of market understanding, tourism knowledge and reliance on government funding.

Nevertheless, it remains that much so-called 'rural' tourism in fact is based in the rural towns and villages or in enclaved resort chains, not in the surrounding rural farmlands. Consequently, many of the benefits of rural tourism are only felt in the towns, and while they also need the economic input that tourism brings, it is often those working on the land that require it even more. With conscious planning and community consultation along with empowerment, this situation can be ameliorated.

From theory to practice: The case of Landcare and tourism in a rural community

The Australian program known as Landcare was created to provide integration between the environment, farming and the community. It resides within the broader framework of environmental conservation, focusing on sustainable production from the land. It encompasses all areas of production and commercial land use such as crops and domestic animals, water quality and supply as well as the broader components of wildlife, scientific values, aesthetics and recreation (Beeton 2002c). The program is community driven from the bottom up, with support coming from the government in terms of seed funding and some basic administration services where needed. There are four basic Landcare principles:

1 Prevention is better than cure.

2 Rehabilitation may not always be the best response to land degradation as it may be too costly in relation to the returns, and alternatives must be considered.

3 Land degradation problems are as much social as technical.

4 Vegetative cover is the key to land protection (Roberts 1992).

While initially established to protect the environment (as illustrated in the four principles above), a significant side benefit is Landcare's ability to provide a force for community cohesion, due to its community based nature. This has resulted in a future-oriented focus enabling rural people to maintain their community and identity, particularly in hard times (Youl 1997).

The concept of rehabilitating land or finding alternative uses for it can become a central part of a rural tourism experience, even simply by providing activities such as guided tours, field days, demonstrations and festivals – all of which occur in the Landcare programs. In one region in Australia, the local Landcare network and Catchment Authority (charged with protecting the water supply in terms of quantity and quality to the region) decided to establish a separate, commercial operation called 'Impact Tours' to handle the range of educational tours associated with the many Landcare projects in which they were involved. It was anticipated that this would encourage urban-rural interaction and create greater support for the projects in both the local and broader communities.

Impact Tours was established with an initial grant of around $80 000, and a Management Committee drawn from the Department of Natural Resources and Environment, the Landcare Network administration, the Catchment Management Authority and local government. They did not include anyone with direct tourism experience apart from the local government tourism officer who was enthusiastic but had little time to contribute to the committee, eventually completely withdrawing from the group. This was a major loss to the group, and one that was not realised nor addressed until it was far too late for any possible recovery.

A person was employed on a consulting contractual basis to get the operation going, and a beautiful, full-colour glossy brochure was developed that discussed the aims of the enterprise and some potential tours. Unfortunately, all of the funding was consumed through this person's salary and the production and printing of the brochure, with no actual research or business planning being done. The tours were developed by the Management Committee without undertaking any market research or seeking advice from the relevant tourism organisations.

The tours they ran were extremely interesting, and those presenting and interpreting the information had great expertise and certainly would have satisfied the rural, educational, industrial tourism and ecotourism markets if they knew about them. As it was, the tours were taken by local landowners who saw them as a service provided by the Catchment Authority, so they were not prepared to pay more than what they had already contributed to the Authority. This community, while central to Landcare and interested in the progress of various projects, was also not aware of the tourism potential for the enterprise, and could only view the tours in light of their own interests. This caused serious financial difficulties for the program, which ran the tour at a loss and did little to encourage any interested tourists, as the committee failed to access any tourism networks.

One of the problems that Impact Tours faced was a lack of planning regarding the tourism pricing and distribution network, along with virtually no knowledge or understanding of its complexity or how to cost and price tourism experiences. This is one of the main causes of rural tourism failure, as they are unused to the concept of paying commissions, and the entire notion of 'distributing' an intangible service is anathema to primary producers used to dealing with tangible agricultural goods. Accessing the complex tourism distribution system (as outlined in an introductory tourism textbook) was not even considered. Compounding the problem was that the Management Committee of the enterprise consisted of public servants who primarily possessed a funding mentality – they kept looking for government funds to support their unprofitable operation rather than working their pricing and distribution system appropriately and undertaking any real market research.

So, an opportunity to include the local community in tourism directly through its Landcare projects has been lost through people thinking that this 'tourism thing' is easy. This lost opportunity may never be recovered. However, the lesson to be learnt here is the importance of understanding the demand and supply sides of any proposed enterprise *in the context of its community* as well as the machinations of the tourism industry in terms of pricing and distribution, at the very least.

Endnote

1   This section is based on a Keynote Address presented by the author to the New Zealand Rural Tourism Conference.

7

Dealing with crisis in tourism communities

Tourism (both as a community development tool as well as its concomitant economic and social effects) is rarely considered news-worthy, unless it is to provide a feel-good story and/or photo opportunity for a politician. However, when a crisis or disaster strikes that affects the business of tourism, particularly in developing and/or remote regions, tourism (or its loss) is front-page news.

'Crises occur at all levels of tourism operations with varying degrees of severity, from much-publicised environmental, economic and political disasters through to internally generated crises such as accidents and sudden illness' (Beeton 2001d, p. 203). As I predominantly use the term 'crisis' in this chapter, it is important to outline the difference between crises and disasters. A crisis is basically self-inflicted on a business via inept management practices or failure to adapt to change; whereas a disaster consists of sudden, unpredictable, catastrophic changes from external forces.

A disaster can be a natural disaster such as an earthquake, flood, fire, hurricane ('cyclone' in the Southern Hemisphere), social disruption including civil war and terrorism, accidents and health emergencies such as SARS, foot and mouth and the Asian bird flu. The crisis relates more to how such disasters (and other events) are handled by the enterprise

– in this case the tourism communities, operations and destinations. So, I primarily use the term 'crisis' when relating to human nature and its shortcomings in dealing with a disaster. In fact, many disasters are compounded by crises.

We can identify crises under three typologies: an immediate crisis with little or no warning, such as an accident that can be difficult to prepare for; an emerging crisis that is slower in developing and whose effects may be influenced by action from the destination or community; while the final one is a sustained crisis that may last for weeks, months or years.

In addition, false rumours can exacerbate or even create a disaster in terms of their effect on tourism – once gained, incorrect negative perceptions and images can be difficult to shift, resulting in an internal crisis. For example, an accident or disaster in one area can affect tourism in other areas as the way it has been reported has affected the general public's perception very negatively. The role of the media in perpetrating such perceptions is significant, as King and Beeton (2006) found when surveying the youth market's perceptions of risky activities. Over half of those surveyed claimed that, after hearing about an accident through the media, their view of the level of risk involved in that particular activity increased, regardless of where and how the accident occurred. This is a particularly risk-accepting market segment, so the influence of the media on overall negative perceptions would be even higher for other, more risk-averse groups.

Natural disaster life cycle

While there are many models that illustrate the cycle of natural disasters, Bill Faulkner suggested one that was later added to by Brent Ritchie. Based on their model, I have come up with an updated crisis and disaster life cycle (see Faulkner 2001; Ritchie 2004). The cycle consists of two phases prior to the disaster occurring and four after it. These stages are:

1 Pre-event
2 Prodormal

... Disaster occurs ...

3   Emergency

4   Intermediate

5   Long-term (recovery)

6   Resolution

The pre-event phase is when action can be taken to prevent or at least avert a disaster from turning into a crisis, particularly those disasters that can be partly foreseen, such as the probability of a bushfire in national parks in summer. The prodormal stage is when it becomes clear that the disaster is inevitable, such as a hurricane moving along a predictable path. It is shortly after this that the disaster actually occurs, and virtually immediately, a state of emergency occurs. This becomes even more apparent as the immediate effects of the disaster are felt, requiring actions to rescue people, animals and property. The fourth, intermediate stage, is when the short-term needs of the people must be dealt with, particularly in restoring or providing utilities and essential services. Long-term recovery then takes effect, which is primarily a continuation of the previous phase, where things take longer to be completed, such as repairs, rebuilding and counselling. Often new sources of income need to be developed or the old ones re-constructed. Finally, routine is restored, or we see a new, improved state of affairs. However, few places return to the way they were – they rarely fully recover, but are in a continual process of recovering, and in some instances see improvement. The catch-cry of Banda Aceh and Thailand after the 2004 Asian tsunami is 'build it better'.

In a special edition on 'Destination Crisis Management' in the destination management periodic publication *Eclipse*, James Kilgour from the Canadian Centre for Emergency Preparedness states that we need to move away from terms such as 'crisis management life cycles'. Instead we should talk about a 'crisis management program' which consists of a series of life cycles, including mitigation, preparedness, response and recovery (Polunin c. 2002). Such planning is discussed in terms of market planning and communications throughout this chapter.

The Education Group of the philanthropic based organisation Business Enterprises for Sustainable Tourism (BEST) held a Think Tank in Jamaica in 2005 on crisis management, 'Managing Risk and Crisis for Sustainable Tourism: Research and Innovation'. The background and nature of BEST is outlined in Case Study 1 in the next chapter (see page 205). However, the education group's stated description/mission is: 'The BEST Education Network (BEST EN) is an international consortium of educators committed to furthering the development and dissemination of knowledge in the field of sustainable tourism' (BEST EN, www.best-educationnetwork.org).

The Education Group runs a series of Think Tanks on contemporary topics and incorporates elements of sustainability into training modules based around the theme. The 2005 Think Tank, in which I participated, also prepared a research agenda on risk and crisis management. A range of papers was presented as part of the process, and much of the following information is from those papers and the work done at the Think Tank and is acknowledged as such where appropriate.

Crises in destination communities

Dealing with natural disasters tends to be the most obvious crisis that communities have to deal with at their destinations. While they can be devastating, there are other forms of disaster that need to be considered too – such as civil war and ongoing internal unrest, terrorism or an incident involving tourists (that may be an accident such as the collapse of a structure, illness or criminal activities such as assault, theft or abduction). There are two basic elements behind all of these: safety and security.

Any or all of these disasters can result in a crisis for a destination and its community, not only in economic terms, but also in terms of self-esteem, power and community cohesiveness. The most empowered community that must rely on outside assistance to handle a crisis, be that from care agencies or services including another nation's (or their own) armed forces, police, judiciary and so on, can easily become dis-empowered and revert to a permanent state of reliance.

In addition, there are elements that amplify the problems facing a destination community dealing with a crisis, which can be positive, negative or a combination of the two. One of the most influential of these amplifiers is the media. How the world's news media presents the status of a disaster and the recovering process has a direct influence on tourists' perceptions and visitation patterns. As noted in the introductory section of this chapter, there are many instances where the media has presented a disaster as more widespread than it really is, effectively turning it into a crisis, even for destinations not initially affected by the disaster itself.

However, not all media reports are negative, and many of the reports following the 2004 Asian tsunami included discussion of not only the effect on tourism to communities that relied upon it, but also to the ways that tourists were contributing to their recovery by returning. Analysis of the global media giant Fox Media's news service, Fox News', reports of the Asian tsunami showed that, while there was an initial focus on the cost of the disaster, later stories began to talk about the need for visitors to return to the affected tourism regions. Consequently, there is some evidence of an incremental shift in how disasters, accidents and incidents at tourist destinations are reported in the news media (Beeton 2005b).

These cases raise questions that require further consideration and investigation, particularly in terms of whether the nature of the report is driven by the type of incident (and degree of preventable 'fault') or whether media groups such as Fox News and others are actually reflecting a change in community awareness of the importance of tourism, both socially and economically. Or are they just looking for more stories due to changes in global communication, where independent sources such as the Internet and digital technology via mobile phones and cameras can often pre-empt traditional media?

The 2005 case of Australian tourist to Bali, Schapelle Corby, brings into stark relief the role of media and travellers' responses. She was found guilty of bringing drugs into Bali. However, she maintains that she is innocent and that her bags had been tampered with. Her plight attracted enormous media attention in Australia, where it is generally felt that her 20-year sentence was excessive. While this is one person out of the thousands of Australians visiting the destination, the intensive media attention to her case precipitated an interesting change in the behaviour of Australian travellers. They were still going to Bali; however, there was an exponential increase in all Australians travelling overseas (not just to Bali) queuing at Australian airports to get their bags shrink-wrapped in an attempt to avoid tampering. In addition, tourists are beginning to understand their importance to communities such as

Bali and many suggested boycotting Bali, believing in their power to influence the legal system and such outcomes. Tourists and tourism are no longer simply frivolous or meaningless pastimes!

Others also acknowledge the power of the media to turn a disaster into a crisis, with consultant Peter Power explaining that:

> The field of mass media communication is where managers feel most helpless. This is the front line where the harshest collisions with the outside world are likely to occur; made worse because a crisis generates episodes made for television, with drama, action and a real story with a beginning, middle and end. The media whirlwind sweeps up the unprepared when it charges through the door. It invades their frame of reference and creates a shock for those in charge. They always suppose ... that if there were a problem, they would decide, with the executive team, what should be said, when and how. But the world suddenly stands on its head: it is the media who know what is happening and executive management is reduced to asking them for information (Power, in Polunin c. 2002, p. 8).

Nevertheless, there are different reactions to perceptions of risk in the eyes of the tourist, depending on whether the media reports actually have a negative or positive influence in terms of tourism. What for one is an unmitigated disaster may for others be the incident that not only makes the holiday memorable, but enjoyable, particularly in the re-telling of the story (Beeton 2001d). King and Beeton found this to be the case with some of those in the youth market, stating that, while the media coverage increases the perception of risk, for a significant proportion of young people (19–35 years old):

> ... the increase in risk encourages contemplation of participation in the future. Perhaps the increase in perceived risk adds kudos to those that participate or even talk about participating ... People are encouraged to participate in a risky activity because of the psychological benefit of receiving recognition for their achievement (King & Beeton 2006).

Therefore, understanding the psychological nature of your market and what truly motivates them is critical to the recovering process.

There is a body of literature about 'dark tourism', which initially meant tourism to sites of atrocities such as the Auschwitz prison camps and the genocide museums of Cambodia, but it can equally relate to an interest in natural as well as man-made disasters. For more information on the phenomenon and the work being done to better define and understand it, go to the website, *The Dark Tourism Forum* (http://www.dark-tourism.org.uk/), which has been established by the University of Central Lancaster. The community needs to decide if they want to encourage or discourage this type of tourism, as the visitors *will* come.

While the news media often has an immediate, powerful influence, professional travel writers also exert significant influence over their readers. Travel writers not only appear in regular Travel sections in newspapers, magazines and on television, but may also write best-selling books on their experiences.

By presenting more than simple information or advertorial, travel writing provides the reader with a personal, emotional account of varying travel experiences. Such publications may exert long-term influence on certain market segments. This in turn brings us to the world of the travel guidebook. Many of these are immediate in their influence due to their websites where current, up to date information can be presented. While this can provide excellent information for travellers, most also have spaces for travellers to write their own, individual perceptions, which may or may not contain what the destination community wants. Examples of these sites are Lonely Planet (http://www.lonelyplanet.com/) and its Thorn Tree site that posts travellers' stories, queries and comments (http://thorntree.lonelyplanet.com/). Another site among many is the Rough Guide travel site (http://travel.roughguides.com/), while the top end traveller is not ignored, with sites presented by prestige publications such as Condé Nast Traveller (http://www.cntraveller.co.uk/) providing information for the more up-market 'better heeled' traveller.

Another significant amplifier is the travel warnings issued by governments to their nationals regarding issues they may face when visiting certain destinations. These can be extremely problematic, as it is a government's responsibility to protect its people, therefore if they are travelling to 'dangerous' places, the government is obligated to notify them of any potential problems. It is the interpretation and extent of the 'danger' that concerns many affected destinations. Many people argue that the warnings create false impressions of the extent of some disasters or safety and security issues, negatively affecting their tourism industry far more than necessary. In late December 2005, the Australian government site, Smart Traveller (http://www.smarttraveller. gov.au) had high level warnings issued for a number of destinations. They advised against all travel to Afghanistan, Burundi, Iraq, the Ivory Coast, Liberia and Somalia, while they also advised people to reconsider their need to travel to Angola, the Central African Republic, Colombia, Democratic Republic of the Congo, Haiti, Indonesia (including Bali), Nepal, Pakistan, Saudi Arabia, Sudan and Yemen. At the same time, the listing for the United Kingdom from the Australian government included the following:

- We advise you to exercise caution and monitor developments that might affect your safety because of the risk of terrorist attack.

- On 7 July 2005, four bomb attacks occurred on the transport system of central London. Security measures remain at heightened levels and British authorities have warned that further attacks cannot be ruled out. (http://www. smarttraveller.gov.au/zw-cgi/view/Advice/United_Kingdom)

In December 2005, the United Kingdom also expressed concern for their nationals travelling to Australia, issuing an advisory containing some specific warnings regarding visiting Australia:

- Australia is a vast country. Journeys need to be planned, particularly if travelling to remote areas.

- You should be aware of the threat from terrorism in Australia. Attacks could be indiscriminate and against civilian targets, including places frequented by foreigners. On 3 November 2005, the Australian government introduced an urgent amendment to the country's counter-terrorism legislation, in response to an assessment by Australian intelligence agencies that a terrorist attack in Australia is feasible and could well occur. Subsequently on 8 November 2005, the Australian police arrested 16 people in Sydney and

Melbourne in a counter-terrorism operation designed to disrupt preparations for a terrorist attack.

- Since 11 December 2005, there have been sporadic outbreaks of violence in Cronulla, Maroubra, Brighton-le-Sands and other areas of south-west Sydney between gangs of youths. Police presence in these areas has been increased, but you should monitor the situation, and exercise caution if visiting these areas – particularly on the local beaches, or at night (http://www.fco.gov.uk).

Are such warnings an overreaction to what are isolated and, in relation to terrorism, simply an interpretation of relatively minor events in Australia? Beirman (2005) queries whether travel advisories are more about making political statements than a genuine tourism risk assessment. Many countries and regions have been highly critical of such travel advisories, yet if a disaster occurs of which the government was even partly aware, they are criticised for not making that knowledge public.

Whether we are looking at the news and current affairs media reporting or that of government organisations, it is clear that they exert significant influence on travel to and from certain destinations and their associated communities, as already noted by King and Beeton (2006). While the media is not the sole source of visitor perceptions, with previous knowledge and the perceptions of friends and relatives also playing a role, its power cannot be ignored. The social construction of 'reality' by the media in terms of tourism experiences is a theme taken up by Beeton, Bowen and Santos (2005), and Bowen and Santos (2005) in the publication, *Quality Tourism Experiences*. The next section looks at how we can manage people's perceptions of a disaster, in the hope that simple perceptions of a place will not precipitate a crisis.

Managing perceptions

In his presentation at the BEST EN Think Tank, David Beirman (2005) considers that it is important to ensure that strategies and tools are in place so that a destination can challenge and ultimately overcome negative, false perceptions as they arise. Of course, it would be irresponsible (to say the least!) to try to change correct perceptions, even if they may be negative.

As well as the news media, travel journalists, travel guides and government travel advisories, other elements that govern how a destination is perceived include private sector tourism marketing cartels, airlines, major hotel chains and travel agents.

Beirman (2005) offers some tactics to influence potential visitors' perceptions, such as having an effective public relations campaign, some advertising muscle through long-term commercial relationships with the media, well-defined lines of communication in the destination and an accessible and knowledgeable spokesperson. Having a spokesperson who is accessible and knowledgeable is crucial – when the media is onto a story, they want to speak to someone immediately, and if they cannot get to the appropriate individual, they will interview (and quote) virtually any person prepared to talk to them. I don't think I need to point out the potential disaster of an inexperienced, uninformed person speaking to the media on your behalf, as we have all seen it – just turn on tonight's TV news and I'm sure you'll find a few examples. Too often I have seen travel agents who sell international travel being presented as 'experts' on their local community in terms of its internal tourism, yet they have nothing professionally to do with that sector. As Henderson confirms:

Journalists will press for the disclosure of as much detail as possible and answers to their question, against a background of confusion and uncertainty in the initial phases of a crisis (Henderson, in Polunin c. 2002, p. 8).

Beirman also recommends the presence and use of an effective website, which must be not only up to date and accurate, but also easy to find and navigate around (Beirman 2005). So many people access the Internet that this is vital, and it is also another way that the news media obtains its information, so there are many reasons to make sure that the site is outstanding and accurate! Used correctly, it can be an exceptional tool.

During Hurricane Katrina in 2005, the entire communications system collapsed in New Orleans, leaving the media to rely on web logs (blogs) of individual survivors for their information. There were many instances where their stories were reprinted verbatim as 'news' in the print media (without any acknowledgement of their source).

When a disaster occurs at a destination, it is important that the community and other stakeholders are allied, presenting common messages. All key stakeholders from the government and the tourism and hospitality industry's private sector need to be involved, as does the local community. This cannot be done if the community and tourism stakeholders are fragmented before the disaster. Occasionally, certain events will bring people and groups together, but simply hoping that it will happen is not an effective or advisable way to operate. Beirman (2005) stresses that the concept of a recovery alliance is equally relevant to national and supranational tourism recovery programs, while I maintain that this also relates to the local, community level.

As with any planning (see also Chapter 3), contingencies need to be developed by determining the most likely threats to the marketability of your destination and training staff and stakeholders to respond to likely scenarios. The community should establish and train a 'ready to go' disaster team that can swing into action as soon as something happens – this can be anything from a local bushfire or bus accident to a national disaster. Such a team may well prevent that disaster from developing into a crisis.

When considering developing such strategies, there are many practical sources that your community may be able to access – think about the organisations that are most prepared for disasters and seek their guidance. The airline industry is one that has always had to plan for incidents and accidents as well as hijackings, so the International Air Transport Association (IATA – www.iata.org) may have something relevant to offer you in its expertise (Beirman 2005). Most countries have a national airline that may also be able to advise you, while there are many others in the travel or tourism field who can also assist. For example, the Pacific Asia Travel Association (PATA) has released a small, but comprehensive booklet on Crisis Management (PATA 2003). The 2003 PATA publication outlines four phases of crisis management: reduction, readiness, response and recovery, providing a series of practical checklists for dealing with each phase.

Communication strategies
So, when does bad news constitute a tourism crisis and how can it be overcome? Peter Tarlow, an international safety and security expert answered this question in the following manner:

There are two types of bad news: the 'single event bad news' and the 'continual event bad news'. In the former, the impact of the event can be overcome with good marketing and publicity, in a short while and with relative ease. In the latter case, a long-term perception can develop in people's minds ... Israel has suffered from continual event bad news, while New York may recover from September 11 with relative ease (Tarlow, in Polunin c. 2002, p. 2).

Tarlow clearly considers not only that communication strategies are critical for many types of crises, but also that a different strategy is required for each.

Beirman has a great deal of experience in dealing with political crises in his role as the founding Director of the Israel Tourism Office (Australasia and South West Pacific). For him, promoting Israel to potential visitors is an ongoing challenge. However, he suggests that there is a range of questions that need to be asked by any destination or community in terms of its crisis recovery strategy. These include:

- Do we market a destination during a crisis?
- Do we only wait to market after the crisis is deemed resolved?
- Centralise or devolve PR management?
- What is the impact of crisis duration on marketing strategy?
- What are our key marketing messages?
- Do we stratify our market for risk management purposes as Israel has done?
- What constitutes a destination crisis? (Beirman 2005.)

Many tactical communication approaches can be taken if there is a crisis and they can help its recovery process, such as the isolation strategy, where the message is that it only happened in a small area, and it is 'business as usual' elsewhere. This is a common approach to many disasters, but needs to be convincing with clear evidence – tourists have many choices of destinations to travel to, so they will go elsewhere if they are unconvinced. As the UN World Tourism Organisation notes, 'good communications based on the principles of honesty and transparency is the key to successful crisis management' (UN WTO c.2002, p. 1).

By teaming up with other organisations and businesses, even those not directly in tourism or your community, the efficacy of the message is reinforced and strengthened.

After the disaster, the destination may require re-imaging (see Chapter 5) in order to counter the (negative) image that the disaster has given the place. This will often be teamed with a blitz of 'recovery' marketing, with messages that the destination is 'back in business'.

Much of the above advice relates to strategic planning and marketing, and as such a crisis management and recovery plan should be included in the destination or community's overall tourism strategy. While not all disasters and incidents are predictable, by having a stated strategy identifying responsible personnel and contacts (hospitals, doctors, nurses, fire brigade, police), including after-hours contact details, many unforeseen disasters can be prevented from becoming crises. In addition, no crisis will be the same, so there needs to be enough scope for those charged with the responsibility of responding to the crisis to be flexible, applying their knowledge base. Ultimately, the crisis will dictate the reaction.

Market responses

By understanding your visitor market, you should be able to stratify visitors according to their propensity to return and when, as well as who is likely to be discouraged or actually encouraged to visit. Beirman (2005) refers to them as the stalwarts who will come anyway, waverers who will respond to a strong marketing communication approach, and the discretionary group who choose a destination on a range of criteria that can be met elsewhere – such as those looking for a resort-style holiday or general outdoor experiences. Beirman does not acknowledge a fourth group, that of the dark tourist mentioned earlier, who is attracted to places of disaster, nor the very small group of travellers attracted to places of danger. Finding and marketing to all (or any) of these groups is easier said than done, as effective crisis management requires information not only on an integrated level to the typologies outlined above, but also in relation to the behavioural differences of different cultures and how they respond to different types of crises.

In a study of various responses of visitation to Scotland after the foot and mouth outbreak in the United Kingdom and to New York after the September 11 attacks it was found that while the French were particularly affected in their reduced propensity to travel to Scotland by the foot and mouth crisis, in contrast, the Germans were more affected by the September 11 events. Americans, however, responded equally to both disasters in relation to their travel to Scotland (Eugenio-Martin, Sinclair & Yeoman, 2004). This is not surprising as the French live in close proximity to the UK and such a contagious disease as foot and mouth has the potential to affect their agricultural base, whereas the Germans are recognised as wide travellers, who may be more influenced by concerns of global terrorism. The Americans have many choices for travel and would be considered more along the terms of Beirman's discretionary group – they can easily change their travel to Scotland to another destination. In addition, after September 11, Americans were advised against all air travel, with many choosing to remain at home.

The tourism group Visit Florida undertook important market research during the various crisis recovery phases of the four hurricanes that hit Florida between August and September in 2004. There were two significant market segments at risk, namely the leisure traveller segment and the professional meeting planners or conference segment. They believed that each group presented different challenges, so undertook research to find out. They did this in three waves, each time following up with a specialised marketing campaign. The primary messages they got from each group were that the leisure travellers did not want to feel abandoned – they wanted to keep travelling to Florida and were not interested in replacing it (different from Scotland). Meeting planners simply wanted their meeting to happen – they understood the risk and had their own contingency plans.

By undertaking research and not assuming that they knew what their main markets were thinking, Visit Florida not only developed an effective marketing communications strategy for 2004, but have used it to assist in their planning for future hurricane seasons.

Uniting or dividing the community?

As mentioned briefly, certain events can actually bring a community together. While there are many examples of situations where local communities have come together to assist those in need, when an entire population is damaged, different responses may occur. One of the most concerning of these to date was seen in New Orleans after Hurricane

Katrina in 2005. This is particularly demonstrated during the intermediate stage of the disaster life cycle. Generally speaking, during the immediate aftermath of a disaster, people are looking out for themselves and their family in terms of accessing the necessities for life, food and water. Once that has been dealt with, they move towards caring for their community, which is often an entirely new community thrown together due to the disaster. This was clearly evident in New Orleans in the days after Hurricane Katrina, and was eloquently expressed by Larry Bradshaw and Laurie Beth Slonsky who were stranded in the town while attending a conference:

> Now secure with the two necessities, food and water; cooperation, community and creativity flowered. We organised a clean up …
> We made beds from wood pallets and cardboard. We designated a storm drain as a bathroom and the kids built an elaborate enclosure for privacy out of plastic, broken umbrellas and other scraps. We even organised a food recycling system… (Bradshaw & Slonsky 2005, www.emsnetwork.org).

This new community of survivors experienced major hardship as they had been barred from the emergency shelters 'for their own safety', and yet were shot at when trying to leave the city. This community formed in a place where traditional power relations and communities had been totally disrupted and destroyed. So, in an environment of community collapse such as New Orleans, new communities arose.

Risks and crises: When safety and security is critical

In addition to the risks posed by disasters, the sources of risk to tourism enterprises include commercial business and legal relationships, economics (such as exchange rate fluctuations), human behaviour (particularly relating to security, accidents and negligence) and management.

Up to now, we have been talking primarily about large-scale disasters, whether they are natural (hurricanes) or man-made (terrorism). While it does not always gain as much media attention, the risk to a person's safety or security is inherent in all tourism activities and is often closely tied in with the host communities. I have referred numerous times to the BEST EN Think Tank that I attended in Kingston, Jamaica in 2005. This turned out to be just the place to discuss crisis and disaster management. Not only has the region had to deal with its own natural disasters such as Hurricane Ivan, Kingston itself is, overall, a relatively unsafe place for visitors.

On my arrival in the early afternoon, I went for a walk to find some food and get my bearings. I was staying in a hotel with other major hotels nearby, so this would be the part of town most set up to cater for visitors. There were a number of fast food outlets and what were clearly nightclubs (not open in mid afternoon). What immediately came to my attention was the presence of private security guards, while the tiny police station appeared unmanned. Each store had at least one if not two guards. While I did not feel threatened during the day, it was clear that this was not a place to wander around at night. In fact, one of the other guests tried to walk 300 metres to a neighbouring hotel at 9 p.m. one evening and was accosted numerous times as well as having to remove people's hands from his pockets! The local news each night reported at least five murders that day – and they were the ones actually reported.

Jamaica has a reputation for being laid back and relaxed. However, an unaware visitor to its capital (and Montego Bay) runs risks. In this instance, the advice from the Australian government's travel advisory site, Smart Traveller, had alerted me to these issues, even though I had initally felt they may have been exaggerating, as has been claimed for numerous travel advisories. The entry on crime in Jamaica at the site was:

Crime

Violent crime, including armed robbery and gang-related violence, is common, particularly in the Old Kingston area. There is also a high incidence of crime in West Kingston, Grant's Pen, Tivoli Gardens, August Town, Harbour View, Denham Town, Hannah Town in Kingston, Flankers and Mount Salem in Montego Bay (excluding resort areas) and Spanish Town.

Petty crime, including pick-pocketing and bag snatching occurs, particularly in Old Kingston.

Walking after dark, including on beaches, can be dangerous due to the increased risk of robbery and assault.

The risk of robbery when travelling to and from Norman Manley International Airport increases at night.

Travellers using unofficial taxis have been robbed and assaulted. We recommend you use taxis authorised by the Jamaican United Travellers' Association (JUTA), which can be ordered from the hotel or by a uniformed attendant at the airport. (http://www.smarttraveller.gov.au/zw-cgi/view/Advice/Jamaica)

In 2005 there were over 1600 murders in Jamaica, averaging out at 57 per 100 000 population, arguably the world's highest homicide rate for a country not at war (*Jamaica Observer*, 28 December 2005; *Jamaica Gleaner*, 28 December 2005). The region has not managed this situation at all well, and while we were there, many media reports on the effect of the high levels of crime on tourism were being run on the front page of the local newspapers. While few tourists are murdered, theft and assault against tourists is relatively common. In an indictment of the city's tourism management, while being aware of our Think Tank, with the Minister for Tourism opening the event, the tourism department did not speak to any of the many international experts attending for assistance.

According to Scott Cunliffe (2005), a destination (community's) risk is the level of exposure multiplied by the hazard and then again by vulnerability, both of which are high for Kingston. He proposes that, as well as these, the risk environment is an amplifying risk factor. This environment is more than simply the physical environment, incorporating the planning environment (experience, resources and political support), economic environment (financial risk-sharing, access to financial support) and the socio-physical environment (built, natural and social). In other words: circumstance, setting and situation. Cunliffe (2005) believes that the key to reducing the impacts of a crisis (and its level of risk) is to develop, and support, community resilience, increasing the community's capacity to cope with the impacts of a disaster, recover and adapt to cope better with future risks.

Estimating damage and loss

Disasters and their recovery cost us all, financially as well as in terms of our communities, changed power relations and reliance on others. Estimating the extent of these costs is not a simple process, but such a mechanism needs to be put into place and tested before any disaster occurs – certainly before the crisis stage sets in. The United Nations, Economic Commission for Latin America and the Caribbean (ECLAC) and International Bank for Reconstruction and Development (The World Bank), has published a detailed handbook on estimating the effects of a disaster (ECLAC 2003). It includes information on general considerations and sources of information for many sectors including tourism. The chapter on tourism also includes a comprehensive, yet easy to read section on estimation of damage and losses. While the focus here is on Latin America and the Caribbean, much of the information can be applied elsewhere.

In this section, they look at the direct damage to assets and indirect losses in tourism-related economic flows and environmental impact as well as the indirect impacts on macroeconomic variables, investment, employment and what they term 'the differential impact on women' (ECLAC 2003, p. 49).

This is an interesting sector to consider, and is certainly relevant in many Caribbean and Latin American countries as women are often the custodians of much of the traditional community culture and also employed in the tourism enterprises. The handbook notes that:

In this regard, the tourism specialist must co-operate closely with the gender and employment specialists to determine three key points:

- Women's share of sector ownership;
- Women's share in the sector's labor force; and
- The possibility of including women in rehabilitation and reconstruction tasks (ECLAC 2003, Sect. III, p. 54).

As well as presenting case study examples, they also provide constructive suggestions as to how to find the information:

The required information may be obtained from censuses, recent household surveys, chambers of tourism statistics and so on. The results of this analysis must be delivered by the tourism specialist both to the macroeconomist and to the gender specialist, who will be responsible for adding the figures from all sectors to determine the differential impact of the disaster on women at the national level (ECLAC 2003, Sect. III, p. 54).

The report is accessible at no charge via the Internet from the ECLAC website: http://www.cepal.org.mx

From theory to practice: How a potential risk became a business crisis

The following commentary is reprinted from a journal article I wrote in response to an earlier, far more positive report of mine on a case study involving a cooperative approach to crisis management that was based primarily on safety and accident prevention. This is about a business-related crisis, not a natural disaster, but illustrates the complex relationship between those elements we can and those we can't directly control, and the risk we run by ignoring the signs of impending disaster. In this instance, a situation where the adventure tourism industry (here the horse riding segment) had become complacent regarding its safety and accident planning. It was not until there was a crisis in the insurance industry and the insurers began to pull out of risky operations such as adventure tourism (or increase premiums exponentially) that the industry regained some of its initial focus on safety issues. So, a crisis in one industry (insurance) precipitated a crisis in another (tourism). In the commentary below, I maintain that this should not have been the situation. Internal mismanagement escalated what may have been a manageable problem into a crisis.

The cost of complacency – Horseback tourism and crisis management revisited[1]

The article 'Horseback tourism in Victoria, Australia: cooperative, proactive crisis management' (*Current Issues in Tourism*, Vol. 4, No. 5) traced the historical development of a partnership between groups perceived to have divergent aims (one to 'protect' the environment, the other to 'use' the environment, and the third to hedge its losses from high insurance payouts). Through a consultative (and at times aggressive) process, common goals were recognised that satisfied each group in terms of environmental protection, business operation, customer safety and crisis management protocols. Through a process of cooperative consultation between the Victorian Tourism Operators Association (VTOA) representing horseback and other public land tourism operators, the public land management agency (Department of Natural Resources and Environment) and insurance companies, an accreditation scheme was developed as a proactive process that could introduce safety standards and crisis management techniques into a diverse and fragmented industry.

My comment that the cooperative development of safety standards for the tourism industry '... has provided the opportunity for accreditation to proceed merely beyond maintaining service quality and standards, ... now encouraging tourism operators to proactively manage their operations in terms of safety and, ultimately crisis management' was a reminder for the industry and those studying it not to become complacent. What was described in the case study was the establishment of what should be an ongoing process. Unfortunately, complacency is exactly what has occurred, with enormous cost to the tourism industry in Australia over the past 12 months. Accreditation was initially driven by the VTOA members themselves – the tour operators. Once established, ongoing effort was required to maintain and develop industry standards within an ever-changing tourism environment. However, the broad membership of VTOA behaved as though this early form of accreditation needed no further development and, in essence, lost interest once the pressing issues of access to public land and affordable public liability insurance had been resolved. The fortunes of the tourism industry outlined in this ongoing case study provide a salutary lesson for industry personnel, academics and students alike.

Challenges facing industry-based programs

When this section in the previous article was written, one important aspect was not included, one that VTOA, the public land management agency and insurance companies also neglected to recognise – that of volunteer burnout. The (voluntary) Board of VTOA was exhausted, with many neglecting their own businesses to establish the accreditation program. Believing that they had set up a sound procedure and strong lobbying regime, the Board members returned to focus on their own businesses and VTOA's regular members also turned back to their immediate operational needs. Many of the members, especially the horseback tourism operators, are small business operations, with only a few staff and little time to look beyond the day-to-day operational issues. The Board of VTOA soon became a rubber-stamp for the actions of the employed secretariat who continued the work commenced by the original Board, but did not have the empowering direct interest of the members. The Association continued to work with government agencies, but spent more time chasing funding from these same agencies. Once they became reliant on such funding, the potential fallout from fighting anything that may be controversial or jeopardise funding was studiously avoided.

Accreditation and crisis management

Crisis management and insurance were closely linked in the original VTOA accreditation scheme, which included specific requirements for different areas of activity. For example, horseback operators had to comply with a minimum guide:client ratio, maintain their equipment and establish basic risk management procedures such as provisions for fatigued riders, the provision of compulsory safety helmets for under 18-year-olds, have reliable communication equipment and so on. First aid qualifications and certificates as well as public liability insurance and proof of staff competency were also compulsory accreditation requirements.

In May 1999, VTOA handed its accreditation program over to a quasi-government/industry body, the Better Business Tourism Accreditation Program (BBTAP). While the Association is represented on the BBTAP, it effectively lost control of its singular most power-ful membership tool, accreditation, resulting in the loss of its vital link with public liability insurance. The program became bogged down in paperwork, with many previously accredited operators opting out of a scheme that they saw as increasingly irrelevant to their operations. The BBTAP scheme is generically business based with no tour operator specific models or minimum activity stan-dards – the main strength of earlier accreditation. As noted in the previous article, one of the major issues of accreditation as it stood prior to handing over to BBTAP was the lack of site visits and assessment of the product as part of accreditation – this has not been addressed.

Consultation between the government agencies also became less confrontational (and less productive), with VTOA relying on grants for special projects to supplement its income, losing its strong lobbying position. Many country based adventure tourism operators became disenfranchised, but remained with the Association in order to benefit from its group insurance scheme. Then, in early 2001, insurance company HIH collapsed. While HIH was not the underwriter for the VTOA scheme, it was a major public liability insurer of risk ventures. After its collapse, other companies reconsidered their position, increasing premiums and moving away from high risk ventures such as adventure (and in particular horseback) tourism.

Then came September 11. Once again, insurance companies (this time on a global basis) tightened their operations, reducing the hope of operators to find alternative insurance. The main insurer of the horseback tourism businesses, SLE Worldwide, withdrew from the tourism market in October 2001 (VTOA 2002a). Operators were faced with enormous jumps in their premiums of up to 1000 per cent, with most horseback operations increasing from $2500 to $20 000 (VTOA 2002a). Being 'accredited' began to lose its significance as all high-risk ventures were seen as 'at risk', which in turn increased the premiums of the low-risk members in VTOA's group scheme, though not to the same extent.

During the last six months of 2001, over 23 horseback operators closed their doors, citing rising premiums as the cause (VTOA 2002a). Even more have closed, but not given a reason. The fallout continues into 2002, with operators who have over 20 years' experience and enviable safety records announcing their closure. Buyers are not in the market for such ventures due to the uncertainty of insurance, rendering them valueless. VTOA attempted to respond, but had little bargaining power or weight to gain affordable levels of insurance. VTOA and the tourism industry in Australia are now in reactive mode, which is proving too late for many operators. Yet, anecdotal evidence has seen domestic tourism rise dramatically over the 2001–2002 summer holiday period, with people holidaying closer to home – demand for adventure tourism experiences is increasing, while supply dwindles.

It would be simplistic to lay the blame with the VTOA secretariat – they continued to perform as they perceived their role to be, but without strong direction and input from the broad membership base and Board were left to do as best they could. The all too human complacency of the Association's members is really the issue. A membership association is only as strong and representative as its active members and Board. It became difficult to get operators to join the Board as they had no personal motivation to do so, until their insurance premiums soared. Eventually, members realised that they had to take control of the situation, with the Board virtually totally replaced in October 2001 and a new Chief Executive appointed in December of that year.

Under renewed pressure from members, the Association eventually responded, releasing a flurry of press releases and letters to members outlining its activities and efforts. In January 2002, in a letter to its members, VTOA announced plans to broaden its level of industry cooperation with other associations in an attempt to pool insurance schemes to render them more attractive, design proposal forms that are easier to understand and develop a simple flow chart of accident reporting procedures (VTOA 2002b) – all issues that had been under consideration in the mid 1990s, before ennui struck.

The industry is now in a position where it has to go back and reintroduce much of the hard-won elements of earlier accreditation standards. Resurrecting their latent lobbying skills and experience, VTOA has begun to produce some tangible results, such as funding from the State Government to assist operators to undertake risk audits and other initiatives to minimise their risk exposure (Major Projects and Tourism 2002). The insurance debate continues at local, state and federal government levels. Let us hope that their efforts are not too little, too late and that the process outlined in the original article develops some momentum.

The lessons that can be learnt from the case study are not dissimilar from those seen in community tourism studies, but this time the 'community' is the tourism operators themselves. The operators must be empowered, retain ownership of their scheme and develop appropriate leadership succession plans. Issues of burnout and complacency need to be addressed before they occur. In order to obtain these goals, strategic planning must be kept simple, be practical, relevant and grounded, otherwise the operators themselves will again become disenfranchised and disinterested. We need to not only learn from past mistakes, but also from past successes and not let the momentum fade away. Those studying tourism are in a position to stand back and assess such cases, and have an obligation to contribute to the ongoing practical development of tourism in general, and crisis management in particular, by sharing our increasing knowledge and understanding of these issues with the industry.

Endnote

1   This article appeared in Beeton (2002d), *Current Issues in Tourism* Vol. 5, No. 5. Reprinted with permission.

8

Developing communities through tourism: Harnessing the forces

The chapters in this book have introduced the concepts of communities and tourism from both theoretical and practical perspectives, considered the relationship between community tourism planning and development and power relations, the complex notion of community and individual empowerment, and looked in detail at tourism in rural areas as well as disaster management and recovery. This final chapter begins by discussing what has become a natural flow-on for many of those involved in tourism and community development, both from a corporate and individual perspective, namely ethical behaviour in terms of corporate responsibility and private philanthropy.

After the first of two case studies in this chapter are some comments on further developing our ways of looking at communities and tourism. Following these remarks is the final case study, which is about a situation in Hawaii where community concerns regarding the impacts of increased tourism were ignored by the tourism authority.

Unfortunately, this is not a positive note to finish on. However, it provides a timely reminder that we must do more than simply pay lip service to the concept of community and we must strive to better understand tourism's role in community development. The book

ſ 'final word' on the notion of *communitas* and a call for
ſc, inclusive planning.

ſd tourism

The teſ ſn *ethics* relates to the study of morality's effect on conduct (moral philosophy) as well as being a system of moral principles governing appropriate conduct (Encarta Dictionary). While principles may differ among cultures, notions of corporate responsibility and philanthropy as presented in this chapter stem primarily from Western philosophy. As the majority of tourists and the multi-national tourism businesses are from the developed world, such ethical beliefs as those found in countries such as the United States, United Kingdom, Australasia and much of Europe relate to tourism and community development as we have discussed in this book.

These notions of corporate responsibility in relation to tourism and community development are introduced in the next section, particularly in terms of ethical behaviour and Corporate Social Responsibility (CSR) and public–private partnerships. Following this, 'Pro-Poor Tourism' is discussed – a concept that is central to this publication as it deals directly with using tourism to aid and develop impoverished communities.

While many of the concepts in this chapter and book relate to tourism businesses, there is also a shift with certain groups of travellers to become more directly involved in philanthropic projects related to their travel experiences. The first case study introduces one such group, Travelers' Philanthropy.

Corporate citizenship and community tourism

In order to meet the requirements of triple bottom line management and reporting as introduced in Chapter 3, many businesses have adopted elements of corporate citizenship and corporate social responsibility (CSR). These elements are discussed towards the end of this section, after a discussion on the place of ethics in business. Public–private partnerships are also presented as an aspect of ethical business practice, which is not new in the tourism industry – however, along with CSR it has only been recently that they have become recognised and articulated as actual goals for an enterprise.

Traditionally, travel and tourism companies (among others) have tended to take a short-term view with a focus on financial profits, leaving the host communities to deal with the consequences of the behaviour. This has placed the responsibility for sustainable development on the host communities and not on the business. As the tourism industry tends to operate on low profit margins, responsible, ethical behaviour in terms of the sustainability of tourism has been seen as a luxury, not a practical business necessity. However, this does not sit with the shift since the late 1980s towards contributing to community responsibility, as in the niche field of ecotourism.

Many global (or transnational) corporations focusing primarily on financial profits wield a high level of economic power over national state governments. But there are increasing calls for corporate ethical business practice that goes beyond simply considering profits. Consumers have begun to make product choices based, at least in part, upon a company's ethical reputation. The World Travel and Tourism Council (WTTC) notes that an increasing number of companies have developed a culture of corporate philanthropy, where they return a portion of their profits to charities and other causes such as environmental protection (WTTC 2002).

Contributing to environmental protection and the local community are among the tenets of ecotourism. However, there is a growing belief that the private sector's role is greater than this and that organisations should be taking a more holistic approach towards their role in the world, becoming corporate citizens. Companies are looking at not only mitigating the environmental effects of various activities, but also the social issues that emanate from the emergence of a global economy. This is particularly relevant for travel (and tourism), which are by their very nature global activities – tourists travel the globe and contribute to the global as well as local economy.

An issue that is regularly raised when the annual reporting of the salaries of senior management of our multinational companies (including airlines and hotels) are presented is whether company profit should support high salaries (in UK up to $1 million for CEOs), or be reinvested on training and development (in the business) and in the tourism product (such as the host communities). While the media is quick to criticise these high salaries, they seem to have limited effect on some companies that continue to focus on profit at the expense of all else, yet the tide is turning as they realise that profits can still be made through fair trading and ethics. For example, satisfied customers with lower levels of 'guilt' in terms of their travel practices will pay a premium if the price they pay covers a fair share for the people they are visiting, who no longer need to degrade themselves through activities such as begging.

An indication of the growing interest in ethical business practice is the emergence of specialist groups and organisations that focus on investing in so-called 'ethical businesses'. For example, in 2000 the Bendigo Bank, a highly successful community banking organisation in Australia, formed an alliance with the Ethical Investment Trust (established in the 1980s) to introduce the country's first ethical investment bank account, the Ethical Investment Deposit Account. A proportion of all money invested in the Ethical Investment Deposit Account is loaned to borrowers screened by the Trustees against the Trust's investment criteria, which embrace social and environmental values. The alliance aims to deliver security for depositor funds, improved opportunities for socially and environmentally based organisations and enterprises to access those funds (http://www.bendigobank.com. au/specials/Ethical.htm).

Bringing together many ethical investment groups is the Ethical Investment Association in Australia (http://www.eia.org.au/). The aim of this group is to promote the concept, practice and growth of ethically, socially and environmentally responsible investing in Australia. Membership of the association is open to any business, organisation or investment professional (excluding listed companies) participating in the ethical investment field and committed to the association's objectives. Their listings include managed funds, financial advisors, superannuation funds, commercial enterprises, government organisations, trusts, not-for-profit organisations and individuals.

However, in spite of the clear connection with tourism as a 'clean' industry and ethical practice, there are no leisure, tourism or hospitality members in EIA, nor does the Bendigo Bank actively promote investment in tourism. One fact that has not encouraged the development of ethical business practices in tourism is that tourism investment is seen as financially risky, so has not been an area that 'ethical investment companies' (or any others) have become involved in.

However, ethical practice can be presented by a company as a quality standard and a point of difference, particularly in the highly competitive travel and tourism sector. This can be presented in terms of Corporate Social Responsibility (CSR).

Corporate citizenship: Corporate social responsibility

There is no simple, single definition of the term 'corporate social responsibility', however, as indicated above, it is more than simply giving money to charities that are more often than not separated from the organisation's core business. CSR is about adopting business practices based on ethical values and managing all aspects of the enterprise in terms of its impact on employees, shareholders, the environment and communities. According to the organisation Tourism Concern:

> Corporate Social Responsibility is of growing importance to
> the Travel and Tourism industry as part of sustainable tourism
> development. With an increasing percentage of customers
> favouring tourism that benefits the local community and
> surrounding environments, this issue is an essential one to
> be addressed by modern progressive management
> (Tourism Concern 2000).

As noted above, taking an ethical stance and promoting an organisation's CSR can be smart business practice, and many of the larger travel companies are starting to include concepts of CSR into their organisation and promotional activities. This is particularly the case with the highly competitive and volatile airline industry. For example, British Airways (BA) now includes a section on 'social performance' in its Environmental Report, where they demonstrate both environmental and community based activities and achievements such as working with communities affected by aircraft noise and sponsoring various environmental and community based awards. They have a Community Relations Department that is responsible for:

... the management of all community investment activity in the UK and further afield. Our aim is to develop strategic partnerships with a range of organisations, which include local community groups and non-governmental organisations (NGOs) such as UNICEF. We believe that it is important to invest in the communities that we fly to and serve – this is done by supporting local events or by giving assistance to community and conservation programmes that have a long-term impact on their communities. Our Community Investment programme is closely aligned to our business priorities and focuses on five key themes: Education and Youth Development, Sustainable Tourism, Environment, Heritage and Supporting our staff. (http://www. britishairways.com/travel/crhome/public/en_)

BA has a Corporate Responsibility Manager who oversees the above activities as well as projects with the airline's subsidiaries, such as British Airways Holidays who have adopted community based projects that are funded by the group at £1 per booking (Tourism Concern 2000). However, BA is yet to attempt to address environmental greenhouse gas issues of air travel itself. Every flight produces carbon dioxide, which contributes significantly to global warming. One single short-haul flight produces roughly the same amount of the global warming gas as three months worth of driving a 1.4 litre car (http://www.carbonneutral.com/shop/results.asp?cat1=Flights). In 2002, UK environmental company The Carbon Neutral Company (previously Future Forests) and responsibletravel.com developed a Carbon Neutral program where the general public (and organisations) can contribute to forestry projects that can offset the effects of their travel.

On the Carbon Neutral website is a calculator that works out your carbon emissions for any flight, based on data from the Edinburgh Centre for Carbon Management. According to the site, a flight from Melbourne to Los Angeles of 12 755 km produces 1.4 tonnes of carbon dioxide, which can be offset by planting two trees or supplying two energy saving light bulbs to a small community in a developing country (http://www.carbonneutral.com/calculators). They also have a calculator and offset program for road travel. There are other similar enterprises being established around the world, including the MyClimate program with

Sustainable Travel International in North America that also estimates the emission costs of their tours as well as flights (see www.NatHab. com). Such opportunities for individuals to contribute to the sustainable future of tourism have certain synergies with the Travelers' Philanthropy case study at the end of this chapter.

Qantas Airlines has developed a 'Sharing the Spirit' community initiative that fosters links with youth and regional communities by bringing sports people to regional centres (such as football clinics) and providing awards for young talent across the arts, science and design. Their cabin crew are encouraged to volunteer for community programs, and the airline has assisted in numerous disaster recovery efforts such as conducting mercy flights for the victims of the 2002 Bali bombings and their families. The benefits of CSR are outlined in a speech given by Qantas' CEO, Geoff Dixon, on receiving the 2003 Queensland Community Foundation Award. Dixon saw the benefits as bringing Qantas closer to its communities and customers, being good for staff morale and building skills and teamwork. He also noted that such activities strengthen the Qantas brand, increasing the staying power of the company, while at the same time strengthening communities. Significantly, Dixon noted that businesses do not exist in a vacuum.

As inferred at the beginning of this chapter, there are some tourism organisations that have been practicing CSR before the term was coined, and Qantas claims to be one such enterprise.

Corporate citizenship: Public–private partnerships

While there have traditionally been difficulties in obtaining funding for tourism ventures, some financial institutions have taken on tourism as part of their community development role. By developing public–private partnerships between the community, local government, local businesses, tourism operators and private sector capital and intellectual property, such organisations are able to leverage the ethical benefits of tourism development in communities. Generally speaking, Public–Private Partnerships (PPP) cover any contracted relationship between the public and private sectors to produce an asset or deliver a service (New South Wales Government 2001).

In an address to the South Asia Sustainable Tourism Forum in February 2005, the president of the Pacific Asia Travel Association (PATA), Peter de Jong, stated that:

> What is needed of course is a convergent path where the public policy framework allows the private sector to enter and compete on an open, transparent and free basis, allowing market-forces to dictate the winners and the losers ... Sustainability in our industry cannot, in our view, be achieved without first recognising that a balance needs to be struck and then working to establish that balance. Ideally that necessitates an open partnership between the public and private sectors (de Jong 2005).

In 2005, the World Tourism Organisation (now known as UNWTO) held a seminar on Public–Private Partnerships in Tourism in Moscow. Speakers included the heads of tourism in Russia, Austria and Spain, private organisations from the UK and France and senior UNWTO officials. UNWTO is a strong supporter and facilitator of PPP.

PPPs have been utilised in over 140 countries worldwide. While there have been significant developments in Europe, Asia and the Americas, many consider Australia and the UK to have developed the most comprehensive PPP strategies and sophisticated financial markets for investment in infrastructure. Prior to 1997, most of the PPPs in Australia were involved in projects such as toll roads, hospitals, prisons, power, seaports and water. Since 1998, there has been an increase in leisure/tourism related partnerships such as airports and rail, with the growth in sustainable urban and community based PPPs coming to the fore from 2003 (Macquarie Bank 2003). Simply put, community partnerships can combine the best skills and experiences of both the private and public sectors. Table 8.1 outlines the benefits and potential risks of PPPs to the public sector.

The government of Ireland considers PPPs to be a significant element of their strategy to facilitate the development of the tourism industry in a balanced manner. They acknowledge that such projects can be used to provide leisure services and amenities at the local level where community members also have access to those facilities developed for tourism through a public–private partnership.

Peter Wright, CEO of Macquarie Bank, acknowledges that regional tourism growth relies on building sustainable communities. He states

Table 8.1 Benefits and risks of PPPs to the public sector

Benefits	Risks
Risk diversification and allocation	Risk variance and assessment at certain phases of the projects
Project delivery	Limited project scoping skills
Enhanced efficiencies (time and cost)	Mitigating risk
Customised to the end user	Political demands and perspectives
Access to wider and deeper funding structures	Maximum risk transfer
Holistic approach between public and private sectors	Macro policy issues
Access to world-class technology	Legal changes, legal structures
Economically sound decision-making	Potential public intervention rights to appeal

Source: Macquarie Bank 2003.

that such 'sustainable communities' will be built in the next wave of Public–Private Partnerships in his organisation, such as the Macquarie Bank Community Partnerships (Macquarie Bank 2003). Macquarie's Banking and Property Group (BPG) is one of the organisation's biggest, most diverse and profitable Groups with over 900 employees across many industry sectors including banking, property, public sector, golf and leisure. In the Asia–Pacific region, Macquarie's Property Group is one of the largest players in property as lender, principal and adviser to both private and public sectors.

The bank considers that regional growth prospects are far greater than for the cities. Where governments have struggled to provide the hard and soft infrastructure necessary to facilitate tourism outcomes, community private–public partnerships can provide the solution for regional tourism growth. They have witnessed many instances where regional tourism has outperformed that of the capital cities over the last five years, and yet as noted previously, leisure assets are still not perceived as an investment of choice. Such assets include hotels and resorts, regional airports, marinas, rail tracks, regional roads and scenic roads, regional attractions, rejuvenation projects and theme parks. Macquarie Bank's stated vision for future community public–private partnership projects includes the creation of community-driven, sustainable community developments that function on an environmental, economic and social scale (Macquarie Bank 2003).

In addition, the World Bank, a source of financial and technical assistance for developing countries, actively supports and promotes partnerships, particularly as the organisation is itself owned by its 184 member countries. Its mission is to reduce global poverty and improve living standards (www.worldbank.org). The Bank does not operate as a commercial banking service, rather as a source of low-interest loans, interest-free credit and grants to developing countries. Over the past 20 years, the Bank's focus and approach has moved towards dealing with more social issues in its partnership roles. These include social services such as health, nutrition and education as well as the more traditional areas of construction and infrastructure development. Consequently, many of the loans are partnerships that provide skills and expertise needed to meet such goals, and include tourism.

PPPs are referred to by many other names, with certain projects and approaches often taking on a specific, descriptive title. One such example, supported by the World Bank, is the *Bulldozer Initiative*, launched in Bosnia and Herzegovina in 2002. It is an example of a public–private partnership that adopted a bottom-up approach by mobilising local businesses to identify issues and lobby for their implementation – the private sector was partnered with local government representatives. The initiative's goal was 'to bulldoze away the roadblocks to a good business climate' (Herzberg 2004, p. 17). As the initiative was focused on small-scale reforms it was able to deliver fast results, with 50 reforms in 150 days. This in turn won the confidence of the private sector, and as a consequence many permanent groups were established.

While PPPs can relate to aspects of tourism and community development in nations such as Ireland and Australia, many such partnerships can be seen in developing countries. One particular type of partnership is that of pro-poor tourism, which is discussed below.

Pro-poor tourism

Because tourism in developing nations is often driven by foreign, private sector interests focused on individual financial gain, it is not well placed to contribute to the reduction of local poverty, rather it promotes it (PPT 2004a). Tourism can disadvantage the poor in terms of increased costs of living, social disruption and disenfranchisement;

however, when managed carefully it can also be a 'power for good' and work to alleviate poverty. Indeed, many of the countries where tourism plays a significant economic role are among the world's poorest and least developed (PPT 2004a).

In an effort to identify the links between tourism and poverty reduction, a review was held in the UK by the Overseas Development Institute (ODI), who coined the term 'pro-poor tourism' (PPT) to refer to the potential of tourism to alleviate poverty. As a result, PPT also became an agenda item on the 1999 United Nations Commission on Sustainable Development (Ashley & Roe 2003).

Since then, pro-poor tourism has come to refer to tourism that results in increased net benefits for poor people, usually (but not exclusively) in developing countries (PPT Partnerships 2004b). Importantly, it is not a *product*, but an *approach* to tourism development and management that enhances the linkages between tourism businesses and poor people in order to leverage and increase tourism's contribution. PPT enables more effective participation in the development of sustainable tourism. Table 8.2 outlines the benefits associated with such practices, illustrating its connection with PPP and general community development.

Table 8.2 Benefits of pro-poor tourism

Economic benefits	Non-financial livelihood impacts	Participation and partnership
Expand local employment and wages	Capacity building, training	Create more supportive policy/planning framework that enables participation by the poor
Expand local enterprise opportunities	Mitigate environmental impacts	Increase participation of the poor in decision making by public and private sector
Tourism service suppliers (food etc.)	Address competing use of natural resources	Build pro-poor partnerships with the private sector
Those who sell to tourists (crafts, art, guides etc.)	Improve social and cultural impacts	Increase flow of information and communication between stakeholders
Develop collective income sources (fees, revenue shares, equity dividends, donations etc.)	Increase local access to infrastructure and services provided for tourists (roads, communications, health care, transport)	Lay the foundation for future, ongoing dialogue

Source: PPT 2004c.

A key element here is that there are many instances where it is the poor of the world who actually own the resources that tourism is based upon, such as natural capital and their cultural festivals and activities. In the past, such ownership has tended to be ignored. However, by acknowledging this particular reality, governments, development agencies and tourism organisations are able to develop strategies to assist many developing communities (Sofield *et al.* 2004).

While the benefits listed above are impressive (and many relate to community development in all parts of the world), there are also potential areas for care or concern, or 'disbenefits' of which we must be aware. These have been summarised by Sofield *et al.* (2004) as:

- Exposure to risk and exploitation – poor communities invariably lack the education and sometimes the worldly knowledge to avoid exploitation by tourism interests

- Adverse impacts on traditional structures resulting in community instability (e.g. intergenerational conflict between young skilled members and untrained elders in a community; between women and men)

- Adverse impacts on cultural elements (e.g. mass production of artefacts, changes in festivals, song and dance to cater to visitors rather than remaining anchored in traditional values, resulting in facile spectacle with deeper meaning pushed aside), commoditisation

- Materialism and individualism replacing collective community based organisation capacities and values.

- Loss of access to natural resources such as coastlines and lagoons, water, forests – where poor communities are dependent upon these for survival they may be particularly threatened by inappropriate tourism development (but equally by mining, agricultural development or urban expansion)

- Physical security may be weakened by tourism development which leads to an increase in outsiders taking up residence, increases in crime, and drugs and prostitution (Sofield *et al.* 2004, p. 6).

However, many of these impacts are not limited to tourism, but tend to come hand-in-hand with modernisation in all its forms, such as the drift from rural to urban areas for work and the impact of television and the Internet on the poor. In fact, as noted elsewhere, tourism can be used to counter some of the same adverse impacts it facilitates. It all depends on our recognition of the possible drawbacks and their subsequent management. A number of strategies that can apply to PPT have been identified, as outlined in Table 8.3. These strategies fall into three distinct categories, namely economic, non-financial livelihoods and participation and partnership (or empowerment).

Table 8.3 Types of PPT strategies

Increase economic benefits	Enhance non-financial livelihood impacts	Enhance participation and partnership
Expand local employment, wages: commitments to local jobs, training of local people.	Capacity building, training.	Create a more supportive policy/planning framework that enables participation by the poor.
Expand local enterprise opportunities – including those that provide services to tourism operations (food suppliers etc.) and those that sell to tourists (craft producers, handicrafts, guides etc.).	Increase local access to infrastructure and services provided for tourists – roads, communications, health care, transport.	Increase flow of information and communication between stakeholders to lay the foundation for future dialogue.
Develop collective income sources – fees, revenue shares, equity dividends, donations, etc.	Address competing use of natural resources.	Increase participation of the poor in decision making by government and the private sector.
	Improve social and cultural impacts.	Build pro-poor partnerships with the private sector.
	Mitigate environmental impacts.	

Source: PPT Partnerships, 2004c.

While it is relatively easy to recognise and recommend strategies such as those outlined above, there are many barriers to the participation of the poor in PPT, as noted in the discussion in previous chapters on empowerment and power relations. These include lack of human capital and finance (or credit), as well as a lack of organisation and market power. In addition, regulations and red tape can exclude the poor from access to opportunities, as well as the limited capacity of many poor communities to understand and meet the requirements of the tourism market, which they also find difficult to access. With government support often targeted to the formal (predominantly foreign-owned) tourism sector, relationships with remote and/or poor local communities are often strained or non-existent (Ashley *et al.* 2000).

Nevertheless, in a further study of PPT, Ashley *et al.* (2001) concluded that, while at times difficult to quantify, PPT can play a significant role in poverty reduction and, in turn, livelihood security. 'For the poor where it happens, PPT is invaluable' (Ashley *et al.* 2001, p. 41). While they are cautious with their results (tourism is NOT the panacea to all the world's problems!), they found five advantages for PPT from the poverty alleviation perspective:

1   It appears possible to 'tilt' the tourism sector at the margin, to expand opportunities for the poor;

2   PPT initiatives have been able to develop two of the key characteristics of pro-poor growth within tourism: increasing demand for goods and services provided by the poor, and increasing their asset base;

3   Current thinking on poverty reduction highlights the need to support diversified livelihoods through the non-farm rural economy;

4   Impacts of PPT initiatives can extend beyond their specific location by contributing to pro-poor change in policies and processes;

5   The existing movement for 'sustainable tourism' which could be harnessed to contribute more to poverty reduction (Ashley *et al.* 2001).

This final point is considered in the first case study in this chapter, and while such encouragement is currently piecemeal, it does have some momentum. The second case study also relates to notions of sustainability (or the lack of) in tourism, but where the community and its environment have been ignored.

Participatory projects such as pro-poor tourism have become increasingly important in the work of the World Bank, and there are many instances of tourism being used as a tool in their projects. In assessing the effectiveness of their support for community based development, the Independent Evaluation Group (IEG) of the Bank noted that

> Projects which involve community participation have increased from less than 5 percent of total Bank lending in 1989 to about 25 percent in 2003. The study finds that these approaches are potentially a powerful mechanism for channeling development assistance to the grass roots level, but highlights several challenges in ensuring effective use of external support (IEG 2005).

For example, one of the World Bank's projects is to strengthen the various cultural industries that they have identified as being 'pro poor'. This includes community based tourism as well as artisans, music and ethno-botanicals. In 2000, the World Bank's Cultural Assets for Poverty Reduction Unit sponsored a workshop to raise awareness as to how low impact tourism projects can be a means to reduce poverty (www.worldbank.org).

As some readers may also be thinking, there are those who consider the term 'Pro-Poor Tourism' to have negative connotations in that it may seem that sounds as if it is more about keeping people poor rather than assisting them to develop. Because of this confusion, others have developed different terms when speaking about poverty alleviation through tourism. The UNWTO has coined the phrase, 'Sustainable Tourism – Eliminating Poverty' (ST–EP) as a more acceptable term. Regardless of the terminology, the aim of reducing/alleviating poverty is the same.

From theory to practice #1: The case of encouraging the philanthropic traveller

The US based group Business Enterprises for Sustainable Tourism (BEST) is an initiative of The Conference Board in association with WTTC and several foundations that provide support. Its mission is to serve as 'a leading source of knowledge on innovative travel industry practices that advance community, business and travelers' interest and support the economic and cultural sustainability of destinations' (www.sustainabletravel.org).

BEST advances business, community and travellers' interests in sustainable tourism by profiling positive cases of cutting-edge business, community organisations and travellers in the field of sustainable and community focused tourism. The organisation has three main areas of activity, namely university level education (discussed in part in the previous chapter in terms of its Think Tanks), community tourism and travellers' philanthropy. It is the last of these, Travellers' Philanthropy, which we focus on in this case study.

Where CSR, PPP and even PPT centre on the businesses related to tourism, Travellers' Philanthropy focuses on the traveller as well as the business, and is based on the premise that individual travellers can make a difference. The term 'travellers' philanthropy' was coined to cover the many ways in which travellers can contribute to the destinations they visit, including making donations to charitable foundations that support those destinations, socially or environmentally. A growing number of civic-minded travellers and travel businesses are giving financial resources, time and talent to further the wellbeing of the communities they visit. This is a powerful demonstration of the emerging voluntary travel movement.

They also have a strong emphasis on encouraging travellers to adopt sustainable practices when they travel, and to leave places better than they found them by preserving irreplaceable natural resources and honouring traditional cultures, as well as acting to advance positive economic development.

The organisation considers that the need for travellers' philanthropy is great, with an estimated 23 per cent of the world's people living in extreme poverty. A study by the Travel Industry Association of America, in collaboration with BEST and National Geographic Traveler, found that more than 55 million US travellers exhibit a high degree of commitment to travel that protects the local environment, engages visitors in the local culture and returns benefits to the community (BEST, www.sustainabletravel. org). Such data augurs well for the future of travel and must be capitalised upon in all aspects of tourism, but particularly when considering its role in community development.

One area of particular interest is BEST's encouragement of individuals to become 'civic travellers', which is the focus of this case study. By promoting the message that travellers enrich their own trips when they seek to contribute to the wellbeing of the places that they visit, BEST has been able to support many positive programs. Though their size, emphasis and approaches may differ, the various programs set up and promoted by Travellers' Philanthropy share a number of common features as outlined in Table 8.4.

Table 8.4 Features of travellers' philanthropy programs

Promote face-to-face, authentic connections between people of different cultures	Establish new partnerships between local businesses and non-profit organisations
Solicit donations and determine needs and projects at the local level	Generate a new stream of cash, goods and volunteer services
Enable local residents to get involved in funding allocation and governance	Engage individual donors – the greatest single source of philanthropic dollars

Source: BEST: www.sustainabletravel.org.

The aim here is to channel resources to grassroots efforts, while offering a new framework for constructive internationalism and global community building, as well as cultural and environmental stewardship. The programs generally occur in destinations where the need for economic development and humanitarian assistance is high, such as developing countries, which brings it in line with PPT and ST–EP.

Through its communications via its website and face-to-face presentations, the organisation demonstrates to travellers the range and extent of projects that they can contribute to and, as outlined in Table 8.5, they are not all necessarily financial.

While the information in Table 8.5 is broad, making travellers aware of what they are achieving is important, as is providing concrete ways that they can make a difference while they are travelling. Examples are provided such as through patronage, gifts of time and talent and charitable contributions. In addition, they encourage travellers to be informed about their destination

Table 8.5 Ways that a philanthropic traveller can contribute

Economic and social sustainability of rural, urban and endangered communities
Protection of cultural and natural assets
Assist in gaining a higher standard of living for local residents
Contribute to their cultural pride
The preservation of a 'sense of place'
By gaining greater cross-cultural understanding, and an appreciation of diversity
Making sure that a higher percentage of tourism revenues stays in the local market (less financial leakages)

Source: Seltzer 2003.

before they go, making realistic suggestions of some valuable resources, such as scanning local newspapers online using www.newstrove.com, a particularly interesting resource. Newstrove is more than a source for local newspapers, however, indexing news content, blogs and websites primarily from the United States, Great Britain, Australia, Canada, New Zealand, India and Israel, as well as English editions of publications from Europe, Asia, the Middle East, Africa and South America. You are able to search it from a particular cultural, religious or political perspective, which provides for some interesting reading!

BEST provides some pertinent and inspiring cases of travellers and enterprises behaving philanthropically. For example, Lindblad Expeditions, an up-market adventure cruise company, has undertaken extensive research into 'persuasive communication' in order to encourage its guests to assist in the preservation of many of the places they visit. They have been particularly successful in protecting and restoring habitat and communities in the Galapagos Islands, one of the world's most unique ecosystems. They are now also working with their guests to protect and develop whale watching on the Baja Peninsula in Mexico.

Another case that BEST promotes is that of a shantytown in Lima, Peru, which is home to many displaced rural peasants. Travel volunteers work on a program that provides some

150 residents with meals – many of whom are elderly and the program provides their only meal for the day. In addition, two couples on a sailing holiday in the Caribbean found that they could not believe the lack of reading material available for island children. They founded 'Boaters for Books', which gathers reading material in North America and ships them to students in the Caribbean. All of these initiatives are contactable via the BEST website (www.sustainabletravel.org).

By promoting these and many other examples of different types of philanthropy, BEST has been able to encourage many travellers to realise what they can do in terms of assisting the places they travel to. They are moving the responsibility for 'responsible travel' on to the actual travellers (or tourists) themselves, not just the travel businesses. It is this type of groundswell support that is able to create movements of change – not only are communities being empowered, but also their guests, the tourists.

Studying communities and their relationship with tourism

In today's ever more rapidly changing environment, we need to keep studying and developing our understanding as to how we can achieve community development and empowerment, with tourism as one of the many tools in the box.

While throughout the book I have suggested many ways that tourism can assist communities, new and innovative concepts and ways to do so are continually evolving. Over the past year, I have become aware of a type of community that is becoming better understood, known as 'authoritative communities'. This new term comes out of the public policy and social sciences areas, coined by the Commission on Children at Risk in relation to improving the lives of children. The report introduces the concept in 'Hardwired to Connect' (Commission on Children at Risk 2003), explaining that children are 'hardwired' for close connections to others. They gain moral meaning through those connections. The authors claim that recent neuroscience studies have shown that children begin with the need for connection with those close to them (parents and other relatives) and then extend out to the wider community. They argue that groups promoting this type of connectedness to strengthen their work and consequent influence are 'authoritative communities'.

> Authoritative communities ... are groups of people who are
> committed to one another over time and who model and pass on
> at least part of what it means to be a good person and live a good
> life (Commission on Children at Risk 2003).

Such communities have traditionally been families, civic and community groups, houses of worship, political clubs and even professional-based associations, however, the report claims that the presence and influence of such groups has weakened over recent times. As tourism can be a tool for community development and engagement, it may also be a tool that can increase the influence of authoritative communities by increasing cohesiveness and empowering its members.

The project has not studied whether connectedness hardwiring persists as we grow older. However, if we desire our community members to be empowered and travellers (and tourism businesses) to act ethically, there may be an opportunity to take the concept of authoritative communities into the wider world. Personal experience in working with various communities has shown that many people are looking for an authority figure to guide them, so if this comes from a respected group from within, it may actually empower rather than restrict them, as in the case of an external authority.

At this stage, this is simply an idea that needs far greater thought, study and application, yet it is one that I believe is worth pursuing. As tourism can also improve lives and work with people (including children), we should have a look at whether the concept of authoritative communities can be applied here, or whether tourism can support authoritative communities, and in turn assist the children in our communities. At the very least, tourism can assist in developing empowered, authoritative communities.

The final case study for this book is one that doesn't quite fit into any specific chapter. However, it is an important case in that it provides a warning that, while there is a great deal of rhetoric surrounding communities, community development, empowerment and so on (including parts of this book), they can still be easily ignored. While the circumstances of this case are a few years old, the issues appear to have not been resolved. Sometimes, it appears that we use our communities when it suits us and ignore them when other imperatives come into play. This is not good enough, and while practical issues can temper pure theory, we are obligated to continue to strive for that perfection of community engagement and development through tourism.

From theory to practice #2: Community? What community? The case of the Hawaii Tourism Authority and the Sierra Club

The Hawaii Tourism Authority (HTA) was formed in 1998 to promote tourism to Hawaii. Its board consists of industry leaders, the majority being non-indigenous Hawaiians, and in 2000, when this case study is set, there was only one indigenous Hawaiian member, who had no voting rights. The HTA's mission is to:

> strategically manage the growth of Hawaii's visitor industry in a manner consistent with our economic goal, cultural values, *preservation of natural resources and community interests*. [own emphasis] (http://www.hawaiitourismauthority.org)

In 2000 the HTA set a goal to add 30 000 visitors *per day* to the islands by 2005 from a total annual base of 6.7 million. This equates to over 10.9 million additional day visits, and while most individuals will stay more than one day, it is still enormous growth in actual visitor numbers. To actively desire such growth is anathema to current global tourism planning and trends. While many in the tourism industry were moving away from mass tourism and chasing more numbers towards encouraging a higher yield (more individual spending and increased length of stay), the HTA's aim for an additional 10 million visitor days certainly appeared misplaced and out of step.

As it turns out, the 2005 figures do not reflect this planned outcome. There was a massive drop in travel to Hawaii after the September 11 terrorist attacks in New York in 2001, which changed the face of tourism, particularly in the US. While this may have played into the hands of those opposing the growth Hawaii was planning for, it does not mean the issues surrounding aiming for such exponential, unregulated growth as in 2000 has actually been resolved.

There were those in the community, particularly the indigenous and environmental communities, who were extremely concerned about the environmental effects such an increase in visitors would have. The Sierra Club, a US-based grassroots environmental organisation founded in 1892 with a Hawaii chapter membership of 4000 people, took up the cause. The Sierra Club's grassroots advocacy has made it among America's most influential environmental organisations.

The Club filed a lawsuit against the Hawaii Tourism Authority in January 2000, requesting that they perform an environmental assessment of their goals, as is required for any physical development. In Hawaii, environmental reviews are required by law on construction projects, and the Sierra Club argued that this should also relate to areas such as tourism promotion, due to the fact that it has measurable effects on the natural environment. The court filing claimed that:

> While the economic benefits which may be derived from the expenditure of these State funds have been established, the countervailing environmental, ecological and social adverse impacts caused by an increased number of visitors were not addressed by Respondent THE HAWAII TOURISM AUTHORITY... (Sierra Club 2000)

The media took up the case, initially presenting the Sierra Club's move as frivolous. However, as many began to think more about tourism and development, the emphasis of the reports began to shift towards the Sierra Club's perspective. As often occurs with such cases, much of the battle was fought in the media, with the CEO of the Hawaii Tourism Authority reported as saying:

> 'To say that there is an inherent environmental responsibility in the marketing of tourism is a bit of a stretch. We could

make the case that every program should have those responsibilities.' Bob Fishman, CEO Hawaii Tourism Authority (Choo 2001).

In the same article, the Sierra Club responded:

'We aren't talking about clear cutting or mining... This is tourism and we should be sharing the work. They should be with us every step of the way.' Jeff Mikulina, Executive Director, Hawaii Chapter, Sierra Club (Choo 2001).

In October 2002, the verdict was passed down, with the Supreme Court dismissing the Sierra Club's petition for an environmental review in a close three to two decision, after what appears to have been 'lively' debate. Interestingly, the two dissenting justices who supported the Sierra Club's petition stated that 'risk occurs when the uninformed decision is made, irrespective of whether the threatened harm will actually occur' (Sierra Club News Release, 23 October 2002).

Regardless of the legal outcome, this case raises numerous concerns about community consultation and corporate social responsibility. Clearly interest groups had not been considered when the HTA proposed its dramatic increased numbers of visitors, creating an opportunity for an influential environmental group such as the Sierra Club to act. I concur with the Sierra Club, believing that it is the responsibility of all tourism marketing organisations to assess the impact of its marketing proposals, socially and environmentally as well as economically.

So, even though they won (by the smallest margin), has the HTA learnt anything from this high profile case? In 2005 the HTA implemented its 10-year Strategic Plan. Hawaii's nominated strengths include one entry relating to the natural environment:

- Brand awareness
- Climate
- Culture and history

- Destination allure and appeal
- High visitor satisfaction
- Natural resources
- People and aloha spirit
- Quality and variety of accommodations
- Safe but exotic
- Variety of activities and attractions
- Geographic isolation (Hawaii Strategic Tourism Plan, 2005–2015, p. 5).

This is surprising, as much of Hawaii is national park, with high level natural attractions such as its volcanoes and beaches. When noting its weaknesses, there is no mention of understanding environmental issues such as carrying capacity, with the list focusing more on business and physical infrastructure issues:

- Geographic isolation
- Inadequate public and private infrastructure
- Insufficient visitor–resident interaction
- Lack of 'new' experiences
- Lack of accurate pre- and post-arrival information
- Lack of stakeholder consensus
- Lag in business tourism
- Visitor expectations and misperceptions
- Volatility of the inter-island transportation services
- Volatility of the national and international airline industry
- Maintenance of public facilities
- Limited awareness and limited access to new experiences
- Lack of professional (certified) guides (Hawaii Strategic Tourism Plan, 2005–2015, p. 5).

The entire plan has a very strong business focus, with only a minor focus on the natural environment. At least there are numerous mentions of the local and indigenous communities, including their ties to the natural environment. However, these ties remain insufficiently dealt with.

The final word

In Chapter 1, I spoke of the term *communitas* as referring to the spirit of community, quoting from Turner that it was 'a whole group of people cross[ing] a threshold and together enter[ing] a liminal time and space – that is, an in-between that is neither past nor present, and a space that is neither here nor there' (Turner 1969, p. vii). I noted that this anthropological perspective is important for those of us wanting to better understand how tourism can assist the development of communities. What I was referring to was the concept that communities do not simply exist in a physical, geographic dimension (such as a town), but more so through the members' shared aspirations. I also noted that community groups may be sharing a profession, belief (religious, political or secular) or interest (creative arts, sport, recreation, conservation groups and so on) and can exist in other dimensions such as 'virtually' through the Internet. While, for ease of discussion, I have often throughout the book referred to communities from a spatial perspective as groups from certain regions, these groups also share certain attitudes and aspirations.

Tourism by accident or design?

While I stress the importance of planning for tourism in order to gain the maximum benefit, there are examples of successful tourism and community development that appear to simply have happened, almost by accident. However, if you look more closely at such cases, you can usually find a 'champion' who has inspired his or her community to work with tourism. There may be no strategies actually written down, but this person (or people) is able to articulate them when pressed. In effect, the planning has been done, and it is rare to find successful tourism in healthy communities without it.

Nevertheless, it certainly is advisable to have strategies in place and written down, as eventually the community leader or champion will leave, either burnt out, moving on or passing away. It is then when a community truly sees if it is empowered and knows what to do next.

Those communities who have had tourism thrust upon them, either by multinational organisations, well-meaning volunteers or the travellers themselves (who simply turn up), face many challenges if they wish to truly benefit from tourism. The negative effects of over-crowding, loss of amenity, environmental damage, increasing prices and so on are incremental – they are not immediately evident. By the time they become issues that the community needs to address, it is often too late to resolve them – once a cultural or environmental aspect is lost, it is extremely difficult to regain.

We cannot afford to wait for tourism to '*do it for us*', as we run the risk of having tourism '*do it to us*'.

Appendix

Communities and ecotourism in the Year of the Outback[1]

When I hear people refer to 'communities and tourism', they rarely articulate what they mean, especially in relation to 'community'. The term itself has become today's latest catchcry – there is talk of 'community ownership', 'community empowerment', and it is used to cover (and sometimes hide) a myriad of areas. Often it is applied without any assurance that we are all thinking about the same type of 'community'.

Communities can be spatially or psychologically defined – we can talk about a community of people living in a town or region, or a community of like-minded folk, such as the 'arts community'. So, what do I mean when I use it?

What I will be talking about today is the broad community based around a rural town or regional area – such a community may contain indigenous groups, settlers, ethnic groups, artists, musicians, writers, farmers, tradespeople, business people and so on. What defines this community is the fact that its members live, work and play in a region that centres on a town such as Charleville. Such a definition may not always be appropriate, and I urge you to think about what you would see as your community – it may involve a group of towns linked by a highway or have a broader or more narrow catchment area or definition than I have nominated.

The title of this paper refers to 'ecotourism', and is a great focus for us to take from a community aspect, also because this year has been declared by the United Nations as the 'International Year of Ecotourism'. So, what makes ecotourism different from many other types of tourism, such as adventure tourism, heritage tourism or nature-based tourism? There are many definitions (of course), but those who promote ecotourism generally subscribe to a number of basic principles that include being based in nature and supporting the environment, both physical and cultural. What I am particularly interested in here is the cultural environment support inherent in ecotourism, with its strong emphasis on providing a return to the community and 'education' of visitors.

The very inclusiveness of ecotourism tends to render the term 'community' superfluous as it is an integral aspect of any true ecotourism enterprise. So, in much of the following discussion I will be referring to tourism and communities, not just ecotourism.

Ecotourism also has the capability to bring the outback environment to life by explaining what people are seeing and experiencing, as well as telling stories about local folklore. This is particularly relevant in a land that to many appears to be monotonous and barren, with scrubby mulga and not much else. By educating visitors to look closer and understand more about this land, they take away not only new knowledge but also a greater respect and love for the outback, that most quintessential part of Australia and of being Australian. The most successful outback tours include at least some educational elements about the natural environment, and many of our most awarded ecotourism enterprises are based in central, inland and northern Australia.

It is also interesting to note that this is also the 'International Year of Culture Heritage' as well as the 'International Year of Mountains'. International years are designated by the United Nations to draw attention to major issues and to encourage action regarding their global importance (UNA-Canada 2002). And of course, in Australia we have nominated 2002 as the 'Year of the Outback'.

Why bother about communities in relation to tourism?

In all the reading, teaching and speaking that has been done on this topic, there tends to be an unspoken 'given' that people should have some ownership of, or say in, tourism that occurs in their communities. However, as wonderful as this sentiment is, there are even more immediate and practical reasons for including the community in all tourism planning and operations, whether they are publicly or privately owned and operated.

As tourists from the highly urbanised developed countries (the main source of domestic and international tourists worldwide) have become more experienced as travellers, they are looking for a different type of holiday than the mass, resort-based holidays of the past. Today's travellers are increasingly interested in new experiences and learning about other cultures while on their holidays. Visitors want to meet local people and feel that they are taking something home with them that is 'authentic', especially in relation to indigenous and rural-based cultures.

This was supported by Rob Tonge at last year's Positive Rural Futures Conference, where he spoke on rural tourism. He stressed the importance of developing links between tourism and communities, along with a need to establish a common vision and partnerships between local government, private enterprise and the wider community. He also noted the changing nature of the visitor market, that has become more 'travelwise' and selective, seeking interactive experiences and contact with local people (Tonge 2001).

So, if a community, or members of that community, resent the tourists that come to their town or region, if they feel that they are being exploited by outside commercial interests and that their privacy is being unfairly invaded, dramatic negative issues could become manifest. Unwelcoming hosts will turn visitors away, as will increases in crime and aggression towards tourists. Even if visitors get the impression that the experience is not fully supported by the local people, they may lose any sense of that important aspect of tourism today – 'authenticity'.

Consequently, even if community members are not directly involved in tourism, they have the power to destroy it by making visitors feel unwelcome and unsafe. It is crucial that communities are included in tourism planning and operations.

Let's consider a letter home from a young traveller visiting an outback town called 'Somewhere Else'.

Dear Mum and Dad,

At last we've made it to Somewhere Else, and it really is 'out back'! We got here on the Matilda Highway (what an evocative name!), which is sealed, so the old van made it. Wish we had air-conditioning though – it's pretty hot. One of the local farmers took about six of us out in a four-wheel drive yesterday. He point-ed out many of the aspects of farming that we've heard about on the news – irrigating the land, salinity issues and the newer crops that they are testing here. Our group included a couple of German backpackers, and their questions generated a lively lunch-time dis-cussion – they knew more than I did about Australia! Even though I usually hate being in 'tour groups', everyone in our small group are independent travellers, just wanting to find out more than they could on their own. I would never have noticed all the things that were pointed out to me if I was on my own. The group is also fun to be with, and the local people are great.

At first, the countryside seemed monotonous – we'd driven through this scrubby mulga for days to get here and we were see-ing even more of it now (at least the vehicle was air-conditioned!). But, our local guide was so knowledgeable and it was obvious that he loved this land, that I began to see it differently.

We spent last night in an old pub that is now run by a retired farming couple – a great night of local ghost stories and unsolved mysteries certainly brought home the severity of the past in this land. (Still not sure how much was true, or just part of the great Aussie humour!) We also spent time star-gazing with some experts who could point out what we were looking at – at last I can recog-nise the Southern Cross! The Germans loved this as the sky is so different from theirs. I can't get over how BIG the skies are in this part of the country. You just feel like you'll be swallowed up.

We were also told about the bilby (you know – like the one you gave me at Easter instead of the usual chocolate bunnies) and how there is a program here to protect them. I didn't realise they were endangered. We hope to speak to some people involved in it tonight and get to meet some bilbies. There is also an area of land that has been revegetated by the local school kids – it'd be great to come back in five years and see how it's going.

I'm sending a couple of things back that I bought in the town – all made from local produce, including a couple of things from the Aboriginal art workshop.

We were only going to stay one night, but we've decided to stay for a couple more – there is so much more to do and see here that we had no idea of. We are camping out tomorrow night and going fishing at dawn at a secret fishing spot. Wonder if they'll blindfold us so we can't give it away? (The guys in the pub reckon they will!)

There's also this gun that the Germans are really interested in seeing – it was one of 10 guns imported from Germany in an attempt to break a really bad drought back about 100 years ago – they hoped that by firing the guns they would cause a change in the atmosphere and bring rain. Guess what? It didn't work!

At last I feel like I'm actually meeting real people and getting a chance to get under the skin of the place. They seem to be even more welcoming and open because we're giving our money to them and not to outsiders, and talk a lot about how important visitors are to them as we make the town more interesting and give the young people more to do.

Love,
Someone's son/daughter

In this letter, the local people (or community) run all the activities, including transport, guiding, the observatory, accommodation, catering and craft sales. The community has also preserved its history, as well as using school projects to revegetate the land. The visitors were educated on some of the history and environmental programs, such as the saving of the bilby.

There are further benefits illustrated in the letter – economic growth, increased pride among residents, jobs for youth and retirees, distribution of tourism revenue throughout the community, improved resource conservation, value-added farming and indigenous products and diversification of the economy. It is also important to note that many of the activities were an adjunct to what was already there (such as farming) – tourism works best within a vibrant, living community.

So, is this ecotourism, and what's the difference between this and other types of tourism? Well, we can call it 'eco' because of its environmental leaning, educational aspects and community focus. However, sometimes we don't really need to call it ecotourism or any other type of tourism – it's the community aspect that is of most importance. It has been argued that the term 'ecotourism' has become little more than a marketing tool. I still see it as being more than that, and in my book I suggest practical methods to conduct tourism businesses in environmentally sound ways as well as providing more discussion on ecotourism per se (Beeton 1998).

Hosts and guests

As noted previously, it is important that all members of the community are happy to have tourism and tourists in their area – they are all hosts, even if they do not deal directly with tourists. Visitors soon sense if they are not welcome and will also warn others to keep away. Consequently, it is crucial that a 'culture of welcome' is fostered through education, interaction and cooperation among the community itself. Tourism has the potential to increase residents' pride in their town as a place worth visiting (and showing off), and there are opportunities to put tourist-generated funds into community projects, increasing the reasons for residents to welcome tourism and tourists.

Stakeholders and community wellbeing

The terms 'stakeholders' and 'community wellbeing' are heard often these days and require some attention. A 'community stakeholder' is really any person who has a vested interest in the community and/or can influence that community. This can go beyond what is considered to be the actual community and can include:

- residents (young, old, employed, unemployed, wealthy, poor)
- retail and trade
- regular visitors
- government
- tourism operators
- hosts and guests.

The concept of 'community wellbeing' goes beyond just looking at the economic benefits of an enterprise to the community, and the term 'triple bottom line' is one that has become part of our daily lexicon (Sustainability 2002). First coined in 1976, triple bottom line includes taking into account the social and environmental effects and benefits as well as economic, further supporting the development of community based tourism. Such inclusive methods are being adopted by commercial enterprises and government departments alike. Tourism Victoria is about to release its latest strategy, which they assure me has a strong focus on the triple bottom line and community wellbeing.

The pros and cons of tourism

Who really benefits from tourism? Clearly accommodation houses, restaurants, tour guides, outfitters such as camping and fishing suppliers, heritage sites and other 'attractions' all benefit. But what about the retired couple living in town or the plumber, doctor, schools, unemployed – do they benefit? Here is a story that may help:

The promoter of a small town country music festival was soliciting sponsorship support from the local plumbing supplier. The supplier was adamant that he received no benefits from people coming to town for a music festival. According to him, the visitors only spent their money at the hotels, cafés and craft shops. As they were talking, his assistant approached him to ask when the new water tank for the pub would be arriving and whether they could also find more portable toilets. The promoter was quick to point out that without the festival the pub would not be able to afford the new water tank and the portable toilets would not be needed at all. The plumbing supplier is now a firm supporter of all festivals in the town and has encouraged others to join him, including the local bank (which nearly closed down). He also now carries a larger range of stock which helped the retired couple when their septic tank died and employs two young trainees on a part-time basis.

There's nothing like a tourism disaster to demonstrate how important tourism is to a region. For example, the Foot and Mouth crisis in England was recognised as a great loss to the agricultural community, yet the potential cost in relation to rural tourism in 2001 is £5 billion (Sharpley 2001). According to the GDP figures, rural tourism in the United Kingdom is worth over four times the value of agriculture, which is only now being appreciated, with the closure of many ancillary rural services not traditionally perceived as being aligned with tourism (ETC 2001; Sharpley 2001).

The recent collapse of Ansett, the public liability insurance issue and even the pilots strike back in 1989 are all local examples of tourism crises that many of you here may relate to.

Tourism can create new jobs (especially for young people), support existing services, bring 'new' money into the town, increase local pride, develop infrastructure, promote conservation and preservation and increase the number of recreational opportunities in the town. For many years jobs in the tourism industry required only moderate formal education and attracted low salaries, with many businesses operating on low profit margins. Increased competition for the tourist dollar and an interest in quality outdoor experiences has increased incomes along with opportunities for those seeking professional careers (Potts & Marsinko c.1995). Ecotourism can provide exceptional opportunities for those who have special insight into their local environments and are willing to professionally provide equipment, guide services, food and lodging.

La Trobe University is working in Central Victoria with a group of small towns on a project called 'Building a Future for the Country'. While it is not solely tourism related, many of these communities see tourism as the answer to their problems of population loss, limited infrastructure and maintenance of public utilities. Many have developed a festival program and are looking at restoring buildings for heritage tourism and see opportunities for ecotourism in the surrounding countryside. However, we are cautious in our approach to these 'opportunities', pointing out that tourism may not have the same relevance to each town and that they need to also consider other options. One town may succeed with a tourism project while another, only a few miles away, may not. While there are great examples of tourism reinvigorating rural communities, it is not always the case. Tourism actually carries with it the seeds of its own destruction – too many visitors may ruin the environment or the quiet nature of the town, it may alter the mix and type of people living in the town, divide the community and so on. A pertinent example of this comes from the UK.

Goathland, in the North Yorkshire Moors was a small town of 300 residents and annual visitor numbers of around 200 000. Visitors came to stay at the small guesthouses and enjoy a relaxed, quiet getaway. The economic basis of the town was built around this image and many retirees also made up the population, enjoying its tranquil atmosphere. Then the town became the site of Aidensfield, the fictitious town in the TV series *Heartbeat*. In a few years, visitor numbers rose to 1.5 million and have now 'settled' at around 1 million each year. The town became crowded and busy, with the traditional visitors opting to stay somewhere else and the new visitors coming only for the day and also staying at other towns. The entire commercial basis of the town was lost, along with its quiet atmosphere that impacted severely on the retirees who were at home during the day. Resentment towards tourists has become evident, and the infrastructure of the town sorely stretched (Demetriadi 1996).

Strategies have been developed to improve the situation, and the TV production company has funded numerous community projects. However, Goathland will never be the same. Last year, the historic railway station was used as the setting for the train station in the Harry Potter movie – at this stage we can only guess what this may bring.

Australia doesn't suffer such enormous visitor numbers as the UK. However, we need to consider these cases and learn from them now, even if we never think it will happen to us. I have been invited to Goathland next year to study this phenomenon and help them with their community and visitor strategies, if I can, as well as learn from their successes and failures.

But, why is it so hard to develop community based tourism initiatives?

If including communities in the tourism decision-making, operational and support processes is so crucial to the development and sustainability of tourism and tourists, why aren't all communities embracing such an approach? You may well find that there are many who have tried, but not succeeded in the first instance, lost heart and given up. Often the strength of a community relies on one or two enthusiastic leaders or 'champions' who carry everyone else along with them. When such people leave the region or just burn out, there is often no one to take their place, and a community that has become so reliant on being led has trouble leading itself. This scenario is repeated time and again and is an excellent reason for such leaders to establish a network that can take on various roles when required. Otherwise, communities continue to seesaw up, down and around, depending on the state of their leadership.

Other issues that challenge the ongoing development of community tourism include:

- lack of community cohesion, divergent goals
- insufficient, 'improper' or no planning and integration
- often a misunderstanding of who actually makes up the community
- the fact that tourism can be introduced and run by outsiders with little community consultation.

The importance of developing a powerful, inclusive vision for your community in terms of tourism cannot be stressed enough. It needs to be strong and clearly defined, because if it's too general it will not be of any use. Once you have that, all decisions, projects and plans can be considered in terms of that vision, and the issues of a leader or champion leaving the community can be ameliorated.

At a workshop for the 'Building a Future for the Country' project, we spent a day developing a vision for the towns involved that is strong, focused and, most importantly, owned by all parties. The vision is:

> To access our community's culture of welcome to help our visitors experience, celebrate and enjoy our local colonial, indigenous and natural heritages and environment, as well as participate in our vibrant cultures.

We were then able to prioritise the desired outcomes that had been identified in the workshop into first and second levels, depending on their 'fit' with the vision. In this way, a tourism strategy that was congruent with the needs and desires of the community could be developed. Now that a vision and some understanding of the issues had been addressed, the community was able to move on to the next steps, listed below.

- Identify and rank specific projects and concepts in the knowledge that they tie in with the broader view of the towns and region
- Conduct a cost-benefit analysis on the highest ranking projects
- Decide whether to proceed with them in light of the analysis.

However, many 'visions' are too broad and vague to be of much use, such as Tourism Queensland's mission statement, that is 'to enhance the development and marketing of Queensland's tourism destinations in partnership with industry, government and the community' (Tourism Queensland 2002a). This vision does not do them justice as Tourism Queensland is far more than a mere marketing organisation, as pointed out elsewhere: '... Our role has expanded to include tourism planning and destination development, making Tourism Queensland a "one stop shop" for tourism operators and anyone interested in tourism' (Tourism Queensland 2002a).

A publicly acknowledged guiding vision (or mission statement) is crucial in that it provides a framework for action and assessment. I'm relieved to say that I do like the Department of Primary Industry's vision shown below, even though it is brief and lacks any 'action' words.

- Innovative food and fibre industries
- Confident communities
- Ecological sustainable use of natural resources (DPI 2002).

Planning assistance

Local, state and federal government all have departments that can assist with the development and planning of community based tourism, with many employing dedicated tourism development and marketing staff. Many arts departments as well as tourism and regional development departments can assist with advice and funding for community tourism projects.

There are many communities throughout the world that are developing community tourism strategies and are willing to share their knowledge. Some excellent community tourism websites include the *Community Tourism Assessment Handbook*, which describes a nine-step process to determine whether tourism development is right for your community (http://extension.usu.edu/wrdc/ctah), *Tourism With Integrity*, an online publication from the Australian Museums and Galleries (http://www.amol.org.au/craft/publications/hcc/tourism.asp) and *21st Century Communities* (http://www.dced.state.ut.us/21century/index.html). Also the *Planeta* website has excellent links and articles on ecotourism in third world communities (http://www.planeta.com). Queensland Tourism also has many relevant resources, and their publication, *Tourism Works for Queensland*, which provides an overview of tourism in general and a brief chapter on community involvement, is available online at http://www.tq.com.au/publications/tourismworks/contents.

Our universities and other educational institutions provide not only students for certain projects, but also research graduates and academics interested in rural communities, many of whom have undertaken studies that may assist you. Universities are also very interested in cooperative research projects with communities.

The last word?

It is crucial that local communities are part of any tourism venture, whether it be as consultants for a commercial venture, or as community-run enterprises. Without the enthusiastic support of the local hosts, tourists will go elsewhere. Ecotourism by its very nature is community focused, committing to employing locals, purchasing local supplies, contributing to community and environmental projects and so on. Ecotourism also has the potential to bring the outback environment to life through its focus on interpretation – telling stories and explaining what people are experiencing.

The most successful tourism enterprises in Australia are not the big resort style developments, but are those that started small, with less than four staff. Local opportunities can start on a small scale, particularly regarding tour guiding, and build as tourism interest builds. Communities must be given the right and opportunity to choose the level and type of tourism they want. Remember, saying 'no' to tourism is also an option.

References

Beeton, S. (1998). *Ecotourism: a practical guide for rural communities.* (Landlinks Press, Melbourne.)

Demetriadi, J. (1996). The Tele Tourists. *Hospitality* October/November, 14–15.

Department of Primary Industries Queensland (DPI). (2002). *Corporate Plan,* 2001–2006. www.dpi.qld.gov.au.

English Tourism Commission (ETC). (2001). Foot and mouth disease and tourism: update from ETC, May 2001. www.englishtourism.org.uk.

Mader, R. (2002). Understanding community tourism. *Planeta,* www.planeta.com/ecotravel/tour/community.html. Accessed March 2002.

Potts, T.D. & Marsinko, A.P.C. (c.1995). *Developing naturally: an exploratory process for nature-based community tourism.* Cooperative Extension Service, Clemson University, South Carolina.

Sharpley, R. (2001). Rural tourism and sustainable development: a governance perspective. *Proceedings of the International Rural Tourism Conference.* SAC Auchincruive, CD-ROM.

Sustainability (2002). The triple bottom Line. Sustainability, www.sustainability.com/philosophy/triple-bottom. Accessed April 2002.

Tonge, R. (2001). Developing rural tourism. *Positive Rural Futures Conference, 2001.* Department of Primary Industries Queensland. www.dpi.qld.gov.au/community/3192.html.

Tourism Queensland. (2002a). Tourism Queensland Website. www.tq.com.au. Accessed April 2002.

Tourism Queensland. (2002b). Queensland Government strategy for growing tourism. Tourism Queensland.

United Nations, Canada (UNA-Canada). (2002). International years. UNA-Canada, www.unac.org/en/news_events/un_days/international_years.asp. Accessed April 2002.

Community tourism web-based resources

Australian Museums and Galleries Tourism With Integrity, http://www.amol.org.au/craft/publications/hcc/tourism.asp

Community Tourism Assessment Handbook, http://extension.usu.edu/wrdc/ctah

Planeta, http://www.planeta.com

Queensland Tourism, Tourism Works for Queensland, http://www.tq.com.au/publications/tourismworks/contents.

21st Century Communities, http://www.dced.state.ut.us/21century/index.html

---

Footnote

1   Keynote presentation to the 2002 Positive Rural Futures Conference, Charleville, Australia.

References

Ap, J. (1992). Residents' perception of tourism impacts. *Annals of Tourism Research* **19**(3), 665–90.

Ashley, C. (n.d.). *Community tourism in Southern Africa: guidelines for practitioners.* (National Resource Management Programme of Southern Africa Development Community, ART, Harare.)

Ashley, C., Boyd, C. & Goodwin, H. (2000). Pro-poor tourism: putting poverty at the heart of the tourism agenda. *Natural Resource Perspectives* **51**, 5 March 2000. (ODI , London.)

Ashley, C. & Roe, D. (2003). *Working with the private sector on Pro-Poor Tourism: opinions and experience from two development practitioners.* (ODI, London.)

Ashley, C., Roe, D. & Goodwin, H. (2001). *Pro-Poor Tourism Report No. 1; Pro-Poor Tourism strategies: making tourism work for the poor; a review of experience.* April 2001. (ODI, London.)

Australian Associated Press (AAP). (1999). Struth! They'll see us as a mob of galahs. *The Age*, 9 January 1999.

Baudrillard, J. (1983). *Simulations.* (Semiotexte, New York.)

Beeton, S. (1998). *Ecotourism: a practical guide for rural communities.* (Landlinks Press, Melbourne.)

Beeton, S. (2000). It's a wrap! What happens after the film crew leaves? An examination of community responses to film-induced tourism. *TTRA National Conference – Lights! Camera! Action!* pp. 127–36. (TTRA, Burbank, CA.)

Beeton, S. (2001a). Smiling for the camera: the influence of film audiences on a budget tourism destination. *Tourism, Culture and Communication* **3**(1), 15–26.

Beeton, S. (2001b). Lights, camera, re-action. How does film-induced tourism affect a country town? In *The Future of Australia's Country Towns.* (Eds M.F. Rogers & Y.M.J. Collins.) pp. 172–83. (Centre for Sustainable Regional Communities, La Trobe University, Bendigo.)

Beeton, S. (2001c). Cyclops and sirens – demarketing as a proactive response to negative consequences of one-eyed competitive marketing. *TTRA 32nd Conference Proceedings, 2001: A Tourism Odyssey*, pp. 125–36.

Beeton, S. (2001d). Horseback tourism in Victoria, Australia: cooperative, proactive crisis management. *Current Issues in Tourism* **4**(5), 422–39.

Beeton, S. (2002a). reCAPITALizing the image: demarketing undesired film-induced images. *TTRA 33rd Conference, CAPITALizing on Tourism Research.* (Arlington, USA.) CD-ROM.

Beeton, S. (2002b). A (de-)marketing approach to enhancing capabilities for film-induced tourism. *ANZAM 2002 Conference Proceedings.* (ANZAM, Melbourne.) CD-ROM.

Beeton, S. (2002c). Entrepreneurship in rural tourism? Australian Landcare programs as a destination marketing tool. *Journal of Travel Research* **41**(2), 206–9.

Beeton, S. (2002d). The cost of complacency – horseback tourism and crisis management revisited. *Current Issues in Tourism* **5**(5), 467–470.

Beeton, S. (2003). Swimming against the tide – integrating marketing with environmental management via demarketing. *Journal of Hospitality and Tourism Management* **10**(2), 95–107.

Beeton, S. (2004a). Rural tourism in Australia – has the gaze altered? Tracking rural images through film and tourism promotion. *International Journal of Travel Research* **6**, 125–35.

Beeton, S. (2004b). Business issues in wildlife tourism: from theory to practice. In *Wildlife Tourism.* (Ed. K. Higginbottom.) pp. 187–209. (Common Ground, Altona.)

Beeton, S. (2005a). *Film-Induced Tourism.* (Channel View Publications, Clevedon.)

Beeton, S. (2005b). Reflecting or directing perceptions? Fox Media's responses to disasters in tourism destinations. In *BEST Education Network Think Tank V.* (Jamaica.) CD-ROM.

Beeton, S. & Benfield, R. (2003). Demand control: The case for demarketing as a visitor and environmental management tool. *Journal of Sustainable Tourism* **10** (6), 497–513.

Beeton, S., Bowen, H. & Santos, C.A. (2005). State of knowledge: mass media and its relationship to perceptions of quality. In *Quality Tourism Experiences.* (Eds G. Jennings & N.P. Nickerson.) pp. 50–71. (Elsevier Butterworth-Heinemann, Burlington, MA.)

Beeton, S. & Pinge, I. (2003). Casting the holiday dice: demarketing gambling to encourage local tourism. *Current Issues in Tourism* **6** (4), 309–22.

Beeton, S. & Valerio, P. (2005). And the rest is history: the rise and rise of destination branding. Unpublished working paper.

Beirman, D. (2005). Critical issues facing destinations. In *BEST Education Network Think Tank V.* (Jamaica.) CD-ROM.

Benfield, R. (2001). 'Turning back the hordes': demarketing research as a means of managing mass tourism. In *TTRA 32nd Conference Proceedings, 2001: A*

Tourism Odyssey. (Eds R.N. Moisey, N.P. Nickerson & K.L. Andereck.) pp. 137–50. (TTRA, Florida.)

Berger, P. & Luckmann, T. (1966). *The social construction of reality*. (Anchor Books, Garden City.)

Blackstock, K. (2005). A critical look at community based tourism. *Community Development Journal* **40**(1), 39–49.

Boorstin, D.J. (1972). *The image: a guide to pseudo events in America*. (Athenaeum, New York.)

Borkowski, N.M. (1994). Demarketing of health services. *Journal of Health Care Marketing* **14**(4), 12.

Bowen, H. & Santos, C.A. (2005). Constructing quality, constructing reality. In *Quality tourism experiences*. (Eds G. Jennings & N.P. Nickerson.) pp. 72–104. (Elsevier Butterworth-Heinemann, Burlington, MA.)

Bradshaw, L. & Slonsky, L.B. (2005). 'Our Katrina experience'. Email transmission. See http:www.emsnetwork.org/artman/publish/article_18337.shtml.

Bramwell, B. (2003). Maltese responses to tourism. *Annals of Tourism Research* **30**(3), 581–605.

Bramwell, B. & Lane, B. (2000). Collaborative tourism planning: issues and future directions. In *Tourism collaboration and partnerships: politics, practice and sustainability*. (Eds B. Bramwell & B. Lane.) pp. 333–41. (Channel View Publications, Clevedon.)

Brown, R.L. (1997). *Ghost dancing on the cracker circuit*. (University Press of Mississippi, Jackson.)

Business Enterprises for Sustainable Tourism (BEST). (2003). *The community tourism summit, BEST Summary Report*. May 13–15 2003. (New York.)

Butler, R.W. (1980). The concept of a tourism area cycle of evolution: implications for management of resources. *Canadian Geographer* **24**, 5–12.

Butler, R.W. (Ed.) (2005). The Tourism Area Life Cycle. Vol. 1 and Vol. 2. (Channel View Publications, Clevedon.)

Butler, R.W. & Hall, C.M. (1998). Imaging and reimaging of rural areas. In *Tourism and recreation in rural areas*. (Eds R. Butler, C.M. Hall & J. Jenkins.) pp. 156–65. (Wiley & Sons, Chichester.)

Carlsen, J. & Getz, D. (2001). Cross-case analysis of family businesses in rural tourism, *CAUTHE Conference*. CD-ROM.

Choo, D.K. (2001). The HTA Versus the Sierra Club. *Hawaii Business Magazine*, March 2001.

Christaller, W. (1963). Some considerations of tourism location in Europe: the peripheral regions – under-developed countries – recreation areas. *Regional Science Association Papers* **12**, 103.

Clements, M.A. (1989). Selecting tourist traffic by demarketing. *Tourism Management* **10**(2), 89–94.

Cohen, E. (1988). Traditions on the qualitative sociology of tourism. *Annals of Tourism Research* **15**, 29–46.

Commission on Children at Risk (2003). *Hardwired to connect. The new scientific case for authoritative communities. A Report to the Nation.* (Institute for American Values, New York.)

Commonwealth Department of Tourism (DOT). (1994). *National rural tourism strategy.* (Australian Government Printing Service, Canberra.)

Cooper, R. (1983). The other: a model of human structuring. In *Beyond Method: Strategies for Social Research* (Ed. G. Morgan.) pp. 202–217. (Sage, London.)

Craik, J. (1991). *Resorting to tourism: cultural policies for tourist development in Australia.* (Allen & Unwin, Sydney.)

Crompton, J. (1979). Motivations of pleasure vacation. *Journal of Leisure Research* **6**, 408–24.

Croy, W.G. & Walker, R.D. (2001). Tourism and film: issues for strategic regional development. In *Conference Proceedings, New dimensions in managing rural tourism and leisure.* (Eds M. Mitchell & I. Kirkpatrick.) CD-ROM. (Scottish Agricultural College, Auchincruive.)

Cunliffe, S. (2005). Tourism risk management for small and medium enterprises. In *BEST Education Network Think Tank V.* CD-ROM. (Jamaica.)

Daly, H.E. & Cobb, J.B. Jnr. (1989). *For the common good: redirecting the economy toward community, the environment and a sustainable future.* (Beacon Press, Boston.)

Dann, G. (1977). Anomie, ego-enhancement and tourism. *Annals of Tourism Research* **4**, 184–94.

Dann, S. & Dann, S. (2004). *Introduction to marketing.* (John Wiley and Sons, Milton.)

De Botton, A. (2002). *The art of travel.* (Hamish Hamilton, London.)

De Jong, P. (2005). Public–private partnerships: linking projects and the private sector. In *First South Asia Sustainable Tourism Forum (SASTF) and Fifth Meeting of the South Asia Subregional Economic Cooperation (SASEC).* Tourism Working Group. February 26–28, 2005, Dhaka, Bangladesh.

Department of Tourism (DOT). (1994). National Rural Tourism Strategy. (AGPS, Canberra.)

Doxey, G.V. (1975). A causation theory of visitor-resident irritants: methodology and research inferences. In *Travel and Tourism Research Association Sixth Annual Conference Proceedings.* pp. 195–98. (TTRA, San Diego.)

Dredge, D. (2003). Tourism community well-being and local government. *Australian Regional Tourism Convention*, 3–6 September 2003.

Drucker, P.F. (1950). Marketing Men Take Over in GE Units. *Business Week* 24 June 1950, pp. 30–36.

Drucker, P.F., Dyson, E., Handy, C., Saffo, P. & Senge, M. (1997). Looking ahead: implications of the present. *Harvard Business Review* **75**(5), 18–26.

Echtner, C.M. & Ritchie, J.R.B. (1993). The measurement of destination image: an empirical assessment. *Journal of Travel Research* **31**(4), 3–13.

Eco, U. (1983). *Travels in hyperreality.* (Harcourt Brace Jovanovitch, San Diego.)

Economic Commission for Latin America and the Caribbean (ECLAC). (2003). *Handbook for estimating the socio-economic and environmental effects of disasters.* (United Nations, Economic Commission for Latin America and the Caribbean (ECLAC) and International Bank for Reconstruction and Development (The World Bank), Madrid.)

Eugenio-Martin, J., Sinclair, M.T. & Yeoman, I. (2005). Quantifying the effects of tourism crises: an application to Scotland. *Journal of Travel and Tourism Marketing* **15**(4), 323–38.

Faulkner, B. (2001). Towards a framework for tourism disaster management. *Tourism Management* **22**(2), 135–47.

Faulkner, B. & Russell, R. (1997). Chaos and complexity in tourism: in search of a new perspective. *Pacific Tourism Review* **1**(1), 93–102.

Fawcett, C. & Cormack, P. (2001). Guarding authenticity at literary tourism sites. *Annals of Tourism Research* **28**(3), 686–704.

Featherstone, M. (1988). In pursuit of the postmodern: an introduction. *Theory, Culture and Society* **5**(2–3), 195–215.

Foucault, M. (1975). *Discipline and punish: the birth of the prison.* (Translated A. Sheridan, 1977). (Allen Lane, London.)

Gibson, C. & Connell, J. (2005). *Music and tourism: on the road again.* (Channel View Publications, Clevedon.)

Gleick, J. (1987). *Chaos: making a new science.* (Heinemann, London.)

Goeldner, C.R., Ritchie, J.R. Brent & McIntosh, R.W. (2000). *Tourism: principles, practices, philosophies.* 8th edn. (John Wiley & Sons, New York.)

Gomera, M. (c.1999). What governments can do for community tourism. *Community Tourism in Southern Africa: Guidelines for Practitioners.* **No. 2.** (Africa Resources Trust, Zimbabwe.)

Graves, L.N. (1992). Cooperative learning communities: context for a new vision of education and society. *Journal of Education* **174**(2), 57–79.

Gudmundsson, S.V. (1999). Airline alliances: consumer and policy issues. *European Business Journal* **1999**, 139–45.

Gunn, C.A. (1988). *Tourism planning.* 2nd edn. (Taylor and Francis, New York.)

Gupta, V. (1999). Sustainable tourism: learning from Indian religious traditions. *International Journal of Contemporary Hospitality Management* **11**(2/3), 91–5.

Hall, C.M. (1998). *Introduction to tourism in Australia: development, dimensions and issues.* 3rd edn. (Longman, Melbourne.)

Hall, C.M. (2003a). *Introduction to tourism: dimensions and issues.* 4th edn. (Hospitality Press, Frenchs Forest.)

Hall, C.M. (2003b). Politics and place: an analysis of power in tourism communities. In *Tourism in destination communities.* (Eds S. Singh, D.J. Timothy & R.K. Dowling.) pp. 99–114. (CABI Publishing, Wallingford.)

Hall, C.M., Croy, W.G. & Walker, R.D. (2003). Imaging and branding the destination. In *Introduction to tourism: dimensions and issues.* 4th edn. (Ed. C.M. Hall.) pp. 316–332. (Pearson Education, Frenchs Forest.)

Hall, C.M. & McArthur, S. (Eds.) (1993). *Heritage management in New Zealand and Australia: interpretation, marketing and visitor management.* (Oxford University Press, Auckland.)

Hall, C.M. & McArthur, S. (Eds.) (1996). *Heritage management in Australia and New Zealand: the human dimension.* (Oxford University Press, Melbourne.)

Hall, S. (1997). The work of representation. In *Representation: cultural representations and signifying practices.* (Ed. S. Hall.) pp. 13–74. (Sage Publications, London.)

Hannigan, J. (1998). *Fantasy city: pleasure and profit in the postmodern metropolis.* (Routledge, London.)

Harris, R. & Leiper, N. (Eds.) (1995). *Sustainable tourism, an Australian perspective.* (Butterworth-Heinemann, Australia.)

Hawaii Tourism Authority. (2005). *Hawaii Tourism Strategic Plan: 2005–2015.* (HTA, State of Hawaii.)

Herbert, D.T. (1996). Artistic and literary places in France as tourist attractions. *Tourism Management* **17**(2), 77–85.

Herbert, D.T. (2001). Literary places, tourism and the heritage experience. *Annals of Tourism Research* **28**, 312–33.

Herzberg, B. (2004). *Competitiveness partnerships: a few guidelines.* (Investment Climate Unit, World Bank, Washington DC.)

Hilty, A. (1996). Tourism and literary connections: how to manage the image created. In *Culture as the tourist product.* (Eds M. Robinson *et al.*) pp. 185–198. (Centre for Travel and Tourism, University of Northumbria.)

Horne, D. (1992). *The intelligent tourist.* (Margaret Gee Publishing, McMahons Point.)

Huang, Y. & Stewart, W.P. (1996). Rural tourism development: shifting basis of community solidarity. *Journal of Travel Research* **34**(4), 26–31.

Ife, J. (1995). *Community development: creating community alternatives – vision, analysis and practice.* (Longman, South Melbourne.)

Independent Evaluation Group (IEG). (2005). *The effectiveness of World Bank support for community-based and -driven development.* (World Bank, Washington DC.)

Iso-Ahola, S. (1980). *The social psychology of leisure and recreation.* (WC Brown, Dubuque.)

Iso-Ahola, S. (1982). Towards a social psychology theory of tourist motivation. *Annals of Tourism Research* **9**, 256–61.

Jack, L. (2000). Development and application of the Kangaroo Island TOMM (Tourism Optimisation Management Model). In *Proceedings of the First National Conference on the Future of Australia's Country Towns, July 2000.* (Centre for Sustainable Regional Communities, La Trobe University, Bendigo.) www.regional.org.au/au/countrytowns/options/jack.htm.

Jacobsen, C. & Cohen, A. (1986). The power of social collectivities: towards an integrative conceptualization of operationalization. *British Journal of Sociology* **37**(1), 106–21.

Jafari, J. (1989). An English language literature review. In *Tourism as a factor of change: a sociocultural study.* (Ed. J. Bystrzanowski.) pp. 17–60. (Centre for Research and Documentation in Social Sciences, Vienna.)

Jafari, J. (1990). Research and scholarship: the basis of tourism education. *Journal of Tourism Studies* **1**(1), 33–41.

Jafari, J. (2002). Retracing and mapping tourism's landscape of knowledge. *ReVista – Tourism in the Americas, Harvard Review of Latin America*, Winter. www.fas. Harvard.edu/~drclas/publications/revista/Tourism, [accessed 1 June 2002].

Jamal, T.B. & Getz, D. (1995). Collaboration theory and community tourism planning. *Annals of Tourism Research* **22**(1), 186–204.

Jamal, T. & Getz, D. (2000). Community roundtables for tourism-related conflicts: the dialectics of consensus and process structures. In *Tourism collaboration and partnerships: politics, practice and sustainability.* (Eds B. Bramwell & B. Lane.) pp. 159–82. (Channel View Publications, Clevedon.)

Janiskee, R.L. & Drews, P.L. (1998). Rural festivals and community reimaging. In *Tourism and Recreation in Rural Areas.* (Eds R. Butler, C.M. Hall & J. Jenkins.) pp. 1–16. (John Wiley & Sons, West Sussex.)

Jennings, G. (2001). *Tourism research.* (John Wiley & Sons, Milton.)

Jennings, G. & Stehlik, D. (2001). Mediated authenticity: the perspectives of farm tourism providers. In *TTRA 32nd Annual Conference Proceedings, 2001: A Tourism Odyssey*, June 10–13 2001, pp. 85–92.

Jopp, M. (1996). Sustainable community tourism development revisited. *Tourism Management* **17**(7), 475–79.

Kayal, M. (2000). Sierra Club sues over marketing of tourism. *Honolulu Advertiser* 13 January 2000.

Kelly, M.E. (2002). *The Community Tourism Newsletter.* November–December 2002. (Community Tourism Development Planning and Design, Gatineau.)

King, R. & Beeton, S. (in-press, 2006). Influence of mass media's coverage of adventure tourism on youth perceptions of risk. *Tourism, Culture and Communications, Special Edition on Tourism and Media.*

Kotler, P. & Armstrong, G. (2004). *Principles of marketing.* 10th edn. (Prentice Hall, Upper Saddle River.)

Kotler, P., Bowen, J. & Makens, J. (2003). *Marketing for hospitality and tourism.* 3rd edn. (Prentice Hall, Upper Saddle River.)

Kotler, P., Haider, D.H. & Rein, I. (1993). *Marketing places.* (The Free Press, New York.)

Kotler, P. & Levy, S.J. (1971). Demarketing, yes demarketing. *Harvard Business Review* **49**(6), 74–80.

Lampel, J. & Mintzberg, H. (1996). Customizing customization. *Sloan Management Review* **Fall**, 21–30.

Lankford, S.V. & Howard, D.R. (1994). Developing a tourism impact attitude scale. *Annals of Tourism Research* **21**, 121–39.

LaPage, W.F. & Cormmier, P.L. (1977). Images of camping – barriers to participation. *Journal of Travel Research* **15**, 21.

Leiper, N. (2002). *Tourism management.* 2nd edn. (Pearson Education, Melbourne.)

Leiper, N. (1999). What is tourism worth? Some alternative approaches and techniques for finding answers. In *Valuing tourism, methods and techniques.* (Eds K. Corcoran, A. Allcock, T. Frost & L. Johnson.) pp. 122–33. (BTR, Canberra.)

Lickorish, L.J. & Jenkins, C.L. (1997). *An introduction to tourism.* (Butterworth Heinemann, Oxford.)

Lyotard, J-F. (1984). *The postmodern condition: a report on knowledge.* (University of Minnesota Press, Minneapolis.)

MacCannell, D. (1973). Staged authenticity: arrangements of social space in tourism settings. *American Journal of Sociology* **79**(3), 357–61.

MacCannell, D. (1976). *The tourist: a new theory of the leisure class.* (Shocken Books, New York.)

Macquarie Bank. (2003). Building sustainable communities: Why bother with the regions? Presentation to *Australian Regional Tourism Convention* by Peter Wright, Chief Executive, 5 September 2003.

Major Projects and Tourism. (2002). $100,000 Bracks Govt program to help adventure tourism. *Media Release.* Victorian Government, 25 January 2002.

Manidis Roberts Consultants. (1997). *Developing a Tourism Optimisation Management Model (TOMM): a model to monitor and manage tourism on Kangaroo Island, South Australia.* (South Australian Tourism Commission, Adelaide.)

Maslow, A.H. (1954). *Motivation and personality.* (Harper & Row, New York.)

McMillan, D.W. & Chavis, D.M. (1996). Sense of community: a definition and theory. *Journal of Consumer Psychology* **14**, 6–23.

Mordue, T. (1999). Heartbeat Country: conflicting values, coinciding visions. *Environment and Planning* **31**, 629–46.

Mordue, T. (2001). Performing and directing resident/tourist cultures in Heartbeat Country. *Tourist Studies* **1**(3), 233–52.

Moscardo, G. & Pearce, P. (2003). Marketing host communities. In *Tourism in destination communities*. (Eds S. Singh, D.J. Timothy & R.K. Dowling.) pp. 253–72. (CABI Publishing, Wallingford.)

Moscovici, S. (1972). Society and theory in social psychology. In *The context of social psychology*. (Eds J. Israel & H. Tajfel.) pp. 17–68. (Academic Press, London.)

Moscovici, S. (1984). The phenomenon of social representations. In *Social representations*. (Eds R.M. Farr & S. Moscovici.) pp. 3–69. (Cambridge University Press, Cambridge.)

Moser, C. (1989). Community participation in urban projects in the Third World. *Progress in Planning* **32**(2), 81.

Müller, D.K. (2001). Literally unplanned literary tourism in two municipalities in rural Sweden. In *Conference Proceedings, New Dimensions in Managing Rural Tourism and Leisure*. (Eds M. Mitchell & I. Kirkpatrick.) CD ROM. (Scottish Agricultural College, Auchincruive.)

Murphy, P.E. (1980). Tourism management in host communities. *The Canadian Geographer* **24**(1), 1–2.

Murphy, P.E. (1981). Community attitudes to tourism: A comparative analysis. *International Journal of Tourism Management* **2 Sept**, 189–95.

Murphy, P.E. (1985). *Tourism: a community approach*. (Methuen, New York.)

Murphy, P.E. (1991). Data gathering for community-oriented tourism planning: a case study of Vancouver Island, British Columbia. *Leisure Studies* **10**(1), 68–80.

Murphy, P. & Murphy, A. (2001). Regional tourism and its economic development links for small communities. In *The future of Australia's country towns*. (Eds M.F. Rogers & Y.M.J. Collins.) pp. 162–71. (Centre for Sustainable Regional Communities, Bendigo.)

Murphy, P. & Murphy, A. (2004). *Strategic management for tourism communities: bridging the gaps*. (Channel View Publications, Clevedon.)

New South Wales Government. (2001). *Working with Government – November 2001, Guidelines for privately financed projects*. (NSW Government, Sydney.)

Northern Territory Treasury. (2000). Budget Paper No. 3 – issues in public finance. *Budget Papers, 2000–2001*. http://www.nt.gov.au/ntt/financial/0001bps [accessed October, 2005].

Nunez, T.A. (1977). Touristic studies in anthropological perspective. In *Hosts and guests: the anthropology of tourism.* (Ed. V.L. Smith.) pp. 207–16. (University of Pennsylvania Press, Philadelphia.)

Oppermann, M. (1997). Rural tourism in Germany: farm and rural tourism operators. In *The business of rural tourism.* (Eds S.J. Page & D. Getz.) pp. 108–19. (International Thomson Business Press, London.)

Oregon Progress Board (1999). *Achieving the Oregon shines vision: the 1999 Benchmark Performance Report.* March 1999. (Report to the Legislative Assembly, Oregon.)

Organisation for Economic Co-operation and Development (OECD). (1994). *Tourism policy and international tourism in OECD countries, 1991–1992.* (OECD, Paris.)

Pacific Asia Travel Association (PATA). (2003). *Crisis: it won't happen to us!* (PATA, Bangkok.)

Page, S. (1995). *Urban tourism.* (Routledge, London.)

Page, S.J. & Getz, D. (Eds.) (1997). *The business of rural tourism.* (International Thomson Business Press, London.)

Pearce, P.L. (1992). Alternative tourism: concepts, classifications and questions. In *Tourism alternatives: potentials and problems in the development of tourism.* (Eds V.L. Smith & W.R. Eadington.) pp. 18–40. (John Wiley & Sons, New York.)

Pearce, P.L., Moscardo, G. & Ross, G.F. (1996). *Tourism community relationships.* (Elsevier Science, Oxford.)

Pizam, A. (1978). Tourism's impacts: the social costs to the destination community as perceived by its residents. *Journal of Travel Research* **Spring**, 8–12.

Plog, S.C. (1974). Why destination areas rise and fall in popularity. *The Cornell Hotel and Restaurant Administration Quarterly* **15**, 13–16.

Polunin, I. (Ed.) (c. 2002). Crisis destination management. *Eclipse.* 6th edn. Moonshine Travel Marketing, Madrid. http://www.moonshine.es/PAGES/ING/ECLI1I html [accessed December 2005].

Port Fairy Folk Festival (PFFF). (2005). Port Fairy Folk Festival, www.portfairyfolkfestival.com/

Porter, M.E. (1980). *Competitive strategy: techniques for analyzing industries and competition.* (The Free Press, New York.)

Porter, M.E. (1998). The Adam Smith Address: location, clusters and the 'new' microeconomics of competition. *Business Economics* **33**(1), 7–13.

PPT Partnerships. (2004a). *Sheet No. 3, PPT and poverty reduction.* (Pro Poor Tourism Partnership, London.)

PPT Partnerships. (2004b). *Sheet No. 1, Defining PPT.* (Pro Poor Tourism Partnership, London.)

PPT Partnerships. (2004c). *Sheet No. 2, PPT strategies.* (Pro Poor Tourism Partnership, London.)

Prentice, R. (1993). Community-driven tourism planning and residents' perceptions. *Tourism Management* **14**(3), 218–27.

Reed, M.G. (1997). Power relations and community-based tourism planning. *Annals of Tourism Research,* **24**(3), 566–91.

Ritchie, B.W. (2004). Chaos, crises and disasters: a strategic approach to crisis management in the tourism industry. *Tourism Management* **25,** 669–83.

Ritchie, J.R. Brent & Crouch, G.I. (2003). *The competitive destination: a sustainable tourism perspective.* (CABI Publishing, Wallingford.)

Ritzer, G. (1993). *The McDonaldization of society: an investigation into the changing character of contemporary social life.* (Pine Forge Press, Newbury Park.)

Ritzer, G. & Liska, A. (1997). McDisneyization and post-tourism – complementary perspectives on contemporary tourism. In *Touring cultures. Transformations of travel and theory.* (Eds C. Rojek & J. Urry.) pp. 96–109. (Routledge, London.)

Roberts, B. (1992). *Land care manual.* (University of New South Wales Press, Sydney.)

Roberts, L. & Hall. D. (2001). *Rural tourism and recreation: principles to practice.* (CABI Publishing, Wallingford.)

Robinson, P. & Boniface, M. (1997). *Tourism and cultural conflicts.* (Oxford University Press, Oxford.)

Rogers, M. (2001). Triple bottom line audit: a framework for community-based action. In *The future of Australia's country towns.* (Eds M.F. Rogers & Y.M.J. Collins.) pp. 135–45. (Centre for Sustainable Regional Communities, Bendigo.)

Ryan, C. (2002). Equity, management, power sharing and sustainability – issues of the 'new tourism'. *Tourism Management* **23,** 17–26.

Saul, J.R. (2005). *The collapse of globalization and the reinvention of the world.* (Viking, London.)

Seaton, A.V. (1998). The history of tourism in Scotland: approaches, sources and issues. In *Tourism in Scotland.* (Eds R. MacLellan & R. Smith.) pp. 1–41. (International Thomson Business Press, London.)

Seltzer, M. (2003). How to be a civic traveler. Presentation to New York University, 12 March 2003, BEST, New York.

Sharpley, R. & Sharpley, J. (1997). *Rural tourism, an introduction.* (International Thomson Business Press, London.)

Sierra Club. (2000). *Petition for declaratory and injunctive relief certificate of service.* Supreme Court of the State of Hawaii, 14 January 2000.

Sim, S. (Ed.) (2005). *The Routledge companion to postmodernism.* 2nd ed. (Routledge, Oxon.)

Singh, T.V. & Singh, S. (1999). Coastal tourism, conservation and the community: case of Goa. In *Tourism development in critical environments*. (Eds T.V. Singh & S. Singh.) pp. 65–76. (Cognizant Communication Corporation, New York.)

Singh, S., Timothy, D.J. & Dowling, R.K. (2003a). *Tourism in destination communities*. (CABI Publishing, Oxon.)

Singh, S., Timothy, D.J. & Dowling, R.K. (2003b). Tourism and destination communities. In *Tourism in destination communities*. (Eds S. Singh, D.J. Timothy & R.K. Dowling.) pp. 3–18. (CABI Publishing, Wallingford.)

Smailes, B. (1999). Mixed reception for $150m ATC campaign. *TravelWeek* **January 20**, 3.

Sofield, T. (2001). Sustainability and world heritage cultural sites: pilgrimage tourism to sacred power places in the Kathmandu Valley, Nepal. In *Hosts and guests revisited: the anthropology of tourism*. (Eds V. Smith & M. Brent.) pp. 257–71. (Elsevier, Oxford.)

Sofield, T. (2003). *Empowerment for sustainable tourism development*. (Pergamon, Elsevier Science, Oxford.)

Sofield, T., Bauer, J., De Lacy, T., Lipman, G. & Daugherty, S. (2004). *Sustainable Tourism – Eliminating Poverty (ST–EP): An Overview*. ST CRC, Gold Coast.

Stephens, U. (2001). *Strengthening Rural Communities*. NSW Premier's Department, Sydney.

Timothy, D.J. & Tosun, C. (2003). Appropriate planning for tourism in destination communities: participation, incremental growth and collaboration. In *Tourism In Destination Communities*. (Eds S Singh, DJ Timothy and RK Dowling.) pp. 181–204. CABI Publishing, Wallingford.

TOMM. (1999). *Annual Report 1999, Tourism Optimisation Management Model*. Kangaroo Island.

TOMM. (2000). *Annual Report 2000, Tourism Optimisation Management Model*. Kangaroo Island.

Tourism Concern. (2000). *Fair trade in tourism, Bulletin 2, Corporate social responsibility*. http://www.tourismconcern.org.uk/fair-trade/index.html [accessed December 2005].

Tourism Forecasting Committee (TFC). (2005). *Tourism Forecasting Committee April Forecasts*. (Tourism Research Australia, Canberra.)

Tourism Victoria. (2005). *Victoria's Tourism Industry Strategic Plan, 2002–2006*. http://www.tourismvictoria.com.au/strategicplan/plan2002_2006 [accessed October 2005].

Turner, V. (1969). *The ritual process: structure and antistructure*. (Cornell University Press, Ithaca, New York.)

UN World Tourism Organisation (UN WTO). (c.2002). *Crisis Guidelines for the Tourism Industry*. UN WTO, Madrid [http://www.world-tourism.org/mkt/committees/recovery/Crisis%20and%20Disaster%20Management%20Guidelines.pdf [accessed December 2005].

Urry, J. (1990). *The tourist gaze: leisure and travel in contemporary societies*. (Sage Publications, London.)

Urry, J. (1995). *Consuming places*. (Routledge, London.)

Urry, J. (2002). *The tourist gaze*. 2nd edn. (Sage Publications, London.)

Vander Kraats, S.A. (2000). Gaining a competitive edge through airline alliances. *CR* **10**(2), 56–64.

Victorian Tourism Operators Association (VTOA). (2002a). Tourism insurance issue: fact sheet. *VTOA Media Release*. 14 January 2002. (VTOA Melbourne.)

Victorian Tourism Operators Association (VTOA). (2002b). *Letter to Members*. 18 January 2002. (VTOA Melbourne.)

Victurine, R. (2000). Building tourism excellence at the community level: capacity building for community-based entrepreneurs in Uganda. *Journal of Travel Research* **38**, 221–29.

Waldrop, M. (1992). *Complexity: the emerging science and the edge of order and chaos*. (Penguin Books, London.)

Weaver, D. & Oppermann, M. (2000). *Tourism management*. (John Wiley & Sons, Australia.)

Wilkinson, K.P. (1991). *The community in rural America*. (Greenwood Press, New York.)

World Travel and Tourism Council (WTTC). (2002). *Corporate social leadership in travel and tourism*. (WTTC, London.)

Youl, R. (1997). Landcare: positive and proven force for rural landscapes. *Parkwatch* September, 190.

Young, G. (1973). *Tourism: blessing or blight?* (Penguin Books, London.)

Index